The Titanic

FOR

DUMMIES®

by Stephen Spignesi

WILEY

John Wiley & Sons, Inc.

The Titanic For Dummies®

Published by
John Wiley & Sons, Inc.
111 River St.
Hoboken, NJ 07030-5774
www.wiley.com

Copyright © 2012 by John Wiley & Sons, Inc., Hoboken, New Jersey

Published by John Wiley & Sons, Inc., Hoboken, New Jersey

Published simultaneously in Canada

For general information on our other products and services, please contact our Customer Care Department within the U.S. at 877-762-2974, outside the U.S. at 317-572-3993, or fax 317-572-4002.

For technical support, please visit www.wiley.com/techsupport.

Wiley publishes in a variety of print and electronic formats and by print-on-demand. Some material included with standard print versions of this book may not be included in e-books or in print-on-demand. If this book refers to media such as a CD or DVD that is not included in the version you purchased, you may download this material at http://booksupport.wiley.com. For more information about Wiley products, visit www.wiley.com.

Library of Congress Control Number: 2011945579

ISBN 978-1-118-17766-2 (pbk); ISBN 978-1-118-20650-8 (ebk); ISBN 978-1-118-20651-5 (ebk); ISBN 978-1-118-20652-2 (ebk)

Manufactured in the United States of America

10 9 8 7 6 5 4 3 2 1

WILEY

About the Author

Stephen Spignesi is a bestselling author of more than 50 books about popular culture, television, film, American history, world history, and contemporary fiction. *The Titanic For Dummies* is his fourth *For Dummies* book. Spignesi is also a novelist, and his psychological thriller *Dialogues* (Bantam) is now available in mass market paperback. Spignesi is a Practitioner in Residence at the University of New Haven in Connecticut where he teaches Composition and Literature, Writing, and courses on Stephen King and the *Titanic*. *The Titanic For Dummies* is the textbook for his course on the history of the great liner. Spignesi is also the founder and Editor-in-Chief of the small press publishing company The Stephen John Press. Spignesi lives in New Haven, Connecticut with his grey cat, Chloe.

Dedication

For Mike Lewis

TITANIC DOGGEREL

By John White

"Unsinkable? Unthinkable!"

The ship designer said.

Nevertheless, it sunk.

But if he'd thunk

It might have occurred to him:

Think or thwim.

The lesson can't be ignored:

Put lifeboats aboard.

Author's Acknowledgments

There are always many people to thank when working on a book of this scope, and certain folks are a must to be singled out and thanked profusely and personally. I had help from many wonderful souls while writing this book and my gratitude knows no bounds. So, my heartfelt love and thanks to:

Valerie Barnes, who makes me better . . .

Mike Lewis, without whom . . .

John White, also without whom . . .

also . . .

my editors extraordinaire Peter Weverka, Joan Friedman, Barbara Shuttle, Alicia South, Jessica Smith, and all the fine folks in the Wiley Dummies division, particularly Melisa Duffy, David Hobson, LeAndra Young, Kathy Nebenhaus, and Kirk Bateman

and . . .

the inestimable Dr. Donald M. Smith, Diane Spinato of the University of New Haven Library, and all my students at the University of New Haven

and . . .

my mother, Lee Mandato, my dear friends Rachel Montgomery, Kathy Marotto, Jim Cole, George Beahm, and Kevin Quigley

and last, but certainly not least . . .

Getty Images, Everett Collection, the terrific people of the Titanic Artifact Exhibition, the fine folks at the Library of Congress, Mayor Ernie Eldridge and Mrs. Eldridge, Douglas Woolley, Joseph Ricker, and Andrew Clarkson.

Publisher's Acknowledgments

We're proud of this book; please send us your comments at http://dummies.custhelp.com. For other comments, please contact our Customer Care Department within the U.S. at 877-762-2974, outside the U.S. at 317-572-3993, or fax 317-572-4002.

Some of the people who helped bring this book to market include the following:

Acquisitions, Editorial, and Vertical Websites

Project Editor: Joan Friedman

Acquisitions Editor: Michael Lewis

Development Editor: Peter Weverka

Copy Editor: Jessica Smith

Assistant Editor: David Lutton

Editorial Program Coordinator: Joe Niesen

Technical Editor: Barbara Shuttle

Senior Editorial Manager: Jennifer Ehrlich

Editorial Manager: Carmen Krikorian

Editorial Assistant: Alexa Koschier

Art Coordinator: Alicia B. South

Cover Photos:
© Mary Evans Picture Library/Alamy

Cartoons: Rich Tennant (www.the5thwave.com)

Composition Services

Project Coordinator: Patrick Redmond

Layout and Graphics: Melanee Habig, Joyce Haughey, Lavonne Roberts, Laura Westhuis

Proofreader: Kathy Simpson

Indexer: BIM Indexing & Proofreading Services

Publishing and Editorial for Consumer Dummies

    Kathleen Nebenhaus, Vice President and Executive Publisher

    Kristin Ferguson-Wagstaffe, Product Development Director

    Ensley Eikenburg, Associate Publisher, Travel

    Kelly Regan, Editorial Director, Travel

Publishing for Technology Dummies

    Andy Cummings, Vice President and Publisher

Composition Services

    Debbie Stailey, Director of Composition Services

Contents at a Glance

Table of Contents

Introduction

. . . .

*F*rom the very beginning, even before she was launched, the *Titanic* was an object of fascination. At the Harland and Wolff shipyards in Belfast where she was built, workers marveled at the size of the ship. When she was launched from Harland and Wolff, about 100,000 people came to see the mighty ship roll down the slipway into Belfast Lough. In Southampton, England, the first stop on her maiden voyage, thousands more came to the docks to see the largest moving object ever built by man. And after the *Titanic* sank to the bottom of the North Atlantic on the sixth day of her maiden voyage, on April 15, 1912, she became an object of fascination for the entire world. Newspapers trumpeted headlines about the tragic ship that was thought to be unsinkable. Newspaper readers devoured every last detail.

After 100 years, the *Titanic* still fascinates the world. The discovery of the *Titanic* wreckage on the bottom of the North Atlantic by Robert Ballard and IFREMER (the French Research Institute for Exploration of the Sea) in 1985 reawakened the public's interest in the *Titanic.* And the blockbuster 1997 James Cameron movie, *Titanic,* with Kate Winslet and Leonardo DiCaprio, thrust the *Titanic* before the public like never before.

The *Titanic* fascinates people because she and her story offer something for everybody. Want a glimpse into how people lived during the Gilded Age? You can get that by reading about the wealthy *Titanic* passengers in first class. Want to see what opulence really is? Take a tour of the upper decks of the *Titanic.* If the technological details of ship building and undersea exploration appeal to you, the *Titanic* may be your subject of choice. Plus it's difficult to imagine anything more dramatic or heartbreaking than the *Titanic*'s last hours. The *Titanic* story offers examples of extreme heroism (and cowardice) under very trying circumstances.

Finally, the *Titanic* offers the opportunity to connect with people who lived 100 years ago — to find out how they lived, to discover what they thought, and to hear their voices. The sinking of the *Titanic* generated many newspaper stories and many pages of eyewitness testimony from investigatory panels and agencies. You can hear the voices of the survivors calling through the years in the newspaper articles and testimonies. I include much of their testimony in this book, so start your journey on the *Titanic* here.

About This Book

I wrote *The Titanic For Dummies* to help you explore what I think is the most fascinating subject of all: the *Titanic* and her story. I didn't write it with the idea that you would read every single page starting with Chapter 1. Of course, you can read the book from front to back if you want, but if you prefer to skip around to topics that tickle your fancy, be my guest.

Skipping around the book is possible because the chapters are modular. In other words, to enjoy it and get the most out of it, you don't have to remember facts from the early chapters to make sense of the later chapters. If you need to know something in a later chapter that I cover in an early chapter, I either define it again or refer you to the chapter with the information you need.

Conventions Used in This Book

To help you navigate this text as easily as possible, I use the following conventions:

- ✔ Whenever I introduce a new term, it appears in *italic*. You can rest assured that I provide a definition or explanation nearby.

- ✔ If I want to share some interesting information that isn't crucial to your understanding of the topic at hand, I place it in a *sidebar*, a gray box that's set apart from the rest of the text.

- ✔ All website addresses appear in `monofont` so they're easy to pick out if you need to go back and find them.

Keep in mind that when this book was printed, some web addresses may have needed to break across two lines of text. If this happens, rest assured that I haven't put in any extra characters (such as hyphens) to indicate the break. So when using one of these web addresses, just type in exactly what you see in this book, pretending as though the line break doesn't exist.

Also, here's an important convention to know about before you start reading: I rarely get precise when referring to the numbers of the *Titanic*'s passengers, survivors, and victims. Instead, I let you know that

- ✔ More than 2,200 people (passengers and crew) were aboard the ship.

- ✔ More than 700 of them survived the ordeal.

- ✔ More than 1,500 of them perished.

Why the generalities? Various sources publish conflicting numbers, and I don't pretend to know which source is correct. The original documents listing passengers and crew members had omissions, inconsistencies, and other errors, which makes it impossible to know with certainty how many people may have perished. Even the number of survivors varies slightly (from 701 to 713, depending on the source). So please don't think I'm being deliberately lax by using these "more than" phrases. I'm simply trying to be aware of and acknowledge the potential inaccuracy of any of these statistics. The reality is that no one knows with certainty the real numbers when it comes to sussing out who lived and died on the *Titanic*.

What You're Not to Read

You may want to know everything possible about the *Titanic*. Or maybe only a handful of subjects interest you. Because I can't be sure what you want to know, I've arranged this book so you can see what to skip if you want only the basics. For instance, throughout this book, I include sidebars: gray boxes that give background information or subsidiary information, or present *Titanic* trivia. You don't have to read what's in the gray boxes if you don't want to. (But I guarantee you'll enjoy it if you do.)

Likewise, the text that appears beside Technical Stuff icons is somewhat technical info that you don't need to understand the topic at hand. You can skip these paragraphs if you want just the basics.

Foolish Assumptions

Pardon me, but I made a few foolish assumptions about you, the reader of this book:

- ✔ You've heard about the *Titanic* (maybe you saw the 1997 blockbuster movie), and you want to know more.
- ✔ You're curious to know the little details about the ship, such as how and why the *Titanic* sank, who sank along with her, and who was rescued.
- ✔ You'd like to know what it was like to be a passenger on the *Titanic* and what the accommodations and amenities on the ship were like.
- ✔ You'd like to hear from the people who survived and what their contemporaries had to say about the *Titanic*.

How This Book Is Organized

The Titanic For Dummies is organized into six parts, and each part focuses on a different aspect of the *Titanic* story. The following sections provide a run-down of the material.

Part 1: The Titanic: A Century of Legend

Part I explores why the *Titanic* has captured the public imagination over the years and how the ship came to be financed, built, and launched. It also describes the larger-than-life people who designed, sailed on, and crewed the ship, including those who survived the *Titanic* sinking. You find out what it was like to be a passenger on the *Titanic,* where and how passengers passed the time aboard the ship, and what food they ate.

Part II: Tragedy at Sea: The Titanic Sinks on Its Maiden Voyage

Part II first takes you on the *Titanic* for the initial four days of her maiden voyage. Then you find out what happened on the night and early morning of April 14–15, 1912, when the *Titanic* sank and those lucky enough to find a place on a lifeboat waited in the frigid waters of the North Atlantic to be rescued. I describe the rescue efforts and the search for survivors, and I provide firsthand accounts of the terrible night. Part II also offers some of the first newspaper accounts of the tragedy and presents findings from U.S. and UK governmental agency reports about the tragedy.

Part III: Exploring Enduring Titanic Mysteries

Part III investigates different theories as to what caused the *Titanic*'s demise. It examines details about what happened aboard the ship on the night and early morning of April 14–15 when the *Titanic* sank. It also describes an eerie 1898 novella, *The Wreck of the Titan,* that seems to prefigure the *Titanic*'s demise in the North Atlantic.

Part IV: The Quest to Recover the Titanic

Part IV describes many different schemes and expeditions to find, recover, or raise the *Titanic*. It starts with schemes proposed soon after the sinking and continues to Robert Ballard's and IFREMER's 1985 discovery of the wreckage. It describes present-day expeditions to salvage artifacts and take photos and videos.

Part V: The Titanic in Popular Culture

Part V examines artifacts that were salvaged from the *Titanic* and explores the question of whether salvaging is ethical. It also looks at popular movies about the *Titanic,* including *Saved from the Titanic,* the first movie made after the sinking (just 29 days after!), and James Cameron's 1997 movie masterpiece.

Part VI: The Part of Tens

No *For Dummies* book is complete without a Part of Tens — a part of short chapters that offer top-ten lists. In this part, you can read about the ten most interesting *Titanic* artifacts, discover ten little-known facts about the ship, and get the names of ten worthwhile *Titanic* documentaries.

And don't forget the appendix at the back of this book. It offers a *Titanic* time-line in case you want to consider the life of the *Titanic* in chronological order.

Icons Used in This Book

To help you get the most out of this book, I've placed icons next to different types of information. They help you find what you're looking for fast. Here's what the icons mean:

You'd be surprised by how many controversies surround the *Titanic.* Should the wreckage site be left alone or explored for artifacts? Did Captain Smith push the *Titanic* too fast across the Atlantic? Where I describe a controversy, you see this icon.

When you see this icon, you know you're reading a piece of information that's especially important. I place this icon in the margin to mark explanations that can improve your understanding of the *Titanic*.

When you see this icon, you know the info next to it describes technical stuff that isn't crucial to your basic understanding of the *Titanic* story. You can skip this material if you're in a hurry or just want the basics.

Where to Go from Here

I wrote this book with the idea that you can start reading pretty much anywhere you want. If you want to read it from start to finish, more power to you. And if you want to dip into its pages here and there, that's fine, too. If you want to flip around, consider what topics interest you most and then have a look at the table of contents or index to find related information.

The *Titanic* is a big subject. You can focus on the ship itself, or you can read about her maiden voyage. Or maybe you're intrigued by all the larger-than-life personalities who sailed aboard the *Titanic* or helped build or finance her. You're invited to read about all these subjects and more at your own pace, starting where you please. Whatever you do, just get started!

Part I

The Titanic: A Century of Legend

The 5th Wave   By Rich Tennant

APRIL 16, 1912 – PATERSON, NJ

The Titanic what?

TITAN

SCAFFOLDS
"You're Safe with Us."

In this part . . .

This part tells the story of the *Titanic* before she set sail for her first and last voyage. It explains how and why the great ship was built and who — from royalty to rats — was on that first fateful voyage. It describes what the *Titanic* looked and felt like to the passengers; you get to climb the Grand Staircase and explore the luxurious promenades, the staterooms, and other areas of the ship. This part also gives my take on why the *Titanic* endures in people's imaginations and why the *Titanic* story is so compelling.

Chapter 1

Why the Titanic Endures

*E*veryone who is intrigued or moved by the story of the *Titanic* has his or her own reason for finding the *Titanic* so compelling. The *Titanic* sank on April 15, 1912. After a century, the fascination with the *Titanic* shows no sign of slowing down. James Cameron's 1997 film *Titanic* is the second-highest-grossing film in movie history. Hundreds of websites are devoted to the *Titanic*. Two dozen documentaries have been made about the ship and its fateful last voyage. As I write these words, countless events around the world are planned to commemorate the 2012 centennial anniversary of the sinking.

All this begs the question: Why does the *Titanic* endure? Why does the ship of dreams continue to intrigue so many people? This chapter takes a stab at answering that question.

Examining Why We Still Care

The *Titanic* maritime disaster continues to intrigue after 100 years because the ship was famous; because the story of the *Titanic*, with all its twists and turns, is irresistible; and because the *Titanic* captured the attention of the entire world when she sank in 1912. Sea travel was never the same after the *Titanic*. In this section, I begin to answer the question of why the *Titanic* endures.

Everyone knows about it

The *Titanic* disaster did not result in the largest loss of life at sea. That sad accolade goes to the sinking of the *Wilhelm Gustloff* during World War II, a tragedy that took more than 9,300 lives.

The *Titanic* also wasn't the largest peacetime maritime disaster. That was the passenger ferry the *Doña Paz;* almost 4,400 people died when the ship collided with an oil tanker off the coast of the Philippines in 1987.

The *Titanic* disaster took the lives of just over 1,500 people. Yet it is without a doubt the single most famous maritime disaster ever. It's famous not just because rich and famous people died or because it sank on its maiden voyage (although that factor certainly contributed to the immediate and ongoing fascination with the disaster). It's also famous because it opened eyes. It awakened people to the awesome power of nature and reminded them that no human-made edifice, no matter how strong or technologically advanced, is immune to the raw force of nature. It also made governments and the shipbuilding industry take a step back and ask, "Are we being as safe as we can?" And the answer, of course, was "No."

The story is irresistible

As a subject of study, the *Titanic* is irresistible. The combination of arrogance on the part of its owners and builders and the fact that the ship sank on her maiden voyage makes it so. However, social arrogance and a cocky certitude in the excellence of a ship were not unique to the *Titanic*'s builders, owners, and passengers. It seems that the single unique element — the most compelling aspect — of the story is that the *Titanic* was on her maiden voyage when she went down.

In thumbnail, the story seems farfetched, if not impossible: The biggest ship ever built sinks on its first voyage. If a writer pitched that idea to a movie studio, he or she might get laughed out of the room. *"Its first voyage? And it's the biggest and allegedly safest ship ever built? Who in the world is going to buy that?"*

But the story of the *Titanic* is true and, for myriad reasons, has become iconic. Editors and publishers used to say that the three most-written-about topics are Abraham Lincoln, Jesus Christ, and the *Titanic.* The same cannot be said about the *Wilhelm Gustloff* or the *Doña Paz,* even though those shipwrecks were much worse than the *Titanic* in terms of loss of life. Only the *Titanic* story has endured an entire century.

The world took notice

When the Mississippi River steamboat the SS *Sultana* sank on April 27, 1865, due to a boiler explosion and claimed 1,800 lives, newspaper attention at the time was . . . let's call it "spare." The Washington, D.C., *Daily National Republican* on April 28, 1865, gave the disaster two paragraphs on its front page. On May 5, 1865, the Burlington, Vermont, *Burlington Free Press* devoted less than 90 words to the explosion. Granted, these newspapers were preoccupied with other events, like Robert E. Lee's surrender, President Lincoln's assassination, and the hunt for John Wilkes Booth. Nonetheless, a maritime disaster simply did not warrant massive coverage, huge headlines, or widespread attention.

That changed with the loss of the *Titanic.* Newspapers trumpeted the collision, the sinking, and the aftermath with an intensity previously reserved for wars and the deaths of major figures on the world stage. Some examples:

> "*Titanic* Reported to Have Struck Iceberg," *Virginia Times-Dispatch,* April 15, 1912
>
> "1,302 Are Drowned or Missing," *Virginia News-Leader,* April 16, 1912
>
> "*Titanic* Disaster," *The London Times,* April 16, 1912
>
> "Over Fifteen Hundred Sank to Death With Giant White Star Steamer *Titanic*," Norfolk, Virginia *Virginian-Pilot,* April 16, 1912
>
> "Fifteen Hundred Lives Lost when *Titanic* Plunges Headlong into Depths of the Sea," *Los Angeles Times,* April 16, 1912
>
> "*Carpathia* Refuses to Give Any Details of *Titanic's* Loss and as Fruitless Hours Go By, Suspense Grows More Maddening," Richmond, Virginia *Times-Dispatch,* April 18, 1912

As I explore in Chapter 9, the demand for news about the *Titanic* was so great that newspapers sometimes reported rumors without verifying whether they were true, as in this classic New York *Evening Sun* headline:

> "ALL SAVED FROM TITANIC AFTER COLLISION"

The sinking of the *Titanic* was a seminal moment in world history. It provided a powerful reminder about man's place in the grand scheme of the natural world: Nature always wins.

The disaster changed sea travel

The sinking of the *Titanic* changed travel at sea for all time. Here are some of the changes that ensued:

- ✔ **Enough lifeboats were carried onboard.** As Chapters 6 and 11 explain, the *Titanic* didn't carry enough lifeboats for her passengers and crew. After the *Titanic,* ships were required to provide one seat for every passenger and crew member on a lifeboat.

- ✔ **The International Ice Patrol (IIP) was established.** This organization monitors icebergs in the Arctic and North Atlantic oceans and broadcasts information about their locations. Not a single accident involving a ship and an iceberg has occurred since the establishment of the IIP. (See the sidebar in Chapter 10 for more information.)

- ✔ **Ship designs changed.** Ships' hulls were made stronger to prevent them from being breached and flooded by objects such as icebergs.

Maybe these reforms and changes to regulations would have been made if the *Titanic* didn't strike the iceberg and sink on April 15, 1912. But it may well have taken the sinking of the biggest ship ever built on its maiden voyage to cause the "sea change" in ship design and ocean travel the world needed.

Tempting Fate with the Word "Unsinkable"

The White Star Line, the company that owned the *Titanic,* never used the word *unsinkable* to describe its biggest ship. The company did, however, put out a brochure about the *Titanic* and her sister ship the *Olympic* that read "these two wonderful vessels are *designed to be unsinkable*" (my emphasis added).

The word *unsinkable* pertaining to the *Titanic* was first used in an article in a 1911 edition of *Shipbuilder* magazine. (The magazine called the *Titanic* "practically unsinkable.")

Whether the White Star Line really thought its ship was unsinkable or gave any thought to the difference between "unsinkable" and "designed to be unsinkable," newspapers soon took up the "unsinkable" refrain. The "unsinkable" tag got stuck to the *Titanic,* and after the ship sank, the White Star Line was accused of "tempting fate" by claiming its ship could not sink.

I submit that a company's actions can't act as a challenge to the forces of nature and that nature isn't in the business of punishing humans for arrogance or tempting fate. It's hard for me to believe that the *Titanic*'s designers and builders thought, "We'll build the biggest ship ever; we'll define her as unsinkable; and we won't put enough lifeboats on the ship because icebergs, storms, and the Atlantic wouldn't dare mess with us!"

Sea superstitions

Maybe the notion that the builders of the *Titanic* "tempted fate" is just part of the long tradition of sea superstitions. Here are some my favorite sea superstitions:

✔ Bananas and women onboard are bad luck unless you put a figure of a naked lady at the bow. (There were hundreds of women — and bananas — aboard the *Titanic.*)

✔ Setting sail on a Friday is bad luck and will doom the voyage. (The *Titanic* avoided this curse by sailing on a Wednesday.)

✔ Black suitcases and people with red hair are bad luck for seamen. (There were certainly both red-haired people and black satchels aboard the *Titanic.*)

✔ Stepping onto a boat with your left foot is bad luck. (How many passengers on the *Titanic* stepped aboard with their left foot and doomed the ship?)

✔ Priests onboard a ship are bad luck. (Fathers Thomas Byles and Joseph Peruschitz were on the *Titanic* and said Mass every day. Uh oh!)

✔ Cutting hair or fingernails at sea is very bad and will bring bad luck. (The *Titanic* had a barbershop and beauty salon where, of course, hair was cut and nails were clipped.)

But this idea that the White Star Line and the *Titanic* builders tempted fate when they built their ship persists. It's one of the reasons that the *Titanic* story is so compelling. People who search for a moral in the tragic events sometimes find one in the "tempting fate" angle. For these people, the *Titanic* was a modern-day Tower of Babel. It was built so big that it challenged the authority of God. It was punished accordingly with an iceberg.

Considering Social Arrogance and Class Structure

As I detail in Chapter 3, the era of the *Titanic* saw a very strict caste structure that was accepted willingly by all involved, from the poorest emigrating steerage passenger to the wealthiest of the wealthy in the first-class staterooms. In the pre–income tax time of the *Titanic*, the wealthy were rich beyond imagination. The government made money on tariffs, property taxes, and other forms of taxation, but private income was not taxed until 1913, a year after the *Titanic* sank.

One intriguing side story of the *Titanic* is the picture it paints of the differences among the social classes in 1912. The wealthy on the *Titanic* were rolling in it (dough, that is). They had an attitude of entitled superiority that everyone accepted, including newspaper reporters. After the *Titanic* sank, newspapers were full of stories about the stoic heroism of the upper classes. Newspaper reporters often painted a picture of the wealthy sacrificing themselves to save others, whether or not everyone would agree with such a depiction. The wealthy were ostensibly not only materially rich, but also morally and ethically rich — this is what would today be called a *meme* (an idea passed from one to another via media and/or the Internet). Oftentimes, memes are misleading, inaccurate, or exaggerated.

However, it is often too easy to assign motive and define attitude in hindsight. We are quick to define the über-wealthy of the *Titanic* era as "arrogant," yet were they? I think a more accurate description of the cultural sensibility of the rich was that they carried a sense of entitlement with them, and such entitlement was accepted by people of all strata of society.

An interesting aspect of the "rich dying on the *Titanic*" story is just how many of the wealthy died, in one place, at the same time. Think of it like this: How extraordinary would it be if the ten richest people in America were all on the same plane and that specific plane crashed with few survivors? That is how amazing it was to have so many of the wealthy on the *Titanic* and to lose so many of them in one accident.

Coming to America: The Immigrant Story

Sometimes in the haste to dwell on the luxury and opulence of the *Titanic,* the third-class passengers in steerage get lost or forgotten. These passengers, who died in far greater numbers than the first- and second-class passengers on the upper decks, were part of the great migration from Europe to America that occurred at the turn of the twentieth century. They pegged their hopes and dreams on getting to the United States, the Promised Land.

The immigrants wanted to participate in the American dream, a term coined by writer and historian James Truslow Adams in his 1931 book *The Epic of America.* He wrote:

> It is not a dream of motor cars and high wages merely, but a dream of social order in which each man and each woman shall be able to attain to the fullest stature of which they are innately capable, and be recognized by others for what they are, regardless of the fortuitous circumstances of birth or position.

The idea of the American dream was alive and well among the hopeful emigrating steerage passengers. Leaving their homelands with essentially everything they owned and the clothes on their back was the biggest decision of their lives. Many scrimped, saved, and borrowed to buy their third-class tickets on the *Titanic.* (As I note in Chapter 4, a third-class ticket cost $15–$40, the equivalent of $350–$900 today.)

Immigrants in third class included about 113 Swedes, 120 Irish, 59 Finns, 27 Russians, 81 Syrians, and 8 Chinese. These immigrants to the United States carried all their worldly possessions with them — and managed to cram these possessions into their narrow third-class berths.

If the *Titanic* had arrived on schedule in New York on April 17, 1912, her immigrant third-class passengers, like immigrants before them, would have marveled at the sight of the Statue of Liberty. They would have been taken to New York Harbor's immigrant inspection station on Ellis Island. If they were fortunate, they would have been admitted to the United States and become Americans.

The *Titanic* story is not just the story of the ship of dreams sinking to the bottom of the North Atlantic. It is also part of an older and ongoing story: the epic journey of people coming to the United States to live the American dream.

Discovering the Titanic Wreck in 1985

"Wreckage." That was the word first spoken when Dr. Robert Ballard and his team of researchers, along with IFREMER (the French Research Institute for Exploration of the Sea), found the wreck of the *Titanic* on September 1, 1985. One of the *Titanic*'s boilers, which had not been seen by human eyes for more than seven decades, was suddenly illuminated and visible on a TV screen. The *Titanic* could hide no more. (Chapter 15 describes the discovery in detail.)

Between 1985 and the present, more people have viewed the *Titanic* on TV at the bottom of the ocean than viewed her during her entire three-year existence, including the building stage and her maiden voyage.

A lot has happened with the wreck since its discovery in 1985. The question of who owns the wreck and the artifacts in the *Titanic* debris field has been a bone of contention, as well as a subject for myriad court cases and court rulings.

Ultimately, ownership of the wreck and the artifacts was awarded to the company RMS Titanic, Inc., the latest incarnation of a company originally formed by the late George Tulloch. This company is the *salvor-in-possession,* the company that the courts recognize as the owner. To remain the salvor-in possession, or *salvor* for short, RMS Titanic, Inc., must remain "in possession" of the wreck. In other words, it must visit the wreck on a regular basis to salvage artifacts or take photographs and video.

How much is too much?

About the wreck of the *Titanic*, the question arises, "How much is too much?" How many photographic visits to the wreck should be made? How many more artifacts should be salvaged? How much effort to raise the wreck should continue?

One school of thought says to leave the *Titanic* alone and treat the wreckage as a gravesite that should never be disturbed. The other school of thought is to get as much — of *everything* — as possible. Take as many pictures and videos as possible. Go down to visit the site as often as possible. Sell trips to the wreck as often as possible. Someday, this school of thought says, the ship will be disintegrated, and it will be too late to collect artifacts or visit.

There is no definitive answer as to which school of thought is correct. For now, RMS Titanic, Inc., is the salvor-in-possession, and anything it wants to do with the wreck is within its legal rights.

After all the ballyhooing by the anti-salvagers and anti-visitors, I would like to ask: How many people who are adamantly against salvaging and submarines visiting the *Titanic* visited *Titanic: The Artifact Exhibition* and watched the *Titanic* documentaries showing incredible footage of the wreck?

As of this writing, RMS Titanic, Inc.'s most recent expedition to the *Titanic* did not salvage any artifacts, but it did come back with something equally spectacular as a piece of the *Titanic* or a passenger's wallet. The expedition, cosponsored by RMS Titanic, Inc., and the Woods Hole Oceanographic Institution, took high-definition photos, video, and 3D video. The plan is to release the footage in a documentary. The imagery is stunning and unlike anything the world has seen before. Vivid, clear, brilliantly lighted photos and film footage show the *Titanic* in all its salvaged glory. For *Titanic* buffs, this new imagery is a thrill beyond measure. Long after her demise, the *Titanic* endures as an object of study and undersea fascination.

Watching Titanic, the Movie

Interest in the *Titanic* got a shot in the arm in 1997 when James Cameron released his *Titanic*, the movie. The movie was the talk of the town well before its release, primarily because of the rumored scope of, and problems with, the film. The movie became a legend before there was a movie to call a legend.

The rumors were legion: Cameron was going to build the *Titanic*. It was going to be the most expensive movie ever made. He was going to reproduce the sinking in ways no one had ever seen before. He was going to yell and scream and be the most difficult director anyone had ever worked with. And the best part about all this rattle and hum is that for the most part, it was true.

Aside from the prerelease talk, there was also ceaseless speculation as to whether anyone would want to go to the movie. After all, the sinking of the *Titanic* can be a depressing subject, and everybody knows exactly how the story ends. Would box-office and DVD sales be adequate for the movie to not only earn out, but also turn a profit?

The smart money, for the most part, was on Cameron. He was, after all, Mr. *Terminator,* Mr. *Aliens,* Mr. *True Lies,* and Mr. *Abyss.* He knew how to make blockbusters, and he knew how to make money. All his previous efforts had been great successes, so the thinking was that if anyone could build and sink the *Titanic* and make money while doing it, it was James Cameron.

But *Titanic* was different on two fronts: cost and production. Rebuild and sink the *Titanic,* no matter what it costs? Seriously? The answer was yes, and that was essentially James Cameron's mission statement. One of the few compromises he made was settling for building the ship at 90 percent of the original. (And knowing Cameron's penchant for accuracy, even that compromise probably annoyed the heck out of him.)

One of the elements that contributed to *Titanic*'s blockbuster success was repeat viewings. The typical repeat viewer rate for all successful movies is 5 percent. In other words, for every 100 people who see a hit movie, 5 will go back and see it again (and, of course, pay again). The repeat viewer rate for *Titanic* was an unprecedented 20 percent. Many believe the high repeat viewer rate was due to the romance angle of the screenplay and, for teenage girls, the presence of heartthrob Leonardo DiCaprio. Some experts claim that 30 to 40 percent of the movie's overall gross sales came from teenage girls. Some girls reported going back to see the movie a dozen or more times. Sony Classical did a study and determined that girls under the age of 14 were the dominant buyers of the film's soundtrack. (That "My Heart Will Go On" sure did the trick, didn't it?)

Perhaps the movie's biggest fan

In March 1998, the Associated Press reported that a 12-year-old Italian girl named Gloria from the town of Caselfranco Emilia had seen Cameron's blockbuster *Titanic* every day since it had opened in December 1997 and that she planned to continue attending the 9 o'clock feature in the only movie theater in town for as long as the movie played there. Gloria, who also had cats named Jack and Rose after the main characters in the film, was enamored with Leonardo DiCaprio's character of Jack Dawson. She told the Italian newspaper *La Repubblica* that "Jack is cuter than Leo, and it's for real, it's a true story. That's what makes it so beautiful."

The theater stopped charging Gloria for admission and even saved a special seat for her for each evening performance. Gloria's mother said she had no problem with her daughter's "hobby." "She's not doing anything bad," the mother said.

A Garry Trudeau *Doonesbury* cartoon from 1998 speaks to this phenomenon. A teenage girl comes home crying from what she said was her 500th screening of *Titanic*. She says to her friend, "Kim, can I ask you a personal question? Have you ever lost a lover to hypothermia?"

Ken Marschall, one of the world's most knowledgeable authorities on the *Titanic* and a painter of meticulously accurate artworks of the ship and the wreck, said he was spellbound as he walked the essentially identical re-creations of the *Titanic*'s staterooms, decks, and other locations on the ship. Cameron was adamant that the ship seen in his movie look exactly like the real *Titanic*. The carpeting was made by the company that made the carpeting for the *Titanic*. So were the lifeboat davits. All the furniture, dishware, cutlery, wall hangings, plumbing fixtures, and other elements of the ship were all reproduced precisely and with the White Star Line logo on them. Cameron's goal was to take viewers back in time and put them on the *Titanic*.

This philosophy and goal also applied to the sinking scene. Cameron reportedly was never satisfied with the sinking scenes in other *Titanic* movies (which I discuss in Chapter 17). Most sinking scenes utilize miniatures, and no matter how they're shot, the results tend to look a bit fake. In large part, the problem occurs because miniaturized ships on real-size water don't work visually, and there is no way to miniaturize water. Cameron solved that problem by, for the most part, not using real water for the "ship at sea" scenes. Much of the water in *Titanic* was digital, which allowed him to scale it down to whatever size looked the most realistic.

Movie budgets were never the same after *Titanic*. Producers and directors wanting more money for their movies could point to *Titanic* and ask, "See what can happen?"

Special effects have never been the same either. Books and entire issues of magazines have been devoted to analyzing and deconstructing the special effects in the movie.

"I'm the king of the world!"

In an iconic scene in James Cameron's movie *Titanic*, Jack Dawson (played by Leonardo DiCaprio) stands at the prow of the ship and shouts, "I'm the king of the world!" After the movie came out, cruise ships became concerned about the number of their passengers duplicating this stunt. Standing on the narrow prow of a cruise ship with the wind blowing, especially with your arms spread wide like Jack Dawson, while you shout "I'm the king of the word!" is dangerous.

In 1998, the Passenger Vessel Association issued what it called "a *Titanic* alert" to its cruise operators: "Keep your crew members alerted to this potential problem and perhaps even close or rope off the extreme bow access area of your vessel."

Chapter 2

Building the Ship of Dreams

In This Chapter

▶ Conceiving the biggest ship ever

▶ Constructing the *Titanic* and her sisters

▶ Looking inside *Titanic*

▶ Examining the *Olympic*

▶ Discovering the plans for the new *Titanic*

The construction of the *Titanic* and her sister ships the *Olympic* and the *Britannic* was, you may say, somewhat routine for a company like Harland and Wolff. By 1909, when it started building the *Titanic,* the company had been building enormous ocean liners for nearly a half-century.

What made the construction of the *Titanic,* the *Olympic,* and the *Britannic* unique in the annals of shipbuilding is that the three ships were intentionally designed to be the biggest and best ever built. Competition was a big factor in the decision to build the three ships. The Cunard Line's *Lusitania* and *Mauretania* were hogging a lot of the transatlantic passenger business. But from the beginning, the focus of the White Star Line (the *Titanic*'s owner) and Harland and Wolff (the *Titanic*'s builder) was always excellence. The idea was to design and build a ship beyond anything ever seen before.

This chapter investigates how the *Titanic* and her sister ships were financed and built. It looks at key milestones in the building and launching of the *Titanic,* explores the *Olympic,* and examines whether a second *Titanic* can ever be built.

Deciding to Build the Titanic

In early 1907, J. Bruce Ismay, chairman and managing director of the White Star Line, and Lord William James Pirrie, chairman of Harland and Wolff, decided to build three new ships. These ships would be called the *Olympic,* the *Titanic,* and the *Britannic* (some say this ship's original name was the *Gigantic*). Ismay and Pirrie had a specific goal in mind: to build the biggest and most luxurious passenger ships that had ever graced the seas. Designing the ships began in June of that year.

Harland and Wolff was the premier shipbuilder of the time. Not only did the company build the bodies of the ships (something all shipbuilding companies did), but Harland and Wolff also built the engines, boilers, and other mechanical components. The shipbuilder was a one-stop shop for building steamships. The White Star Line chose Harland and Wolff to build the three ships for this reason. The company was the perfect match to the White Star Line's vision of building a high-quality ship because Harland and Wolff would control every aspect of the ships' construction. After all, every manufacturer knows that the more you do yourself, the more control you have over the final product and the more attention you can pay to quality.

Competing with the Cunard Line

The White Star Line had a commercial motive for building the *Titanic* and her sister ships: competition from the Cunard Line. Along with the White Star Line, the Cunard Line was a leading conductor of passengers between Europe and North America. At the time, the Cunard Line had commissioned the building of two ships that were going to be the epitome of the shipbuilding art: the *Lusitania* and the *Mauretania*. These two "superliners" were built with financial help from the British government. They were launched in 1906 (the *Mauretania*) and 1907 (the *Lusitania*).

The White Star Line had to counter with something bigger, better, and more luxurious than the Cunard Line's two prized liners. Ismay and Pirrie, rather than surrender to the Cunard Line's temporary dominance of the sea lanes, decided to raise the bet: They would build three ships that would outshine the Cunard Line's two.

Accommodating wealthy passengers

One of the most important features of the White Star Line's three new steamships would be unimaginable luxury and opulence. Nothing but the best would do for the *Olympic,* the *Titanic,* and the *Britannic.* The world was, after all, in the Gilded Age, and the wealthy were more than willing to live in the lap of luxury no matter the cost.

American multimillionaires were fortunate to be living in an era before income taxes — a time when they didn't pay a penny of income tax on their vast fortunes. How else would they have been able to afford a £870 ticket (approximately $100,000 in today's dollars) for a voyage on the *Titanic*?

The financial and social elite were the White Star Line's main clientele. The company ordered Thomas Andrews, its chief designer (and also William James Pirrie's nephew), to design ships that would make the wealthy feel like they were traveling the ocean in the finest hotel they could imagine. The *Titanic* offered the moneyed flawless personal service; pleasurable amenities; the best food and drink; and facilities like a swimming pool, an exercise room, and a library.

Making more room for steerage passengers

The *Titanic* was unique in the higher quality of the accommodations it provided for third-class, or steerage, passengers. The third-class cabins were nowhere near as nice as the second- or first-class cabins: The toilets were communal, and the cabins were in the lower decks, where the rocking of the ship was more likely to cause seasickness and where heat from the boilers was more noticeable. Still, the food in third class was good and plentiful. Andrews, the *Titanic*'s chief designer, also made sure that third-class passengers had open areas in which to lounge and read. For many of the immigrants who traveled in steerage, the living conditions on the *Titanic* were better than the conditions in the homes they left to come to America.

The *Titanic* was bigger than any other ship ever built. And to their credit, the designers and builders didn't devote all the extra square footage to the first- and second-class passengers. The space allocated to third-class passengers was bigger as well.

Lining up funding for the construction of the ship

After deciding on the opulence of the newest fleet of ocean liners, the White Star Line had to start thinking in terms of financing. At $7.5 million, the cost to build the *Titanic* was staggering. Who had that kind of money? The answer: Financier and banker John Pierpont Morgan and his International Mercantile Marine Company, which was the trust that purchased the White Star Line in 1902.

J. P. Morgan, the steel magnate who rescued the United States from the Panic of 1907, wanted to get into the passenger-ship business. Morgan's company had the capital and saw a huge profit potential in building the biggest ship ever to set sail. Because the ship would be able to compete with the Cunard Line's *Lusitania* and *Mauretania,* it would give the International Mercantile Marine Company a leg up in the competition for transatlantic travel.

A big part of the cost of building the *Titanic* was, of course, the payroll. To build the ship would require three years and more than 11,000 workers.

Building the Ships at Harland and Wolff

Harland and Wolff was formed in 1861 in Belfast (in what is now Northern Ireland). The company built its first ship for the White Star Line in 1870. Altogether, Harland and Wolff built about 70 ships for the White Star Line and more than 150 renowned ships in its history, including the *Titanic, Olympic, Britannic, Baltic, Celtic, Adriatic, Germanic, Majestic,* and *Doric.*

Thomas Andrews, a talented young naval architect and draughtsman, supervised the drawing of the plans for the trio of sister ships: the *Olympic,* the *Titanic,* and the *Britannic.* Andrews did a five-year apprenticeship in the drawing office of Harland and Wolff before becoming manager of construction at the age of 28. The unanimous consensus was that Andrews was well-liked and was superb at his job. Andrews, who worked on the design of the *Titanic* with Pirrie and with Alexander Carlisle, knew every inch of the ship and, until the night he died, was constantly looking for ways to make improvements.

Andrews was aboard the *Titanic* as it sank and decided to go down with "his" ship. He was a Gilded Age scientist and a gentleman who accepted full responsibility for everything he set his hand to. The most telling legacy of Andrews is probably this: He wanted 36 more lifeboats, a double hull, and watertight bulkheads that went all the way up to B deck on the *Titanic.* He was overruled, but these safety measures probably would have saved the ship. And the additional lifeboats would surely have saved more lives.

Harland and Wolff hired an additional 5,300 workers to build the trio of ships, bringing its entire workforce to 11,300 employees. Because the three ships were so big, the company had to do the following:

- Tear down the three massive gantries it had used to build steamships in Belfast for decades and convert them into two even larger gantries so that the ships' three wide hulls would fit. A *gantry* is the large scaffolding-like frame that encloses a ship when it's being built or serviced; see Figure 2-1, which shows the *Titanic* under construction.
- Build newer, larger slipways for each ship. A *slipway,* or *slip,* is the shore ramp on which a ship is moved to and from the water.

Shipbuilder magazine and *Engineering News* followed the ships' progress. Even before she launched, the *Titanic* was an object of interest to people around the world. The early news coverage of the *Titanic* may have been the fountainhead of the *Titanic* obsession that rages today.

Dracula author visits the construction site

In 1907, none other than Bram Stoker, author of the 1897 Gothic horror novel *Dracula,* visited the Belfast site where the *Olympic* and the *Titanic* were being built. He wanted to see for himself the two massive ships that were in progress.

Stoker described the Harland and Wolff shipyard as "the biggest and finest and best established" in the world. He raved that "there is omnipresent evidence of genius and forethought; of experience and skill; of organization complete and triumphant."

He was also impressed by the speed with which the workers got paid. According to Stoker, Harland and Wolff paid all employees their wages of $10 a week every Friday afternoon — and the entire payout took only ten minutes.

Figure 2-1: The *Titanic* in a dry dock at the Harland and Wolff shipyard in Belfast.

© F J Mortimer/Getty Images

In a January 12, 1911, article, *Engineering News* complained about the size of the *Titanic*. In the article "The *Olympic* and *Titanic* Near Completion," the publication examined the problem of piers being too short for the White

Star Line's leviathans. According to the article, the hulls of the ships were 882½ feet long, and the newest dock in New York was 100 feet too short. The dock's length would be dangerous to passing ships because it meant that the ocean liners would jut out from the dock 100 feet. Under no circumstances, the editors of *Engineering News* felt, should the "overburdened taxpayers of New York City" foot the bill to lengthen the piers just because a steamship company built enormous ships.

The *Olympic* was launched from the Harland and Wolff shipyards on October 20, 1910; the *Titanic* was launched on May 31, 1911. The *Britannic* was launched February 26, 1914.

Taking a Titanic Tour

With her black hull, gracefully tilted funnels, and multiple decks and promenades, the *Titanic* was a vision to behold. She was elegant, yet utterly and undeniably powerful.

Many of today's cruise ships, designed to hold as many passengers as possible and provide their passengers with movie theaters, casinos, and restaurants, are described as "boxy" and "unattractive." The *Titanic*'s lines were quite the opposite: as you can see in Figure 2-2, the ship, even in port, looked sleek and beautiful.

Harland and Wolff today

The invention of the jet airplane in the 1930s hurt Harland and Wolff. These new jet airplanes could carry passengers between Europe and America in a matter of hours instead of days. As a result, the demand for giant steamships, Harland and Wolff's specialty, fell significantly in the mid-twentieth century. Even with help from the British government, Harland and Wolff knew it had to diversify in order to survive.

To create more business for itself, the company branched out into oil tankers and bridges, marine engineering, offshore construction, and ship repair and conversion work. It built close to a dozen U.S. aircraft carriers and a dozen oil tankers. Diversifying has kept the company fiscally healthy. In fact, Harland and Wolff, now called Harland and Wolff Heavy Industries, Ltd., is active today and is reportedly involved in the plan to construct a modernized version of the *Titanic* called the SS *Titan*. (See the section "Building a New Titanic" later in this chapter for more details on the plan to build the SS *Titan*.)

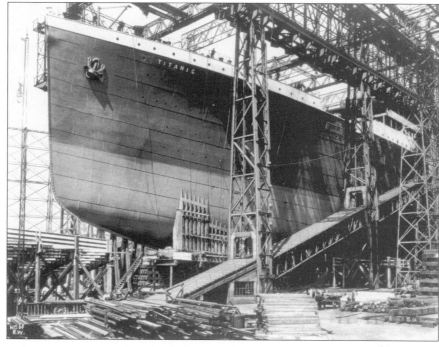

Figure 2-2:
The *Titanic* under construction in a photograph taken June 10, 1911.

Table 2-1 takes you on a tour of the *Titanic*'s ten decks, starting from the topmost and going to the bottommost deck. (For a description of the rooms mentioned in this table, visit Chapter 4.)

Table 2-1	*Titanic*'s Ten Decks	
Deck	*Description*	*Rooms*
Boat	The lifeboats were stored here. The entrance to first class via the Grand Staircase was also located on this deck.	Wheelhouse, captain's quarters
Promenade (A)	First-class passengers used this deck.	Reading and Writing, Lounge, a first-class smoking room, Verandah Café, Palm Courts
Bridge (B)	First-, second-, and third-class passengers had the use of this deck. The third-class promenade was located here on a poop deck.	À la Carte Restaurant, Café Parisien, a second-class smoking room

(continued)

Table 2-1 *(continued)*

Deck	Description	Rooms
Shelter (C)	This deck held 148 first-class staterooms, the purser's office, the surgery office, and the barbershop. The foot of the Grand Staircase was located here.	Crew's mess, the library (for second-class passengers), a third-class smoking room
Saloon (D)	This was the largest deck, with first- and second-class cabins, kitchen galleys, and an open space for third-class passengers.	First-class reception room, first-class dining saloon, second-class dining saloon
Upper (E)	This deck ran the entire length of the ship. It had cabins for second- and third-class passengers; cabins for the crew; and "Scotland Road," a corridor that stretched the length of the ship.	
Middle (F)	This deck had most of the third-class accommodations, with some second-class passengers also assigned to cabins here. The swimming pool and Turkish baths were for first-class passengers.	Third-class dining saloons, swimming pool, Turkish baths
Lower (G)	This deck had additional third-class cabins and facilities for storing food.	Squash court, post office
Orlop	This deck was basically a cargo hold. It had chutes for shoveling coal into the Tank Top deck below it.	
Tank Top	This deck comprised the inner lining of the bottom of the ship.	

The *Titanic* was built with 16 watertight compartments. They were labeled from A to P, ran from the bow to the stern, and were separated by 15 *bulkheads:* dividing walls between the chambers. The bulkheads all reached as high as E deck, and eight of them — A, B, K, L, M, N, O, and P — climbed as high as D deck. Why didn't they go all the way up to beneath A deck, which would make each compartment *truly* watertight? That would have been inconvenient and would have required taking up space in the passenger decks, as well as limiting easy crew access to any deck in the ship. A dozen of the bulkheads had watertight doors that could be closed locally or from the bridge.

As I explain in Chapter 6, the watertight compartments were key to the ship's sinking. As the *Titanic* went down by the head, the first four watertight compartments quickly filled up, and water spilled over into subsequent compartments. The *Titanic* could float with the first four compartments flooded. But when water filled the fifth compartment and beyond, the ship was doomed.

Titanic Milestones: From Launch to Loading

In this section, I provide you with a look at the birth of the *Titanic,* from the laying of her first keel plate to her disembarkation from Southampton, England, on April 10, 1912.

 ✔ **March 31, 1909:** Harland and Wolff workers lay down the keel of the *Titanic* in Yard 401.

   Ships are constructed starting with the *keel,* the long beam that forms the spine of the ship and that runs from the bow to the stern; after the keel is laid, the beams, deck plates, and hull plates are fitted.

 ✔ **April 1910:** The *Titanic* is fully framed.

 ✔ **October 19, 1910:** The plating of the *Titanic* (accomplished by assembling 1-inch-thick sheets of steel) is complete. Hydraulic riveting is used to give the best-quality plating for the ship.

 ✔ **May 31, 1911 (12:13 p.m.):** *Titanic* is officially launched from Harland and Wolff Slip Number 3. The *Titanic*'s launch lasts 62 seconds and is witnessed by more than 100,000 people. Twenty-three tons of tallow, train oil, and soft soap are used to lubricate her slip and ease her entry into the water. Eighty tons of cable and three anchors on each side control her speed. Five tugs tow the *Titanic* to a deep-water berth for her *fitting out* (the phase when final construction of the ship, mostly of the interior, is completed).

 ✔ **January 1912:** Sixteen wooden lifeboats and four collapsible Englehardt boats are fitted on board.

 ✔ **March 31, 1912:** The outfitting of the *Titanic* is complete.

✔ **April 1, 1912:** Scheduled sea trials for the *Titanic* are postponed due to strong northwest winds.

✔ **April 2, 1912 (6 a.m.):** Five tugs tow the *Titanic* down Victoria Channel to Belfast Lough for sea trials. The trials include maneuvering the ship at different speeds, evaluating the performance of the helm, and performing an emergency stop. The *Titanic* travels less than a half mile at 20 knots before coming to an emergency stop.

✔ **April 2, 1912 (7 p.m.):** The *Titanic* returns to Belfast Lough. The Harland and Wolff observers disembark. The ship is awarded her passenger certificate.

✔ **April 2, 1912 (8 p.m.):** The *Titanic* departs Belfast under the command of Captain Edward J. Smith and proceeds to Southampton, England. (Captain Smith, known as the "millionaire's captain," has logged about 2 million miles aboard White Star Line ships.)

✔ **April 3, 1912:** The *Titanic* arrives at Southampton and docks at Berth 44.

✔ **April 4, 1912:** Workers begin preparing to load the *Titanic* with cargo and supplies for her maiden voyage, which is scheduled for six days hence.

✔ **Friday, April 5, 1912:** The loading and preparations for receiving of passengers continue. Photographs of the *Titanic* in her berth are taken, and hundreds come to the docks to see her. The public isn't allowed on board.

✔ **April 6, 1912:** A British coal strike is settled. The shortage of coal had made it necessary for the *Titanic* to load 4,427 tons of coal from the *Olympic* and five other International Mercantile Marine steamships docked at Southampton.

✔ **April 6, 1912:** The majority of the *Titanic*'s crew arrives at the docks. Most crew members are drawn from the British Seafarer's Union and the National Sailors' and Firemen's Union.

✔ **April 7, 1912 (Easter):** No work is performed on the *Titanic*.

✔ **April 8, 1912:** Foodstuffs are loaded onto the *Titanic*. The ship's chief designer, Thomas Andrews, oversees all activity and remains onboard until 6:30 p.m., after which he returns to his office.

✔ **April 9, 1912:** The *Titanic* passes its final day in Southampton. One of the few photographs of Captain Smith on the bridge of the *Titanic* is taken by a London photographer. All the officers spend the night on board and keep regular watches.

✔ **April 10, 1912 (11:45 a.m.):** The *Titanic*'s mighty triple-toned steam whistle blows three times. Twenty minutes later, the great vessel casts off and is towed from the Southampton dock by six tugboats.

Taking a Look at the Olympic, the Titanic's Sister Ship

The *Titanic* and the *Olympic* (along with the *Britannic*) were referred to as "sister ships" and were almost identical in design, outfitting, size, and other elements. Here are two major initial differences between the two ships:

- The Promenade (A) deck on the *Olympic* was wide open; on the *Titanic* it was enclosed.

- The windows on the Promenade deck on the *Olympic* were irregularly spaced; on the *Titanic,* they were evenly spaced.

Other minor differences existed between the ships, but most were internal and not visible to the casual observer. The *Olympic* — known as "Old Reliable" — launched eight months before the *Titanic.* Andrews, who designed the sister ships, traveled on the *Olympic* to determine what changes needed to be made before the *Titanic* set sail on her own maiden voyage.

Given the ships' similarities, you may wonder what happened to the *Olympic* after the *Titanic* sank. You've come to the right place. The following sections show you how the White Star Line dealt with the *Olympic* in the years after the sinking.

Refitting the Olympic

Six months after the *Titanic* sank, the September 25, 1912, *Chicago Examiner* carried a story titled "*Olympic* To Be Rebuilt." It read, "The White Star Line announces definitely that the steamer *Olympic,* sister of the *Titanic,* will come to Belfast from Southampton for renovation. She will be made identical with the new ship *Britannic,* now building. The *Olympic* is due at Southampton October 5."

The story was true. In October 1912, the White Star Line "benched" the *Olympic.* The company had no choice. The flaws in the *Titanic*'s design that caused its sinking were known worldwide. The White Star Line couldn't continue to sail the *Olympic* without refitting her — and making sure that the world knew she had been refitted. The changes and improvements made to the *Olympic* specifically addressed what went wrong with the *Titanic.*

The White Star Line refitted the *Olympic* in the following ways to make her a safer ship that was less likely to suffer the terrible tragedy that her sister ship suffered:

- ✔ Enlarged the lifeboat davits to accommodate more lifeboats, ensuring that every passenger would have a seat if the ship were abandoned.

- ✔ Installed 64 additional lifeboats. They were placed in 32 locations (two high) along the Boat deck.

- ✔ Added a new watertight skin to the boiler and engine rooms.

- ✔ Extended some of the most vulnerable watertight bulkheads up to B deck, creating *true* watertight compartments.

- ✔ Added extra plating and riveting to the hull to make it stronger.

Retiring the Olympic

The *Titanic* sailed for a few days. The *Britannic* sailed for three years, was commissioned as a hospital ship in World War I, and then struck a mine and sank. The *Olympic,* however, served for 24 years, beginning in 1911. She was officially retired in February 1935.

How does a shipbuilder "retire" a ship? Does it get dry-docked and serve as a nautical museum of sorts, offering new generations a chance to see the great seagoing vessel inside and out and experience what it was like to walk its decks and gaze out the windows? Hardly.

In most cases, retired ships are dismembered. They're taken apart and sold for scrap. The *Olympic* was retired in Southampton, England, in 1935 after sitting abandoned for six months. The White Star Line sold her as scrap to John Jarvis for $500,000. He then sold her to Thomas Ward & Sons ship breakers. (Ship breakers do exactly what the name implies — they break apart and dismantle retired ships.) The *Olympic*'s superstructure was dismantled in England, but her hull was taken apart in Scotland. Her interior components were auctioned off in a nine-day auction consisting of almost 4,500 lots of goods.

Building a New Titanic

A *Titanic* replica existed for many years — it was called the *Olympic* (as I explain in the previous section). And now, a century after the sinking of the *Titanic,* talk of building and sailing another *Titanic* replica has garnered people's attention. The *Titanic* craze has become so widespread that people who wouldn't think it wise to sail on a replica of a doomed ship now embrace the idea of vicariously traveling back in time to the days when great ships like the *Titanic* sailed the seas.

Picturing Titanic's Grand Staircase

Countless *Titanic* buffs, historians, book and magazine readers, and movie and documentary watchers have seen the famous black-and-white photo of the *Titanic*'s Grand Staircase and marveled at its beauty. The glorious stately swoop of its beautiful stairs and the magnificent clock at its first landing have long captivated *Titanic* followers.

I don't mean to burst any bubbles, but this iconic photo doesn't show the *Titanic*'s Grand Staircase. In fact, no photos of that particular staircase exist. The famous photo (presented in Chapter 4 of this book) shows the *Olympic*'s Grand Staircase. The reason for this is that very few actual photos of *Titanic*'s interior were taken, either by the White Star Line or by passengers. After the sinking, media and White Star had to make do with photos of the *Olympic*. Reportedly, the two Grand Staircases were identical.

However, an exact replica of the *Titanic* can't actually be built today because what was state-of-the-art in 1912 is now hopelessly obsolete. Regulatory laws have changed dramatically as well. Fulfilling today's environmental and regulatory requirements would make changes to the ship that would render it completely different from the original *Titanic*. If an exact duplicate of the *Titanic* from stem to stern were built, it would be completely illegal to board and sail.

But this fact hasn't stopped people from thinking about how to build a modernized version of the *Titanic*. And from this thinking has emerged a comprehensive plan to build a new *Titanic,* the SS *Titan.* This ship may be the ship that comes closest to duplicating the *Titanic* experience at sea.

Introducing the SS Titan

Joseph Ricker and the team behind the building of the SS *Titan* (including none other than builders Harland and Wolff) are seemingly doing it right. Of all the myriad proposals to build a new *Titanic,* most of which have been abandoned, it seems that Ricker's plan may have a decent chance of succeeding.

Since he was 5 years old, Ricker was fascinated by the *Titanic*. He also always wanted to help sick children after losing a close childhood friend to leukemia. Here's where the two passions came together: After seeing James Cameron's *Titanic* in 1998, he decided to form a company "which would bring *Titanic* into the 21st century through a newbuild named *Titan,* while the massive profit potential of such a project could fuel my desire to help many children worldwide with their various unfortunate issues."

On October 14, 2007, Ricker's 40th birthday, he woke up and asked himself, "What will I do for the rest of my life?" The answer was simple: the SS *Titan*. Ricker then filed incorporation papers with the State of Minnesota for The SS *Titan* Foundation. On October 27, 2008, the official website (`www.sstitan.org`) went live.

Getting Harland and Wolff onboard

At his request, Ricker received a proposal for the initial design for the *Titan* from Harland and Wolff Heavy Industries, Ltd., in early 2009. In April of that year, he pitched the idea of the *Titan* to none other than *Titanic* artist extraordinaire Ken Marschall, who agreed to work with Harland and Wolff and help with the design process.

Ricker believes that the typical traveler for the *Titan* "will be anyone who has an interest in the *Titanic,* the great ocean liners of the first 50 or so years of the 20th century, and your basic cruisers. The untapped market for those wanting to experience life at sea is seemingly unlimited, and we intend to capitalize on that growing market." Ricker says the overall reaction from the *Titanic* community has so far been overwhelmingly positive, with few detractors.

Ricker intends to retrace the *Titanic*'s sailing for the *Titan*'s first voyage across the Atlantic. You can read about this initial itinerary, along with other project information, at the foundation's website.

Chapter 3

From Royalty to Rats: Who Sailed on the Titanic

*F*our groups of people sailed aboard *Titanic:* first-class passengers, second-class passengers, third-class passengers (who traveled in steerage), and crew members.

Although all of them were aboard the same ship, they lived quite differently. From where they slept to what they ate to what parts of the ship they were allowed to visit, a distinct sociological and cultural line divided the passengers and crew of the *Titanic.* As has often been said, in America you become notable for what you achieve. In Great Britain, especially at the beginning of the twentieth century, you were notable for your family lineage. This social paradigm was obvious, and it was enforced, even on transatlantic voyages.

This chapter provides brief biographies of many notables aboard the *Titanic,* from the high and mighty in first class, to the ones who are famous for surviving the ordeal, to the crew, to the orchestra leader and bell boys.

Riding in Steerage with the Third-Class Passengers

U.S. immigration laws played a role in the design of the *Titanic* and all other steamships with routes that took them to American harbors. For health reasons, immigrants had to be housed separately from other passengers; the separation prevented lice and communicable diseases from spreading to the upper decks from steerage.

The majority of the 700-plus steerage passengers were emigrants looking forward to a new life in the United States. Most were British, Irish, and Swedish, but some came from other nations, including Norway, Finland, Bulgaria, Syria, and Sweden.

Only 25 percent of the *Titanic*'s third-class passengers survived, and of that 25 percent, only a fraction were men. By contrast, about 97 percent of first-class women survived the sinking of the *Titanic*.

What does steerage mean?

The term *steerage* originally referred to the part of the ship below-decks where the steering apparatus was located. However, over time, the term came to refer to the part of a passenger ship below-decks where third-class passengers were housed.

Most Americans whose ancestors arrived in the United States at Ellis Island came as passengers in steerage. Traveling in steerage was the cheapest ticket you could get, but steerage accommodations could be brutal.

In 1911, the United States Immigration Commission, in a report to President William Howard Taft, had this to say about steerage:

> The open deck space reserved for steerage passengers is usually very limited, and situated in the worst part of the ship, subject to the most violent motion, to the dirt from the stacks and the odors from the hold and galleys . . . the only provisions for eating are frequently shelves or benches along the sides or in the passages of sleeping compartments. Dining rooms are rare and, if found, are often shared with berths installed along the walls. Toilets and washrooms are completely inadequate; saltwater only is available.

> The ventilation is almost always inadequate, and the air soon becomes foul. The unattended vomit of the seasick, the odors of not too clean bodies, the reek of food and the awful stench of the nearby toilet rooms make the atmosphere of the steerage such that it is a marvel that human flesh can endure it . . .

> Most immigrants lie in their berths for most of the voyage, in a stupor caused by the foul air. The food often repels them . . . It is almost impossible to keep personally clean. All of these conditions are naturally aggravated by the crowding.

Looking at steerage accommodations

On the *Titanic,* third-class passengers shared common bathrooms, ate in dining facilities with other third-class passengers, and slept in cabins four to a room. By the standards of the day, the accommodations on the *Titanic* for third-class passengers were excellent. In fact, the *Titanic* provided nicer living conditions than many of the steerage passengers were accustomed to at home. It was said that the *Titanic's* third-class accommodations resembled other steamships' second-class accommodations.

Third-class cabins on the *Titanic* had running water and electricity. Steerage passengers were provided with meals, which were a wonderful perk; most steamships that carried steerage passengers at the time required them to bring their own food. Passengers could clean up in their cabins in a washbasin. However, only two bathtubs served all 700-plus third-class men and women.

Bunk beds in third class had mattresses, pillows, and blankets, but no sheets or pillowcases. This fact wasn't a problem because most third-class passengers, who were leaving their native lands forever to start over in America, had all their belongings with them, including their sheets and pillowcases. For these passengers, anything that the ship provided was a bonus that made the voyage more pleasant.

Where did they eat?

Third-class passengers ate three meals a day in two common dining rooms called the *dining saloons.* These rooms were located on F Deck between the second and third funnels, exactly two decks below the first-class dining room.

Third-class passengers did not get individual tables; they ate on rows of tables lined up next to each other. Combined, the two third-class dining saloons could hold only around 475 people, so diners were served in two seatings. (See Chapter 4 for details on the food served on the *Titanic.*)

How did they pass the time?

The *Titanic* provided the General Room, where steerage passengers could sit, read, play cards, and otherwise pass the time. Steerage passengers weren't allowed into the areas of the ship boasting other entertainments, like the gymnasium or the pool, but they could have their own parties and dances. (The party scene in James Cameron's 1997 movie *Titanic* offers a perfect example of the spontaneous gatherings in third class, complete with fiddle players and plenty of beer.)

Interestingly, all the sitting surfaces in the General Room were made of wood. (Lice can't find a home on slatted benches the way they can in fabric and upholstered surfaces.)

Third-class men also had access to a smoking room complete with spittoons. (A *spittoon,* in case you ever need one, is a metal bowl into which tobacco chewers spit.)

Sharing steerage with rats

Yes, there were rats on the *Titanic,* even though it was a brand-new ship. Before the ship put to sea in April 1912, it sat at the dock for quite some time. Rats got onto the ship and into the *Titanic*'s food stores by way of the ship's mooring cables. Eventually, rat guards were placed on all mooring ropes; they prevented (to a point) rats from infesting the ship's cargo hold and third-class cabins.

Rats found a home primarily in the steerage section of the ship. All the third-class cabins were very low in the ship, so the rats migrated and congregated there. I can find no survivor reports of rats in the first- and second-class accommodations.

If you saw James Cameron's 1997 film *Titanic,* you saw dozens (perhaps hundreds) of rats running down the hall as water flooded a corridor. This scene was definitely realistic and possibly a tad understated. Considering the size of the *Titanic,* the amount of time it sat at dock, the sheer volume of its cargo, and its myriad spaces for rats to give birth and hide, the ship most certainly carried a very large rat population.

Meeting the Famous Onboard the Titanic

Intercontinental travel in 1912 was quite an event. The only way to get from America to Europe or Europe to America was by steamship, and it took a long time. Ships of the era served as temporary homes for the richest and most notable, as well as the meek and humble.

The famous flocked to the *Titanic.* With ocean travel the *only* way to get from continent to continent, the wealthy were drawn to the ship touted as the single most luxurious and greatest steamship ever built.

This section looks at the *Titanic* travelers whom today we'd describe as having household names, some of whom are shown in Figure 3-1.

72 THE SPHERE [APRIL 27, 1912

The Personal Side of the "Titanic" Disaster.

Lady Duff-Gordon (Madame Lucile)

Who was rescued and has given a vivid account of her experiences

Mr. B. Guggenheim

One of the American millionaires lost on the *Titanic*. He was the fifth of the seven sons of Meyer Guggenheim and a member of the famous family of bankers, miners, and smelters. Mr. Guggenheim was born in 1865

Mr. J. Wesley Woodward

The 'cellist of the *Titanic*'s band, which at first played merry tunes to keep up the passengers' courage and then finally played "Nearer, my God, to Thee" as the vessel sank with them. They played on until the inrush of water swept over them

Lady Rothes, Saved from the "Titanic"

She has been resting at the Ritz-Carlton Hotel in New York after landing from the *Carpathia*

Lady Duff-Gordon, who left in one of the last boats, said that panic had begun to seize some of the remaining passengers by the time her boat was lowered. "Everyone seemed to be rushing for that boat. A few men who crowded in were turned back at the point of Captain Smith's revolver, and several of them were felled before order was restored. I recall being pushed towards one of the boats and being helped in."

Captain Arthur Henry Rostron, R.N.R., commander of the *Carpathia*, is a son of the late James Rostron, Astley Bridge, Bolton, Lancs. He was educated at the Bolton High School and the Bolton Church Institute, and later went on board the Conway, naval training ship in the Mersey. He was taken into the service of the Cunard company and for a long time was chiefly employed in the Mediterranean. He is an officer in the Royal Naval Reserve and recently got his commission as commander in the R.N.R. He has decorations for long service and the King's medal for his safe conveyance of troops to South Africa during the South African War. Captain Rostron is comparatively young—forty-three years.

The Young Wireless Operator who Assisted Phillips, the Chief Operator, During the Crisis

Mr. Bride, like most of the operators on board ships, is quite young. He assisted Phillips very efficiently during the critical hours on the *Titanic*

Mr. Bruce Ismay, Chairman of the International Mercantile Marine

Who was saved from the *Titanic*

The Countess of Rothes showed great courage during the hours in the boats. An A.B. of the *Titanic* says: "There was a woman in my boat as was a woman. She was the Countess of Rothes. I was one of those who was ordered to man the boats, and my place was in No. 8 boat. There were thirty-five of us in that boat, mostly women, but some men along with them. I was in command, but I had to row and I wanted someone at the tiller. When I saw the way she was carrying herself and heard the quiet, determined way she spoke to the others I knew she was more of a man than any we had on board, and I put her in command. I put her at the tiller, and she was at the tiller when the *Carpathia* came along five hours later." Several ladies proved themselves to be efficient oarswomen.

Managing Director of Messrs. Harland and Wolff, the Builders of the "Titanic," Not Rescued

Mr. Andrews was another of the high officials intimately concerned with the fortunes of the *Titanic*. He was on board, but is not among the survivors

Mr. J. Wesley Woodward, 'cellist in the *Titanic* orchestra, was formerly in the Eastbourne municipal band and afterwards joined the Duke of Devonshire's Eastbourne orchestra. He was on board the *Olympic* when that steamer collided with H.M.S. *Hawke*. His portrait is given at the head of the page.

On the Bridge at the Moment of Contact

Mr. Murdock was the officer in charge at the moment the *Titanic* encountered the ice floe. He was not rescued, and the manner of his death is at present uncertain

Notable Men on the "Titanic"

Captain Archibald Butt, military aide to President Taft
Mr. Charles M. Hays, president of the Grand Trunk Pacific Railroad, with his family
Mr. Benjamin Guggenheim of the mining brotherhood
Mr. George Widener, American millionaire of Philadelphia, and his son, Harry (see p. 84)
Mr. F. D. Millet, the noted artist (see p. 79)
Mr. and Mrs. Isidor Straus
Mr. J. Thayer, vice-president of the Pennsylvania Railroad
Mr. Henry B. Harris, American theatrical manager
Colonel Washington Rœbling, the American engineer
Mr. Jacques Futre'le, novelist and journalist

The Captain who Rescued the 705 Survivors

Captain Arthur Henry Rostron, R.N.R., is commander of the *Carpathia*. He immediately steamed towards the *Titanic* and eventually rescued the 705 passengers

Figure 3-1: The *Titanic*'s famous faces and names.

Colonel John Jacob Astor IV

Colonel John Jacob Astor IV, a real estate millionaire, sailed on the *Titanic* with his pregnant 18-year-old wife (he was 48). Astor went down with the *Titanic* and ended up covered in soot from head to toe when the forward funnel fell and crushed him. His wife, Madeleine, survived.

Regarding the accumulation of wealth, Astor once remarked that "a man who has a million dollars is almost as well off as if he were wealthy." This remark — made more than a century ago, mind you! — paints a picture of how the rich perceived wealth (and perhaps still do).

Astor was eulogized as a hero for going down with the ship after seeing to the safety of his pregnant wife. He requested a place on the lifeboat with his wife, but from all accounts, when he was turned away, he calmly accepted his fate.

In Chapter 14, where you can see a picture of Astor, I tell a story about Astor's grief-stricken son, Vincent, who desperately wanted to raise the ship's wreckage so he could find his father's body. As the sidebar "Recovering Astor's body" in this chapter shows, the son's plan proved unnecessary.

Madeleine Astor

Madeleine Astor was Colonel Astor's wife. After her husband's death aboard the *Titanic,* Mrs. Astor inherited a $5 million trust fund and the use of her husband's residences on the condition that she never remarry. She eventually relinquished her inheritance so she could marry — and divorce — twice more. She died in Palm Beach, Florida, in 1940 at the age of 47. Some histories report that she committed suicide.

J. Bruce Ismay

J. Bruce Ismay was the chairman and managing director of the White Star Line. He was the person who sketched the first plans for the *Titanic* on a dinner napkin at Lord William James Pirrie's mansion in 1907 (see Chapter 2).

To this day, some people believe that Ismay behaved like a scoundrel on the night the *Titanic* sank. He left aboard one of the last collapsible lifeboats, shirking his responsibilities as a gentleman and White Star executive by leaving the ship when hundreds of passengers, many of them women and children, were still aboard. Ismay swore there were no more passengers on the deck when he was offered a place in a lifeboat.

Recovering Astor's body

The body of John Jacob Astor IV was recovered from the North Atlantic a week after the *Titanic* went down. It was taken aboard the *Mackay-Bennett,* a cable ship hired by the White Star Line to recover bodies from the ocean. The initials *J. J. A.* sewn into the shirt collar of the recovered corpse enabled rescuers to identify Astor's body. Following is the rescuers' description of the body:

NO. 124. - MALE. - ESTIMATED AGE, 50. - HAIR AND MUSTACHE, LIGHT.

CLOTHING - Blue serge suit; blue handkerchief with "A. V."; belt with gold buckle; brown boots with red rubber soles; brown flannel shirt; "J. J. A." on back of collar.

EFFECTS - Gold watch; cuff links; gold with diamond; diamond ring with three stones; £225 in English notes; $2440 in notes; £5 in gold; 7s. in silver; 5 ten franc pieces; gold pencil; pocketbook.

FIRST CLASS.

NAME - JOHN JACOB ASTOR.

In 1998, Ismay's great-nephew Michael Manser told *People* magazine that his uncle acted honorably on the *Titanic.* Regarding his great-uncle's depiction in the 1997 movie *Titanic,* where he is portrayed as something of a villain, Manser said the filmmakers portrayed his great-uncle that way because they had "to have a baddie in the film."

Providing another spin on Ismay's behavior on the *Titanic,* in 1934, survivor Edith (Rosenbaum) Russell wrote the following in her diary:

> I went out on the boat deck and stood in a direct line of light with Mr. Bruce Ismay. . . . He called out, "What are you doing in this boat? I thought all women had already left!" And [then] he cried out, "If there are any women around come over to this staircase at once!" I walked over to Mr. Ismay, who pushed me swiftly down the narrow iron staircase. . . . Bruce Ismay certainly saved my life, and I don't doubt that he saved many more.

See Chapter 10 for Ismay's statement in self-defense to the media.

Francis Davis Millet

Francis Davis Millet was a well-known American artist who perished on the *Titanic.* He was born in Massachusetts and attended Harvard University. Millet served as a war correspondent during the Russian-Turkish War. He had also worked for his surgeon father as a surgeon's assistant during the Civil War.

J. P. Morgan cancels

J. P. Morgan was an American transportation millionaire, the founder of U.S. Steel, and the owner of the White Star Line. In effect, because he owned the White Star Line, Morgan owned the *Titanic*. Morgan had his own first-class suite and promenade deck on the *Titanic*. He was booked on her maiden voyage but canceled at the last minute. Apparently, business affairs required him to stay in Europe a bit longer.

Conspiracy theorists pointed to Morgan's cancellation as evidence that the *Titanic* had been switched with the *Olympic* in order to collect insurance money on the *Titanic*'s damaged sister ship. The conspiracy theory goes something like this: The *Olympic*, it seems, had been badly damaged. Rather than repair it, the White Star Line, owner of the *Titanic* and the *Olympic*, switched one boat for the other, painted the name *Titanic* on the *Olympic* and vice versa, sank the *Olympic* on purpose in the North Atlantic, collected the insurance money on the sunken ship, and ended up with insurance profits from the sinking and a healthy new ship. Like most conspiracy theories, this one was long-winded, hard to explain, preposterous, and untrue.

Morgan was at his French chateau during the period following the *Titanic*'s sinking. When tracked down by a reporter and asked about the financial losses as a result of the loss of the great liner, he said, "Oh, someone pays, but there is no such thing as money losses in existence."

Millet reportedly helped women and children into lifeboats before perishing. His body was recovered and identified. He is buried in Massachusetts.

In 1998, a British painter named Douglas Edwards told *The Washington Post* that he believed he was the reincarnation of Millet, something he learned during a hypnotic past-life regression session in the mid-1980s. During this session, he told the *Post*, he kept repeating the phrase, "Black water. Don't have a chance." He also revealed that he had been afraid of water since he was a child and that even at an early age the name *Titanic* upset him. "I know it sounds very absurd, doesn't it?" he told the *Post*. "After all, you can't see the air, now can you? But it is there."

Millet's most well-known works are his large murals that adorn many governmental and municipal buildings throughout the United States. Many are still on display (some having been completely restored) in cities such as Cleveland, Ohio, and Baltimore, Maryland.

Isidor and Ida Strauss

Isidor Straus was a first-class passenger and the millionaire founder of the Macy's department store chain. Strauss remained on the *Titanic* and was last seen sitting with his wife on deck chairs waiting for the end to come.

Ida Strauss, Isidor's wife, chose to remain on the *Titanic* and die with her husband rather than get into a lifeboat without him. "We have been living together for many years," she reportedly said to her husband. "Where you go, I go."

Lucy Noël Martha Leslie, Countess of Rothes

The Countess of Rothes, Lucy Noël Martha Leslie, a first-class passenger, was placed in Lifeboat 8 and survived the sinking. (*Rothes* is a title in the peerage of Scotland.) Thomas Jones, seaman in charge of the lifeboat, said that the countess "had a lot to say, so I put her to steering the boat." As noted in *Encyclopedia Titanica,* Jones's comment was apparently not a sarcastic one. Jones was presumably impressed with the countess's leadership skills and put her in charge of steering the lifeboat for that reason.

Margaret Tobin (Molly) Brown

Margaret Tobin Brown (see Figure 3-2), known to the world as "the unsinkable Molly Brown" (even though no one called her Molly until after her death), was the wife of the Colorado mining kingpin J.J. Brown. Ms. Brown took charge of Lifeboat 6 and threatened to throw Quartermaster Robert Hichens overboard when he refused to allow her and the other women in Lifeboat 6 to row back to the site of the *Titanic*'s sinking to look for survivors in the water.

Brown's fearless courage soon became the stuff of legend, and it wasn't long before the sobriquet "unsinkable" became attached to her name. In 1932, 20 years after surviving the *Titanic,* she died in New York of a stroke at the age of 65.

Figure 3-2: Margaret Tobin Brown, who after her death came to be known as Molly.

© *Everett Collection*

After her death, she became the subject of a hit Broadway musical and film called — what else? — *The Unsinkable Molly Brown.* See Chapter 17 for info on the movie of the same name.

Major Archibald W. Butt

Major Archibald W. Butt was a military aide to President William Howard Taft. He was returning to the United States on the *Titanic* after an extended diplomatic and recuperative stay in Italy. Butt was last seen standing quietly on the *Titanic*'s deck at about 2 a.m. on April 15. He was remembered for dying bravely and stoically, like the soldier he was. In a letter sent to his sister-in-law just before the *Titanic* sailed, the major wrote, "If the old ship goes down, you'll find my affairs in shipshape condition."

Dorothy Gibson

Dorothy Gibson, a 22-year-old singer, model, and silent-movie star, survived the sinking of the *Titanic* and went on to star in a silent film called *Saved from the Titanic* (also known as *I Survived the Titanic*). Gibson's was the first movie made about the disaster. The film was released on May 14, 1912, just one month after her rescue. In the film, Gibson wore the same dress, sweater, gloves, and black pumps she had been wearing when she was pulled from Lifeboat 7, the first boat launched. Gibson was one of the first people saved.

Saved from the Titanic was filmed aboard the *Titanic*'s sister ship, the *Olympic.* The movie presented footage of the *Olympic* being towed into her berth in New York as footage of the *Titanic* being towed from her berth in Southampton.

Saved from the Titanic has been lost, and no copies have surfaced as of this writing. Gibson died of a heart attack in 1946 in Paris at the age of 56.

Colonel Archibald Gracie IV

Colonel Archibald Gracie IV, a first-class passenger, wrote a best-selling account of the sinking and his subsequent rescue called *The Truth About the Titanic.* Gracie's book, unfortunately, was published after his death. Gracie died in December 1912. (Gracie had earlier written a book of Civil War history called *The Truth About Chickamauga.*)

Gracie's *Titanic* book meticulously chronicles the launching and passenger contingents of every one of the *Titanic*'s lifeboats. Gracie was the second of the *Titanic*'s survivors to die. (The first was 3-year-old Eugenie Baclini, a Lebanese immigrant, who died in August 1912 from meningitis.)

The Unsinkable Molly Brown's Titanic insurance claim

A $20,000 necklace, 20 gowns, $300 worth of lingerie, and 14 hats? Molly Brown certainly traveled in style. After the disaster, she submitted an insurance claim totaling $27,887 for possessions that went down with the *Titanic*. Here is the itemized insurance claim she filed for payment for her lost property:

- Street Furs: $300
- Ermine Collarette: $75
- Ermine Opera Cape: $500
- Brussels Lace Gown: $375
- Persian Overdress: $175
- 6 Dinner Gowns ($75 each): $450
- Green Lace Gown: $175
- 1 Sealskin Jacket: $700
- 4 Gowns ($200 each): $800
- 1 Necklace: $20,000
- Odd Laces: $200
- 1 Pearl Brooch: $150
- 14 Hats: $225
- 6 Lace Shirtwaists: $75
- 6 Embroidered Waists, Lace: $140
- Silk Hosiery: $75
- Lingerie: $300
- Souvenirs (Egypt): $500
- 3 Crates Ancient Models for Denver Museum: $500
- 2 Japanese Kimonos: $50
- 1 Black Satin Gown: $150
- 1 Blue and White Serge Gown: $75
- 3 Satin Evening Gowns: $450
- 1 Irish Lace Gown: $150
- 3 Dozen Gloves: $50
- 1 Hat: $35
- 6 Shoes (10 Each): $60
- 4 Tailored Gowns and 2 Coats: $500
- 3 Shoes: $36
- 1 Evening Wrap: $150
- 4 Evening Slippers: $16
- Brown Velvet Gown: $200
- Brown Velvet Coat: $100
- 2 Black Gowns: $150

Benjamin Guggenheim

Benjamin Guggenheim, a wealthy industrialist and heir to the Guggenheim mining fortune, is remembered for saying as the *Titanic* sank into the icy Atlantic, "We're dressed in our best and are prepared to go down like gentlemen." (One can't help but wonder if the valet who accompanied him had anything to say about the decision to "go down.") Legend has it that Guggenheim and his valet smoked cigars and sipped brandy while awaiting their deaths.

Guggenheim is also supposed to have said, "I think there is grave doubt that the men will get off. I am willing to remain and play the man's game if there are not enough boats for more than the women and children. I won't die here like a beast. Tell my wife . . . I played the game out straight and to the end. No woman shall be left aboard this ship because Ben Guggenheim is a coward."

Getting to Know the Crew of the Ship of Dreams

Many members of the *Titanic*'s crew who survived became celebrities. Their appearances and testimonies at the UK and U.S. inquiries (see Chapter 10) were covered in the press. Many wrote books and gave speeches. Following is a look at some of the more notable crew members, both those who survived and those who didn't.

Edward J. Smith: Captain on the verge of retirement

Captain Edward J. Smith, the commander of the *Titanic,* was known as the "millionaire's captain" for his popularity with his wealthy transatlantic society passengers. Passengers would deliberately seek out ships he was helming so that they could travel with him. He had major charisma and inspired confidence in his passengers, some of whom were the wealthiest people in the world. It is believed that Captain Smith's Europe-to-America trip on the *Titanic*'s maiden voyage would have been his final voyage as a sea captain because he planned to retire after successfully docking the *Titanic* in New York.

In 1880, Smith joined the White Star Line; he received his first command, the *Republic,* seven years later. He served with distinction in the Boer War, transporting English troops twice to South Africa.

Smith went down with the *Titanic,* and questions still linger about his judgment and decisions during the ship's brief maiden voyage. The main question concerning Captain Smith is this: Why, after several iceberg warnings from other ships, did he steer full speed ahead into an ice field at night? (Turn to Chapter 6 for the full rundown of the wireless messages the *Titanic* received in the hours leading up to the collision.)

Smith left a wife and daughter. After his death, his wife, Eleanor, issued the following statement:

> To my poor fellow sufferers —
>
> My heart overflows with grief for you all and is laden with sorrow that you are weighed down with this terrible burden that has been thrust upon us. May God be with us and comfort us all.
>
> Yours in sympathy,
>
> Eleanor Smith

Captain Smith's body was never recovered, and differing accounts of his end became part of the *Titanic*'s legend. See Chapter 12 for a discussion of Captain Smith's last moments and final words.

Harold Godfrey Lowe

Harold Godfrey Lowe was the *Titanic*'s fifth officer. He is remembered for two dramatic acts as the *Titanic* foundered:

- ✔ Lowe fired his pistol to prevent men from crowding a lifeboat when women were still aboard the vessel (see Chapter 12).
- ✔ Lowe was the only lifeboat commander who went back to the site of the sinking to rescue passengers in the water. He was able to pull from the water four men, one of whom, William Hoyt, died in the lifeboat. (See the sidebar "Pulled from the sea too late.")

Pulled from the sea too late

William F. Hoyt was pulled from the sea into a lifeboat by Fifth Officer Harold Godfrey Lowe, who had gone back looking for people to save. Hoyt, a lace importer from New York, was a big man; it took quite an effort to pull him into the lifeboat.

Hoyt had been dragged under when the *Titanic* sank below the surface but was eventually released as the ship began to break up on its way toward the bottom. However, Hoyt sustained serious injuries when he was dragged under. He died as a result of internal injuries caused by the pressure he was subjected to. Said Fifth Officer Lowe, "After we got him in the boat we took his collar off so as to give him more chance to breathe, but unfortunately, he died. He was too far gone when we picked him up."

He is also remembered for two statements he made at the U.S. Senate Subcommittee *Titanic* Hearing (the American investigation into the disaster, which I detail in Chapter 10):

- ✔ Lowe told the senators that he had fired his pistol because two men had tried to jump into a lifeboat. About one of the men he remarked, "I do not know whether he was an Italian or what, but he was of the Latin races anyhow." He later apologized to the Italian government for this statement. (See the sidebar "Harold Lowe's apology to the Italian government.")

- ✔ When Senator William Alden Smith asked him what an iceberg was composed of, Lowe's somewhat impudent answer was "Ice, I suppose, sir."

Lowe's heroism did not serve him well after the *Titanic*. He was appointed third officer on the *Medic,* a minor position, and then served as a commander in the Royal Navy during World War I. Lowe then retired to his native Deganwy, Wales, although he did serve in a minor capacity during World War II. He died in May of 1944 at age 61.

Even though Lowe rarely spoke of his actions during the *Titanic* tragedy, his deeds were remembered. In his eulogy, he was honored as "a man who made up his mind what his duty was and did it regardless of personal consequences."

Harold Lowe's apology to the Italian government

For his false assertion that an Italian man had donned woman's clothes in order to be admitted on a lifeboat, Harold Lowe issued an apology, as follows:

This is to certify that I, Harold Godfrey Lowe . . . fifth officer of the late steamship *Titanic,* in my testimony at the Senate of the United States stated that I fired shots to prevent Italian immigrants from jumping into my lifeboats.

I do hereby cancel the word "Italian" and substitute the words "immigrants belonging to the Latin Races." In fact, I do not mean to infer that they were especially Italians, because I could only judge from their general appearance and complexion, and therefore I only meant to imply that they were of the types of the Latin races. In any case, I did not intend to cast any reflections on the Italian nation.

This is the real truth, and therefore I feel honored to give out this present statement.

H.G. Lowe

Fifth Officer late "Titanic."

Washington, D. C., *April 30, 1912*

Frederick Fleet

Frederick Fleet was the 24-year-old *Titanic* lookout who first spotted the fatal iceberg. He shouted, "Iceberg right ahead."

After his rescue, Fleet complained about not being given binoculars for the crow's nest. With the binoculars, he believed, he might have spied the iceberg sooner. (See Chapter 11 for more on the missing binoculars.)

Fleet continued sailing until 1936, when the Great Depression shut down much of the world's sea trade. He went to work in a Harland and Wolff shipyard until his retirement in 1955. He then sold newspapers ("just to while away the time") on a Southampton, England, street corner.

On January 10, 1965, Fleet committed suicide by hanging himself in his garden. I discuss the circumstances of his suicide in Chapter 7.

Fleet was buried in an unmarked grave in Southampton. Through the efforts of the *Titanic* community, Seaman Fredrick Fleet now has a headstone on his grave.

Charles H. Lightoller

Second Officer Charles H. Lightoller was the *Titanic*'s senior surviving officer. Lightoller directed the loading of the lifeboats on the port side. He was diligent about interpreting the "women and children first" rule of the sea to mean "women and children only," sending off lifeboats half full rather than allowing men to board. Many people believe that lives were lost unnecessarily because of his interpretation of this rule. (Truly, if you were a male aboard the *Titanic,* your fate could easily have rested upon your choice of walking to port or starboard when the time came to evacuate.)

Lightoller ultimately was sucked under when the *Titanic* sank. He was held against the grating of a giant funnel until a rush of expelled hot air threw him clear of the ship and saved his life. Lightoller hung onto a collapsible until he was rescued.

Lightoller wrote an autobiography, *Titanic and Other Ships,* in which he devoted six chapters to his *Titanic* ordeal.

"Lights," as he was sometimes called, defended J. Bruce Ismay, the chairman and managing director of the White Star Line, at the U.S. Senate Subcommittee *Titanic* Hearing that investigated the disaster (see Chapter 10). He was subsequently accused of whitewashing the actual events of that night. He later served as a commander with the British Royal Navy during World War I. After the war, Lightoller became a successful chicken farmer but returned to the sea in World War II when he used his private yacht, the *Sundowner,* to assist in the evacuation of Dunkirk.

Lightoller held Captain Smith in very high regard; he believed that Captain Stanley Lord of the *Californian* was greatly to blame for the loss of the lives that night (see Chapter 7). The U.S. Senate Subcommittee *Titanic* Hearing was, Lightoller believed, "nothing but a complete farce."

Lightoller died in December 1952. In his book, Lightoller wrote this passage about the moments shortly after the *Titanic* sank:

> To enter into a description of those heartrending, never-to-be-forgotten sounds would serve no useful purpose. I never allowed my thoughts to dwell on them, and there are some that would be alive and well to-day had they just determined to erase from their minds all memory of those ghastly moments, or at least until time had somewhat dimmed the memory of that awful tragedy.

Joseph Boxhall

Joseph Boxhall was the *Titanic*'s fourth officer and the crewman who calculated her position the night of the collision, wired her position to the *Carpathia,* and later testified about having seen a ship in the distance that did not respond to the *Titanic*'s requests for assistance.

From Boxhall's testimony, it was determined that he had seen the *Californian* and that his calculations fixing their relative positions had been correct. (See Chapter 7 for a discussion of the controversy regarding the delayed response from the *Californian* after the wreck.) At the U.S. Senate Subcommittee *Titanic* Hearing, he told Senator William Alden Smith, "When you take stars you always endeavor . . . to take a set of stars. You take two stars for latitude, and two for longitude, one star north and one star south, one star east and one star west. If you find a big difference between eastern and western stars, you know there is a mistake somewhere. But, as it happened, I think I worked out three stars for latitude and I think I worked out three stars for longitude [and] they all agreed."

Boxhall, who was 28 at the time of the sinking, ultimately attained a command position with the British Royal Navy but never achieved the rank of captain. He retired from maritime duty in 1940 at the age of 56. In 1958, when Boxhall was 74, he served as technical advisor on the film adaptation of Walter Lord's bestselling book about the disaster, *A Night to Remember.*

Boxhall died in 1967 at the age of 83. His ashes were scattered over the site of the *Titanic*'s sinking, near the location — 41°46'N, 50°14'W — that he was certain he had calculated correctly as the *Titanic*'s position on that terrible night.

Thomas Andrews

Thomas Andrews was the chief designer for Harland and Wolff and also the nephew of Lord William James Pirrie, Harland and Wolff's chairman. Andrews, perhaps more than any other man, was responsible for the construction of the *Titanic.*

Andrews was a tireless worker who often arrived at the shipyard at four in the morning to begin his workday. Andrews went along on the *Titanic*'s maiden voyage (in first-class cabin A36, on the port side between the first-class smoking room and the first-class lounge) to make a final inspection and note any changes necessary. It wasn't long after departing Southampton that Andrews decided to convert part of the A deck Reading and Writing Lounge into more first-class staterooms.

Andrews's secretary, quoted in *Titanic, Triumph and Tragedy,* by John P. Eaton and Charles A. Haas (W. W. Norton & Company), once wrote of her boss:

> He would put himself in their places such as racks, tables, chairs, berth ladders, [and] electric fans, saying that except he saw everything right he could not be satisfied. He was always busy, taking the owners around the ship, interviewing engineers, officials, managers, agents, sub-contractors, discussing with principals the plans of new ships, and superintending generally the work of completion.

On the eve of sailing day, Andrews wrote a note to his wife in which he told her, "The *Titanic* is now about complete and will I think do the old Firm credit tomorrow when we sail."

On Sunday evening, April 14, 1912, Andrews was so engrossed in studying the *Titanic*'s plans that he didn't notice the ship's collision with the iceberg. Andrews was subsequently summoned to the bridge and, after a short tour of the ship with Captain Smith, came to the conclusion that the *Titanic* was doomed and that she would sink within two hours at most.

In the time remaining before the ship foundered, Andrews worked diligently to load as many people into lifeboats as possible. He also moved through the ship, opening stateroom doors and instructing people to get into the boats. In *"Unsinkable": The Full Story of RMS Titanic,* by Daniel Allen Butler (Stackpole Books), Andrews is quoted as shouting, "Ladies, you must get in at once!" to one group of hesitant passengers. "There is not a minute to lose! You cannot pick and choose your boat. Don't hesitate. Get in, get in!"

But even with such stalwart and heroic behavior to his credit, there can be no doubt that Andrews was operating in a state of utterly devastating shock. The unthinkable had become his final reality.

Andrews was last seen by Steward John Stewart in the first-class smoking room adjacent to his cabin. He stood dazed with his arms crossed, staring at a painting called *Plymouth Harbor* that hung above a fireplace. His lifebelt lay on a card table. Reportedly, Stewart said to Andrews, "Aren't you even going to try for it, Mr. Andrews?" Andrews did not reply. It was the last anyone saw of Thomas Andrews, the designer of the *Titanic*. His body was never found.

Harold Bride

Harold Bride was a junior Marconi operator on the *Titanic* who made it into a lifeboat and survived. (The other Marconi operator, Jack Phillips, did not.) Bride told his story to *The New York Times* from the *Carpathia* after being rescued. See Chapter 8 for Harold Bride's account of the *Titanic* disaster and a picture of him being helped off the *Carpathia*.

Robert Hichens

Robert Hichens was the *Titanic*'s quartermaster and the man who was at the wheel when the *Titanic* collided with the iceberg. Hichens was the helmsman who physically carried out First Officer William Murdoch's order "Hard a-starboard" (which was in response to Frederick Fleet's warning "Iceberg right ahead"). Hearing the order, Hichens turned the *Titanic*'s wheel in an attempt to avoid a head-on collision with the iceberg. Hichens's action managed to turn the *Titanic* 22.5° (two compass points) to port but did not prevent the steamer from striking the iceberg.

Shortly thereafter, on Second Officer Lightoller's orders, Hichens took charge of Lifeboat 6 (on the port side), where he did not do himself proud. With Hichens in Lifeboat 6 was Canadian Major Arthur Peuchen. Hichens immediately began ordering him around in an attempt to confirm and assert his authority over the major. Peuchen then attempted to take charge, ordering Hichens to turn over the tiller and row, but Hichens refused. A few minutes later, Captain Smith, shouting through a megaphone, ordered Hichens to return for more passengers. Hichens, perhaps for the first time in his maritime career, disobeyed a direct order from his commanding officer.

"No, we are not going back to the boat," he told the Lifeboat 6 occupants. "It's our lives now, not theirs."

After the *Titanic* sank, the women in Lifeboat 6 (which was designed for 65 passengers and held only 28) pleaded with Hichens to go back and try to rescue people from the water. Hichens refused, warning them that their boat would be swarmed by desperate people in the frigid water and that they would all die if they went back. "There's no use going back," he coldly shouted at them, " 'cause there's only a lot of stiffs there." (At the U.S. Senate Subcommittee *Titanic* Hearing, Senator William Alden Smith said that Hichens was quoted as saying, "We are to look out for ourselves now, and pay no attention to those stiffs.")

One of the women in Lifeboat 6, however, was the "unsinkable" Molly Brown (as she would come to be known after her rescue). Brown was a force to be reckoned with. The indomitable Mrs. Brown grabbed the tiller out of Hichens' hand and ordered the women in the boat, many of whom were eager to find husbands and fathers among the men in the water, to start rowing. When Hichens stood up and made a move to grab the tiller from Brown, she warned him that she would, indeed, throw him overboard. Hichens backed down but started whining that they were doomed and would never survive. When Brown told him to shut up, he swore at her and was chastised by a stoker. This silenced Hichens. He made no further attempts to command his fellow lifeboat passengers.

After the disaster, the White Star Line gave Hichens the position of harbormaster at Cape Town, South Africa. Hichens reportedly told a British seaman that the White Star Line had paid him off and given him his new job in order to keep him quiet about certain events that took place on the *Titanic*'s bridge the night she sank. What these "events" were has never been disclosed or discovered.

Donald Lynch, in *Titanic: An Illustrated History* (Hyperion Books), wrote that "it is more likely that the White Star Line didn't know what to do with the man who had steered the *Titanic* into an iceberg. Sailors were notoriously superstitious, and Hichens, though innocent of any responsibility for the disaster, was probably unwelcome aboard other ships."

Wallace Hartley

Wallace Hartley was an accomplished violinist and the director of the *Titanic*'s eight-man orchestra. As the *Titanic* sank, his selfless courage and leadership inspired his fellow musicians to continue playing in an attempt to calm the panicked passengers. Hartley and his bandmates did not survive the sinking.

Hartley had been engaged to marry and had actually considered skipping the *Titanic* voyage. He ultimately opted to go in hopes of making contacts among the well-heeled passengers that might result in future work.

Forty thousand mourners attended Hartley's funeral on Saturday, May 18, 1912.

On Friday, May 24, 1912, a memorial concert in honor of the *Titanic* bandsmen was held at the Royal Albert Hall in London. The concert boasted the largest orchestra that had ever performed in the Albert Hall — more than 500 musicians. Selections performed included Chopin's "Funeral March"; the program concluded with the 10,000 members of the audience singing in unison "Nearer, My God To Thee," the hymn purported to be the last piece played by the band before their deaths. (See Chapter 12 for more on the unresolved mystery of the band's final song.)

The people of Colne, Lancashire, England, Hartley's hometown, erected a memorial in Hartley's honor.

The 50 bell boys

One of the legends about the *Titanic*'s sinking is that the ship carried 50 bell boys who tended to the first-class passengers and that they all perished when the ship went down. On a ship, a bell boy is someone who carries luggage and otherwise attends passengers, similar to a bellhop.

The bell boys, aged 14 to 16 or so, were said to have gathered on deck for a final smoke before going down with the ship. They are remembered as being true self-sacrificing heroes because not one of them tried to get into a lifeboat. The legend holds that they considered themselves expendable and knew that the passengers' lives were more important than their own.

This legend has survived a century. On a December 1996 broadcast of *The Charlie Rose Show,* Peter Stone, who wrote the book for the musical *Titanic* (see Chapter 17), recounted the story of the 50 bell boys and said that their story was to him one of the most moving stories of the sinking.

And moving it would be . . . if it were true.

An examination of passenger and crew rosters proves that 50 bell boys were not onboard. In fact, there weren't even five bell boys. There were three: W. A. Watson (age 14), Alfred Barrett (age 15), and Clifford Henry Harris (age 16). They all perished.

Chapter 4

Life Onboard: From Breakfast and Lunch to Steerage and Bunks

For first-class passengers anyway, the *Titanic* was as much a luxury hotel as a steamship. It offered all the amenities of a five-star hotel: luxury suites, a swimming pool, and a Turkish bath.

This chapter gives you a tour of the *Titanic* so you can experience the ship of dreams for yourself. It takes you to all ten decks on the ship, from the Boat deck at the top where well-heeled first-class passengers strolled and took the air, to the lower decks where third-class passengers huddled in their narrow berths. On the way, you visit all the places on the ship that made the *Titanic* special, such as the gymnasium, smoking rooms, and first-class lounge.

I also take you behind the scenes for a look at the victualling crew — the stewards, cooks, and scullions who worked so hard to serve the day-to-day needs of the *Titanic*'s passengers.

Finally, this chapter focuses on the dining saloons and restaurants on the *Titanic*. They really knew how to eat in those days, as you'll soon find out.

Taking the Grand Tour of the Titanic

How comfortable your sleeping quarters were, what you ate, and how you passed the time on the *Titanic* depended on what kind of ticket you purchased: a first-, second-, or third-class ticket. What's more, where you could set foot on the ship also depended on your ticket. Certain parts of the ship were meant solely for first-class passengers. Certain parts were forbidden to all but the crew members. Certain parts of the ship — namely, the smoking rooms and Turkish bath — were reserved for male passengers.

But no matter what type of ticket you held, traveling aboard the *Titanic* was a delightful experience. Even the *Titanic*'s third-class accommodations were a cut above those on other ships. It was said that the *Titanic*'s third-class accommodations were equivalent to second-class accommodations on other ships.

Where do you want to go aboard the *Titanic?* The Grand Staircase? The Turkish baths? In this part of the chapter, I take you there. This section gives you a grand tour of the ship of dreams. Before the tour starts, however, I show you how to find your way around the *Titanic.* I thought you might like to know how many decks there were and what was on each deck so you don't get lost.

Finding your way around the ship

Table 4-1 lists the ten decks on the *Titanic,* starting with the uppermost deck (called the *Boat deck* because most of the lifeboats were stored there) and ending with the Tank Top deck, the lowest deck in the ship. The table shows what was located fore, amidships, and aft on each deck. *Fore* means toward the front of the ship, *amidships* means in the middle, and *aft* means toward the back. In the table, *1st, 2nd, 3rd,* and *crew* indicate what parts of the ship were accessible to first-class passengers, second-class passengers, third-class passengers, and crew members. Also, the *poop deck* was an exposed deck that formed the roof of an aft cabin on the ship.

Table 4-1	The Ten *Titanic* Decks		
Deck	**Fore**	**Amidships**	**Aft**
Boat	Officer's bridge (crew)	Promenade (1st)	Promenade (2nd)
		Gymnasium (1st)	
Promenade (A)	Reading and Writing Room (1st)	Lounge (1st)	Smoking room (1st)
			Verandah Café (1st)
			Palm Courts (1st)
Bridge (B)	Forecastle deck (crew)	Suites, cabins (1st)	À la Carte Restaurant (1st)
			Café Parisien (1st)
			Smoking room (2nd)
			Promenade (poop deck) (3rd)

Deck	Fore	Amidships	Aft
Shelter (C)	Crew mess (Crew)	Cabins, state-rooms (1st)	Library (2nd)
			Smoking room (3rd)
		Crew mess (Crew)	General room (3rd)
		Purser's office (Crew)	
Saloon (D)	Open space (3rd)	Dining saloon (1st)	Dining saloon (2nd)
	Cabins (3rd)		Kitchen galleys (crew)
		Reception room (1st)	
		Cabins (1st)	
Upper (E)	Cabins (3rd)	Cabins (2nd)	Cabins (2nd)
		Cabins (Crew)	Cabins (3rd)
Middle (F)	Cabins (3rd)	Dining saloon (3rd)	Cabins (2nd)
			Cabins (3rd)
		Swimming pool (1st)	
		Turkish baths (1st)	
Lower (G)	Storage rooms (crew)	Boiler rooms (crew)	Squash court (1st)
			Post office (crew)
	Engine rooms (crew)		
Orlop	Cargo rooms (crew)	Boiler rooms (crew)	Engine rooms (crew)
	Baggage rooms (crew)		Cargo rooms (crew)
	Mail room (crew)		
Tank Top	Boiler rooms (crew)	Boiler rooms (crew)	Boiler rooms (crew)
	Engine rooms (crew)	Engine rooms (crew)	Engine rooms (crew)

To get from deck to deck on the *Titanic,* first-class passengers could use an elevator or the Grand Staircase (see Figure 4-1). The Grand Staircase rose from the first-class dining room and reception room on the Saloon deck (D) to the Boat deck, the uppermost deck on the ship. In the daytime, an iron-and-glass dome at the top of staircase let in natural light that flooded the staircase's candelabra, oak paneling, and other ornate details. The Grand Staircase was the *Titanic*'s pièce de résistance and an important passageway from deck to deck. Even at the bottom of the ocean it serves an important purpose: The best means for submersibles to explore the interior of the *Titanic* wreck is to use the Grand Staircase.

Figure 4-1:
The Grand Staircase of the *Olympic,* which was identical to the *Titanic*'s.

© Mary Evans/ONSLOW AUCTIONS LIMITED/Everett Collection

Visiting the suites and cabins

Table 4-2 lists the prices passengers paid for different accommodations on the *Titanic*. At approximately $100,000 a pop in today's dollars, you can see why the world's richest and most elite sailed on the *Titanic* — only they could afford the parlor suites. For the immigrants who traveled in third class, the cost of a berth was no small sum either. The immigrants were poor, and raising that kind of money (approximately $350 to $900 in today's dollars) for passage to America was difficult in the early 1900s.

Table 4-2	Prices for *Titanic* Accommodations	
Accommodation	*Price*	*Approximate Price in Today's Dollars*
First-class parlor suite	£870/$4,350	$100,000
Berth in first-class cabin	£30/$150	$3,500
Berth in second-class cabin	£12/$60	$1,375
Berth in third-class cabin	£3–£8/$15–$40	$350–900

First-class parlor suites and cabins

First-class accommodations were located amidships, where the rocking of the ship was less keenly felt and passengers were less likely to get seasick. They were decorated opulently in different period styles: Queen Anne, Louis XVI, and Georgian.

The parlor suites came with wardrobe rooms, private baths, and in some cases private promenades. All first-class accommodations were equipped with telephones, heaters, special gimbal lamps that were designed not to tip over in choppy seas, table fans, and (of course) call bells for summoning the steward.

If the parlor suite didn't suffice, a wealthy family could purchase several first-class cabins adjacent to one another and open the interconnecting doors between the cabins to have a suite of their own.

Second-class cabins

In second class, passengers slept in berths built into the walls of the cabins. At two to four berths per cabin, privacy was hard to come by, although a passenger could close the curtain around his or her berth. Each second-class cabin had a washbasin and a chamber pot to be used in case of seasickness. Second-class passengers used communal bathrooms. Figure 4-2 shows the comfy, homelike atmosphere of a second-class cabin.

Third-class cabins

Third-class passengers slept on bunk beds in crowded quarters at six to a narrow cabin. Like second-class passengers, they shared bathrooms, but the number of people sharing a bathroom was much higher in third class: Only two bathtubs were available for all 710 third-class passengers, one for the men and one for the women. In those days, many of the poor believed that frequent bathing could cause respiratory disease; therefore, most third-class passengers likely didn't lament the lack of bathtubs.

Figure 4-2: A *Titanic* second-class two-berth stateroom.

Exploring decks and rooms on the Titanic

It must have been a real pleasure for *Titanic* passengers to wander from place to place on the ship, discovering what was around the next corner. This section takes you to the Boat deck, Turkish baths, smoking rooms, and other points of interest on the *Titanic*.

Boat deck

The Boat deck was the uppermost deck on the *Titanic;* it was so named because lifeboats were stored there. The Boat deck offered the only real open space on the ship. First- and second-class passengers could stroll, rest on benches, play *quoits* (a game similar to horseshoes), or simply lose themselves in quiet contemplation on the Boat deck. (Third-class passengers did their promenading on the Bridge [B] deck, on a platformlike poop deck located at the aft of the ship. However, they were obliged to share this crowded space with cargo and equipment.)

Sixteen of the *Titanic*'s 20 lifeboats were fastened to the Boat deck. The Boat deck was the scene of confusion and terror on the night the *Titanic* sank, as frantic passengers were loaded onto the lifeboats and lowered some 70 feet to the frigid waters below.

Gymnasium

First-class passengers had the use of the *Titanic*'s state-of-the-art gymnasium, which was located on the Boat deck. Besides the usual dumbbells, rowing machines, stationary bicycles, and *Indian clubs* (heavy wooden clubs shaped like bowling pins that were popular at the turn of the twentieth century), the gymnasium provided a mechanical horse for honing your equestrian skills and a mechanical camel to work your abs and back muscles. The cost to use the gymnasium was one shilling (about 25 cents), to be paid to Thomas McCawley, the on-site gymnasium steward, who dressed in white flannels.

Unlike today's gyms, where men and women exercise together, the *Titanic* gymnasium was segregated. According to a strict schedule, men, women, and children could exercise only during prescribed hours.

Smoking rooms

The early twentieth century had its "designated smoking areas" too; they were called *smoking rooms.* A man who felt the urge to smoke on the *Titanic* took his cigar, cigarette, or pipe to one of the ship's three smoking rooms and lit up. Smoking was not forbidden in other parts of the ship, but unless you were in a smoking room, smoking indoors was considered bad manners in 1912. For a woman to smoke was considered very, very bad manners, no matter what room she was in!

The first-class smoking room, on the Promenade (A) deck, modeled after a London men's club, was dark and intimate, with mahogany paneling and leather chairs. A deck below (on the Bridge, or B, deck), the second-class smoking room had a linoleum floor and furniture upholstered in green Moroccan leather. The third-class smoking room, another deck below (on the Shelter, or C, deck), was austere compared to the other smoking rooms; it had wooden benches and chairs.

It almost goes without saying, but alcoholic beverages were imbibed in all three smoking rooms, and all three smoking rooms doubled as card parlors.

Reading and Writing Room

The female counterpart to the smoking rooms was the Reading and Writing Room (see Figure 4-3), located on the Promenade (A) deck and available to first-class passengers. This room's comfortable chairs, white paneling, bay window, and fireplace made for a relaxing place to write a letter or read a novel.

Figure 4-3: A Reading and Writing Room, one of *Titanic*'s luxury rooms.

The Lounge

First-class passengers also had the Lounge, a luxurious room on the Promenade (A) deck meant for socializing. This rich, oak-paneled room had alcoves where passengers could talk to one another with a degree of privacy. Lounge decorations were modeled after the Palace of Versailles. Coffee, tea, and liquor were served in the Lounge.

Verandah Café and Palm Courts

Also on the Promenade (A) deck, first-class passengers could avail themselves of the Verandah Café and Palm Courts. The large windows, wicker furniture, trelliswork, potted plants, and checkered floors in these rooms suggested being in the English countryside. First-class children favored the Verandah Café and often went there to play together.

Library

Although it was called the Library, this expansive room really served as a lounge for second-class passengers. In his *The Loss of the S. S. Titanic,* published in 1912 (and republished most recently by Mariner Books), survivor Lawrence Beesley wrote this about the Library:

I can look back and see every detail of the library that afternoon — the beautifully furnished room, with lounges, armchairs, and small writing or card tables scattered about, writing-bureaus around the walls of the room, and the library in glass-encased shelves flanking one side — the whole finished in mahogany relieved with white fluted wooden columns that supported the deck above. Through the windows is a covered corridor, reserved by general consent as the children's playground, and here are playing the two Navratil children with their father — devoted to them, never absent from them.

Swimming pool

The *Titanic* offered its first-class passengers a heated saltwater swimming pool. It was located on the Middle (F) deck. Passengers could change in the dressing rooms and take showers in the stalls along the side of the pool.

The *Titanic*'s swimming pool was only the second swimming pool built into an ocean liner. The first was built on the *Olympic,* the *Titanic*'s sister ship.

Turkish baths

The *Titanic* boasted exclusive, first-class-only Turkish baths. Male passengers who paid the $1 fee could visit the rooms with hot, temperate, and cool temperatures; a steam room; a private toilet; and even a shampooing room. The Turkish baths also offered a freshwater drinking fountain (made of marble). The Turkish baths featured ornate tiles in the Arabic style and comfortable lounge chairs where passengers could rest.

Squash court

For vigorous exercise, the *Titanic* offered its first-class passengers the use of a squash court. After paying the attendant two shillings (about 50 cents), you were given a racquet, a ball, and an opponent or two if you didn't bring your own. The squash court was located on the Lower deck. To the players' backs was an observation gallery where spectators could watch the games. (*Squash,* similar to racquetball and handball, is played by two or four players with racquets and a small hollow ball.)

Dining on the Titanic: Food, Glorious Food!

A warning: As you read about the food served on the *Titanic,* your mouth may water. You may experience severe hunger pangs. If you are currently dieting, reading the following pages is not recommended.

This section looks at the food served on the *Titanic,* the different dining rooms and restaurants, the food preparers, and the food servers. First, it shows you how much food is required to stock a seagoing hotel for seven days.

Stocking a seagoing hotel

To give you an idea of what feeding more than 2,200 passengers and crew for a seven-day voyage entails, Table 4-3 presents a list of the foodstuffs that the *Titanic* carried when she left Southampton for her maiden voyage on April 10, 1912. Notice how many potatoes the *Titanic* carried — 40 tons (80,000 pounds)! It's hard to imagine that many potatoes, much less imagine that many stored in a luxury liner. The *Titanic* also carried an ample supply of liquor to keep her passengers in good cheer: 1,500 bottles of wine, 20,000 bottles of beer, and 850 bottles of *spirits* (distilled beverages such as brandy, gin, and whisky). In an indication of how culinary tastes have changed since 1912, the ship also carried 1,000 pounds of sweetbreads. You don't see *sweetbreads* — the thymus gland of the cow — on many modern menus.

Table 4-3	Foodstuffs Carried on the *Titanic*
Food Item	*Amount*
Beverages	
Beer	20,000 bottles
Coffee	2,200 lbs.
Mineral waters	15,000 bottles
Spirits	850 bottles
Tea	800 lbs.
Wines	1,500 bottles
Dairy	
Butter	6,000 lbs.
Condensed milk	600 gallons
Cream	1,200 qts.
Eggs	40,000
Ice cream	1,750 qts.
Milk	1,500 gallons
Dry goods	
Cereals	10,000 lbs.
Flour	200 barrels
Rice, dried beans, and so on	10,000 lbs.
Fruits and vegetables	
Asparagus	800 bundles
Grapefruit	50 boxes
Grapes	1,000 lbs.

Food Item	Amount
Fruits and vegetables	
Green peas	2,250 lbs.
Lemons	16,000
Lettuce	7,000 heads
Onions	3,500 lbs.
Oranges	36,000
Potatoes	40 tons
Tomatoes	2.75 tons
Meat, poultry, and fish	
Bacon and ham	7,500 lbs.
Fish	11,000 lbs.
Meat	75,000 lbs.
Poultry and game	25,000 lbs.
Salt and dried fish	4,000 lbs.
Sausages	2,500 lbs.
Sweetbreads	1,000 lbs.
Sugar and preserves	
Jams and marmalades	1,120 lbs.
Sugar	10,000 lbs.

Meeting the food preparers and servers

The victualling crew was responsible for looking after passengers, preparing food, and serving food. The *Titanic* had 385 people in the victualling crew (75 survived the sinking). About a third were tasked with food preparation and service; to find out what the other two thirds did, see the following section.

Among the food preparers and servers on the *Titanic* were bakers, butchers, chefs, cooks, confectioners, kitchen porters, pantrymen, *scullion and scullery maids* (what today are called dishwashers), and *stewards and stewardesses* (what today are called waiters and waitresses). These victualling crew members prepared food and delivered it to the dining saloons, the crew's mess hall, the lounges, cafés, smoking rooms, and first-class suites and cabins. They had to cover a lot of territory.

Perhaps the most unusual job in the victualling crew belonged to 26-year-old Peter W. Fletcher. His job was to go from deck to deck playing the White Star Line's traditional meal call on his bugle. The song was a patriotic English ballad, "The Roast Beef of Old England."

Introducing the rest of the victualling crew

The rest of the victualling crew did the jobs that today are associated with a five-star luxury hotel: They carried and stowed baggage, shined and polished shoes, pressed clothes, made beds, cleaned cabins, and stocked pantries. In addition, every saloon and smoking room depended on the victualling crew to pour drinks, tidy up, and sell postcards. The lounge, library, crew's mess, squash court, swimming pool, and Turkish baths also depended on the victualling crew to keep going. All first-class suites and cabins had a call bell that the passenger could ring to summon a member of the victualling crew. The roster of the victualling crew even included a barber (the *Titanic* had two barber shops).

Most members of the victualling crew were "stewards" of one kind of another. Stewards didn't usually make a lot of money, but most stewards in first and second class were rewarded with tips. There were four basic types of stewards aboard the *Titanic,* which I describe next.

Bath stewards

Bath stewards took care of supplying and cleaning the communal bathrooms. They supplied fresh towels, bathmats, soap, and sponges, and also kept the tubs, fixtures, and floors spotless.

Some first-class passengers had their own personal bath stewards. These private stewards knew how hot or cold to make the water, how many towels to use, what types of soaps and toiletries to use, and other personal requirements. All the passenger had to do was show up at the bathroom. The bath steward would stand outside and not budge until the passenger was finished bathing.

Bedroom stewards

There were bedroom stewards for each class of passengers. The elite bedroom stewards were, of course, the first-class stewards; they had to take care of only five or fewer bedrooms. In many cases, a first-class bedroom steward knew the passengers from other ships and voyages.

There were 35 first-class bedroom stewards aboard the *Titanic.* Only six — Alfred Crawford, Charles Cullen, Andrew Cunningham, Henry Etches, William Faulkner, and Alfred Thessinger — survived the sinking.

The second-class bedroom stewards were responsible for up to ten bedrooms at a time; their workload was double that of the first-class stewards. None of the 12 second-class bedroom stewards aboard the *Titanic* survived the sinking.

The third-class bedroom stewards had to take care of 25 bedrooms or more. There were 44 third-class bedroom stewards aboard the *Titanic*. Surprisingly, nine of them survived the sinking.

Glory-hole stewards

The glory-hole stewards had what was undoubtedly one of the nastiest jobs on the ship: They were responsible for cleaning all the common toilets in all three classes and the crews' quarters.

Linen stewards

Linen stewards were responsible for supplying fresh linens of all kinds to all onboard.

Note: There was no laundry service on the *Titanic* because the ship was an express liner. It would never be at sea long enough for its passengers to require newly washed clothes. There was a room, however, to store dirty linens until the ship docked.

Dining in first class

Breakfast, lunch, and dinner were included in the price of a first-class ticket on the *Titanic*. First-class passengers willing to pay extra could also dine in the elegant À la Carte restaurant or the Café Parisien.

First-class dining saloon

The enormous first-class dining saloon was located on the Saloon (D) deck next to the Reception Room (where diners sometimes paused for an aperitif before dinner). Diners sat in armchairs at tables that sat two, four, or six and ate from fine china emblazoned with the White Star Line logo. The dining saloon could seat more than 500. At 6:00, the dinner hour, it was the place to show off the sparkling jewelry and fashionable dress you purchased in Paris. It was the place to see and be seen.

Here are examples of the offerings from the breakfast, lunch, and dinner menus from the first-class dining saloon, taken directly from the original menus:

Breakfast menu (April 11, 1912)

Baked apples; fresh fruit; stewed prunes; Quaker oats; boiled hominy; puffed rice; fresh herring; Finnan haddock; smoked salmon; grilled mutton kidneys and bacon; grilled ham; grilled sausage; lamb collops; vegetable stew; fried, shirred, poached and boiled eggs; plain and tomato omelets to order; sirloin steak and mutton chops to order; mashed, sauté, and jacket potatoes; cold meat; Vienna and Graham rolls; soda and sultan scones; corn bread; buckwheat cakes; black currant conserve; Narbonne honey; Oxford marmalade; watercress

Lunch menu (April 14, 1912)

Consommé fermier; cockie leekie; fillets of brill; egg a L'Argenteuil; chicken a la Maryland; corned beef; vegetables; dumplings;

From the Grill: Grilled mutton chops; mashed, fried, and baked jacket potatoes; custard pudding; apple merinque; pastry;

Buffet: Salmon mayonnaise; potted shrimps; Norwegian anchovies; soused herrings; plain and smoked sardines; roast beef; round or spiced beef; veal and ham pie; Virginia and Cumberland ham; Bologna sausage; brawn; galantine of chicken; corned ox tongue; lettuce; beetroot; tomatoes;

Cheeses: Cheshire, Stilton, Gorgonzola, Edam, Camembert, Roquefort, St. Ivel, cheddar

Dinner menu (April 14, 1912):

Various hors d'oeuvre; oysters; consommé Olga; cream of barley; salmon, mousseline sauce, cucumber; filet mignons Lili; sauté of chicken, Lyonnais; vegetable marrow farcie; lamb, mint sauce; roast duckling, apple sauce; sirloin of beef; chateau potatoes; green peas; creamed carrots; boiled rice; parmentier and boiled new potatoes; punch Romaine; roast squab and cress; cold asparagus vinaigrette; pâté de foie gras; celery; Waldorf pudding; peaches in chartreuse jelly; chocolate and vanilla éclairs; French ice cream

À la Carte restaurant and Café Parisien

Besides the first-class dining saloon, first-class passengers could dine in the elegant 140-seat À la Carte restaurant (nicknamed "The Ritz") or the Café Parisien. These restaurants were next to each other on the Bridge (B) deck. Meals taken at these restaurants were not included in the price of a first-class ticket and had to be paid for out of pocket.

By contrast to the first-class dining saloon, where diners ate from a fixed menu, diners at the À la Carte, as the restaurant's name implies, could order items separately from the menu. The crystal chandeliers in the À la Carte were designed especially to hang without swinging very much so that diners would be less distracted by the rocking motion of the ship while eating.

The Café Parisien served food from the same menu as the À la Carte. It offered diners large picture windows for viewing the ocean. Weather permitting, these windows could be rolled down so that passengers could dine in the open air.

Both restaurants were owned and managed as a private concession by Gaspare Antonio Pietro Gatti, better known as Luigi, an Italian immigrant to England and a well-regarded London restaurateur. Gatti had his own staff of chefs, waiters, and kitchen help whom he paid from his own pocket; they were not employees of the White Star Line. Most were Italian or French nationals. Gatti perished with the *Titanic,* as did all but three of his 66-member restaurant staff.

Dining in second and third class

In the second-class dining saloon, located on the Saloon (D) deck, diners ate at large rectangular tables, often with strangers. The saloon provided starched white linen tablecloths and napkins. It could hold 394 diners. Interestingly, the diners sat in swivel chairs fastened to the floor, the idea being for the chairs to swivel and offset the rocking of the ship.

Here are examples of breakfast, lunch, and dinner menus from the second-class dining saloon:

Breakfast menu (April 11, 1912)

Fruit; rolled oats; boiled hominy; fresh fish; Yarmouth bloaters; grilled ox kidneys and bacon; American dry hash au gratin; grilled sausage; mashed potatoes; grilled ham and fried eggs; fried potatoes; Vienna and Graham rolls; soda scones; buckwheat cakes; maple syrup; conserve; marmalade; tea; coffee; watercress

Lunch menu (April 12, 1912)

Pea soup; spaghetti au gratin; corned beef; vegetable dumplings; roast mutton; baked jacket potatoes; roast mutton; roast beef; sausage; ox tongue; pickles; salad; tapioca pudding; apple tart; fresh fruit; cheese; biscuits; coffee

Dinner menu (April 14, 1912)

First course: Consommé with tapioca

Second course: Baked haddock with sharp sauce; curried chicken and rice; spring lamb with mint sauce; roast turkey with savory cranberry sauce; green peas; puree turnips; boiled rice; boiled and roast potatoes

Third course (desserts): Plum pudding; wine jelly; coconut sandwich; American Ice Cream; nuts, assorted; fresh fruit; cheese; biscuits

In the third-class dining saloon, located in the Middle (F) deck, diners sat at long tables that could seat 20. They hung their hats, coats, and scarves on hooks attached to the walls. The saloon was large and spare. It could seat 473, which means that two seatings were necessary to accommodate all 710 passengers in third class.

The food was hardy and wholesome. Here is the fare served in the third-class dining saloon on April 14, 1912:

Breakfast: Oatmeal porridge and milk; vegetable stew; fried tripe and onions; bread and butter; marmalade; Swedish bread; tea; coffee

Lunch: Bouillon soup; roast beef and brown gravy; green beans, boiled; potatoes; cabin biscuits; bread; prunes and rice

Dinner: Rabbit pie; baked potatoes; bread and butter; rhubarb and ginger jam; Swedish bread; tea

Part II
Tragedy at Sea: The Titanic Sinks on Its Maiden Voyage

In this part . . .

This part takes you aboard the *Titanic* for her first and last voyage. You experience the *Titanic*'s Sailing Day, when she departed Southampton to cheers and celebration, and her first few days of smooth sailing. This part examines why the *Titanic* struck the iceberg. It describes the heroic efforts of the crew to rescue passengers, what it was like to be on the *Titanic* in her last hour, and what it was like to watch the great ship sink from a lifeboat.

This part also depicts the search for survivors at sea and presents newspaper accounts of the tragedy, first-hand accounts of the terrible night, and reports by investigatory agencies.

Chapter 5

Four Days of Smooth Sailing

. . . .

. . . .

T he denizens of Southampton, England, were accustomed to seeing big ships in the harbor and new ships being launched. Southampton was England's primary embarkation point for ships leaving to the United States and Canada. Still, what the citizens of Southampton saw on April 10, 1912, when the *Titanic* launched her maiden voyage was truly remarkable. The *Titanic* was the largest moving object ever built by man. (Be sure to check out Figure 5-1 later in this chapter for a look at the great ship docked at Southampton.)

This chapter looks at the first four days of the *Titanic*'s fateful voyage, beginning with its launch from the docks at Southampton. I also briefly note what occurred on the ship's fifth day at sea when it struck an iceberg in the North Atlantic — a subject I explore in detail in Chapter 6.

Getting an Overview of the Voyage

The *Titanic*'s maiden voyage lasted just five days — she sank 2 hours and 20 minutes into her sixth day. Table 5-1 briefly outlines the *Titanic*'s journey. As the table shows, she increased her speed as the voyage progressed.

Table 5-1	Events of the *Titanic*'s Maiden Voyage	
Day	*Date (1912)*	*Events*
1	Wednesday, April 10	Departs Southampton, England at 1:30 p.m. At 6:30 p.m., arrives in Cherbourg, France, to take on passengers and mail. Departs Cherbourg at 8:10 p.m.
2	Thursday, April 11	Arrives in Queenstown, Ireland, at 11:30 a.m. to take on passengers and mail. Departs at 1:30 p.m.
3	Friday, April 12	By noon, travels 464 miles from Queenstown for an average speed of 20.98 knots (about 24 mph).
4	Saturday, April 13	By noon, travels 519 miles from her position the previous noon for an average speed of 20.91 knots (about 24 mph).
5	Sunday, April 14	By noon, travels 546 miles from her position the previous noon for an average speed of 22.05 knots (about 25 mph). After noon, travels 258 miles for an average speed of 22.11 knots. Collides with an iceberg at 11:40 p.m.
6	Monday, April 15	Sinks in the North Atlantic at 2:20 a.m.

Day 1: The Titanic's Sailing Day

In the *Titanic* era of transatlantic travel, when traveling by ship was the only way to cross the ocean, Sailing Day was a big deal. The launch of a new steamship was an event of pomp and pride, of excitement and enthusiasm. People from all walks of life came to the docks to watch the new ship being christened and gaze as it took its first slow strides on its long walk across the water. (Interestingly, for all its standing in the world of giant steamships, the White Star Line broke tradition by never christening its boats; see Chapter 19.) Figure 5-1 shows the ship docked at Southampton.

Read on to find out about the *Titanic*'s first official day, when she departed Southampton and visited France.

© National Maritime Museum/Everett Collection

Figure 5-1:
The *Titanic*
docked
at South-
ampton.

Departing from Southampton, England

On Wednesday, April 10, 1912 — Sailing Day — at 7:30 a.m., Captain Edward J. Smith boarded the *Titanic* and received the *sailing report,* an overview of current weather and tide conditions, from Chief Officer Henry Wilde. Shortly thereafter, J. Bruce Ismay, the chairman and managing director of the White Star Line, also boarded the *Titanic* and began touring the ship. Between 9:30 a.m. and 11:30 a.m., three boat trains from Waterloo Station near London arrived at Southampton carrying first-, second-, and third-class passengers for the *Titanic.*

At 11:45 a.m., the *Titanic*'s triple-toned steam whistle blew three times — a very loud roar of a C note — and 20 minutes later, the great vessel cast off.

The tugboats *Hector, Hercules, Neptune, Ajax, Albert Edward,* and *Vulcan* towed the *Titanic* from the Southampton dock. You may notice that five of the six tugboats were named after Roman gods; the sixth was named after Edward II, King of the United Kingdom of Great Britain and Ireland, King of the British Dominions, and Emperor of India, a potentate who may well have been more powerful than the aforementioned Roman gods.

The cost to travel on the Titanic

Sometimes the sheer cost of a ticket on the *Titanic* gets lost in the stories, legends, and myths. Traveling on the *Titanic* was an expensive proposition. A first-class ticket in 1912 cost close to $4,500. In today's dollars, that comes to almost $100,000. Imagine taking a sea voyage today that costs $100,000! Wherever they came from, whatever language they spoke, the *Titanic*'s first-class passengers had one thing in common: They were all, without exception, very, very rich. Even third-class passengers, a group made up mostly of European immigrants to America, had to fork over between $15 and $40 for a ticket in steerage, a sum equal to between $350 and $900 today. For most America-bound immigrants, the trip on the *Titanic* cost their life savings, plus whatever they could borrow from family and scrounge from friends.

The movement of the water displaced by the *Titanic* when she launched caused the six mooring ropes of the nearby liner *New York,* then tied up at Berth 38, to snap. Survivor Lawrence Beesley, in his book *The Loss of the S.S. Titanic* (Mariner Books), called the sound made when the ropes snapped "a series of reports like those of a revolver."

As the *Titanic* moved past the *New York,* backwash from her starboard propeller caused the stern of the *New York* to swing toward the *Titanic.* It appeared as though the two massive ocean liners, the *Titanic* and the *New York,* would collide. But quick action on the part of Captain Gale, commander of the tugboat *Vulcan,* to tow the *Titanic* away from the *New York;* an immediate "full astern" order from *Titanic* pilot George Bowyer; and an order from Captain Smith to lower the *Titanic*'s starboard anchor to just above the waterline all combined to avert what would have been a disastrous collision.

Titanic steward George Beedem wrote in an April 11, 1912, letter to his wife:

> As we left today the American boat *New York* broke her moorings & drifted right across our bows[,] missed the *Oceanic* by about a foot . . . it was a narrow squeak for all of us.

The *Titanic*'s suction was indeed powerful. Southampton authorities would later learn that a sunken barge in the harbor had been dragged 800 yards across the harbor bottom as the *Titanic* moved toward the open sea.

The near collision delayed the *Titanic*'s departure by more than an hour and a half. Rather than leave around noon, she left Southampton at 1:30 p.m. Some people watching from the docks considered the *Titanic*'s near collision with the *New York* an inauspicious portent of bad luck. Second-class passenger Thomas Brown remarked to his daughter Edith (who survived and later reported her father's words), "That's a bad omen."

Arriving in Cherbourg, France

After an 89-mile trip across the English Channel, the *Titanic* arrived in Cherbourg, France, at 6:30 p.m. Because the docks weren't large enough to accommodate the massive ship, the *Titanic* dropped anchor in Cherbourg Harbor. Passengers, luggage, and mail were ferried to the ship aboard two White Star Line vessels, the *Nomadic* and the *Traffic.*

Altogether, 274 passengers (142 first-class, 30 second-class, and 102 third-class) boarded. First-class passengers boarding at Cherbourg included Colonel and Mrs. John Jacob Astor IV (she five months pregnant), American mining magnate Benjamin Guggenheim, and the "unsinkable" Margaret (later called Molly) Brown. Second-class passengers who boarded included American illustrator Samuel Ward Stanton. Third-class passengers boarding were of Syrian, Croatian, Armenian, and other Middle Eastern nationalities. Twenty-two passengers disembarked at Cherbourg. They had paid £1.50 (first class) and £1 (second class) for their cross-Channel excursion.

A bit more than an hour and a half after arriving in France, the *Titanic* departed from Cherbourg at 8:10 p.m., bound for Queenstown, Ireland.

During the voyage to Queenstown, the *Titanic*'s chief designer, Thomas Andrews, and a nine-man crew from Harland and Wolff, the ship's builders, worked with the engineering crew to make sure that all the ship's systems were working properly. As the *Titanic* traveled to Ireland, Andrews supervised a successful emergency test (complete with jarring alarm bells clanging) of the watertight doors.

Day 2: The Titanic Visits Ireland

At 11:30 a.m. on Thursday, April 11, after an uneventful 14-hour journey down the English Channel and into St. George's Channel, the *Titanic* dropped anchor in Queenstown harbor off the coast of Queenstown (now called Cobh), on the south coast of Ireland. Like Cherbourg, Queenstown did not have a dock large enough to accommodate the biggest ship in the world. The *Titanic* had to anchor 2 miles offshore.

The tenders *America* and *Ireland* immediately ferried 113 third-class passengers, 7 second-class passengers, and 1,385 sacks of mail to the *Titanic.* Seven passengers disembarked in Ireland, and one crew member, a *fireman* (which means a coal stoker) named John Coffey, deserted. Coffey deserted by hiding in a pile of mailbags being transported to shore. He was from Queenstown and apparently signed on to the *Titanic* in Southampton with the express purpose of getting a free ride home. Coffey was 23, married, and entirely uninterested in traveling to New York; he wanted to get to Queenstown to be with his wife. (Coffey died in 1957 at the age of 68. Deserting his fireman's post on the *Titanic* bought him 45 years.)

One of the seven passengers who disembarked in Ireland was Francis Browne, 32, a Jesuit student priest and avid photographer. Browne took the last surviving photographs from aboard the *Titanic,* including the only known photograph of the wireless room. In an oddly foreboding black-and-white photo that Browne took, Marconi operator and *Titanic* survivor Harold Bride is seen from behind. He is wearing headphones and is seated in front of the wireless. Browne also took the last known photograph of Captain Smith. In the photo, he stands on the starboard wing of the bridge and looks down the *Titanic*'s side.

Prior to leaving Queenstown, the *Titanic* raised the American flag above her deck to signify that her next port of call was in the United States.

At 1:30 p.m., the *Titanic* raised her starboard anchor for the final time and departed Queenstown harbor for New York. Irish passenger Eugene Daly, who had boarded the *Titanic* at Queenstown, played "Erin's Lament" on his uilleann pipes as the Irish coast slowly withdrew from the ship. See Figure 5-2 for what is believed to be the last photo ever taken of the *Titanic*.

Figure 5-2:
The last
photo of the
Titanic.

© Father Browne/Universal Images Group/Getty Images

The fourth funnel face

The *Titanic*'s fourth funnel was used as a vent for the kitchen. In Queenstown, as passengers waited for the *Titanic* to depart, many of them saw a soot-blackened face peering out of the fourth funnel. It was a stoker who had climbed the ladder inside the funnel. Seeing the black face stare out of the giant funnel disturbed some of the passengers. Later, survivors said that the face was an ominous symbolic harbinger of bad things to come.

Days 3 and 4: Smooth Sailing

On Friday and Saturday, days 3 and 4 of her maiden voyage, the *Titanic* steamed across the Atlantic at a speed of about 21 knots (24 miles per hour), and all was well. After the tragedy, survivors would tell of a foreboding or dreadful feeling that their ship was doomed, but what the survivors probably felt was seasickness. Or disorientation at suddenly being in unfamiliar surroundings. Or wonderment at finding themselves for the first time in the middle of an ocean with nothing to gaze at but sky and water. Except for a stubborn coal fire in Boiler Rooms 5 and 6 (rooms fed by Coal Bunker 10), days 3 and 4 of the *Titanic*'s first and last voyage passed smoothly. (Coal fires were not uncommon on coal-fired ships, and the passengers never learned about the fire; see the sidebar "The coal fire in Bunker 10.")

The weather was good, with mild temperatures, light winds, a clear sky, and excellent visibility. Passengers strolling on the Boat deck, the uppermost deck on the *Titanic,* could see far out to sea. Many, like the Englishman Lawrence Beesley, were deeply moved by their first experience of being at sea. Beesley later wrote in *The Loss of the S. S. Titanic:*

> It was a beautiful sight to one who had not crossed the ocean before (or indeed been out of the sight of the shores of England) to stand on the top deck and watch the swell of the sea extending outwards from the ship in an unbroken circle until it met with the sky-line with its hint of infinity: behind, the wake of the vessel white with foam where, fancy suggested, the propeller blades had cut up the long Atlantic rollers and with them made a level white road bounded on either side by banks of green, blue, and blue-green waves that would presently sweep away the white road, though as yet it stretched back to the horizon and dipped over the edge of the world back to Ireland and the gulls, while along it the morning sun glittered and sparkled.

The coal fire in Bunker 10

On Saturday, April 13, the coal fire in Bunker 10 was finally put out. The fire had likely begun when the *Titanic* was still in port at Southampton. It wasn't considered a serious hazard. Smoldering coal fires were not uncommon on steamships. Firemen and trimmers wetted down the coal and shoveled the flaming coal into the boilers. By orders from the ship's engineers, none of the passengers — especially the folks in steerage who slept one level above the coal bunkers — were told about the fire.

Some conspiracy theorists contend that the coal fire weakened the bulkhead wall, which hastened the ship's subsequent break and flooding. But no evidence exists to support this theory.

In the smoking rooms, card players looked up from their games when the day's run — the number of miles the *Titanic* traveled the previous day — was posted. They speculated as to whether the *Titanic* would reach New York on Tuesday night or Wednesday morning. Passengers anxious to reach the United States or anxious about being at sea hoped the ship would continue to increase its speed; passengers who enjoyed the refinements of the luxury liner hoped she would slow down so they could spend an extra half day aboard.

To pass the time, passengers read books and magazines available in the Library and in the Reading and Writing Room. They read the *Atlantic Daily Bulletin,* which was the *Titanic*'s daily newspaper that printed news, advertisements, and menu offerings from the three dining saloons.

The *Titanic*'s orchestra, under the direction of violinist and bandleader Wallace Hartley, played on the Boat deck and in the Lounge. The sound carried down the Grand Staircase and could be heard by second- and third-class passengers below decks.

In third-class steerage, many immigrants heard English spoken for the first time. Knowing that this language was the language of America, their new home, they listened carefully to the words, hoping to make any sense of them.

Behind the scenes, keeping a low profile, the victualling crew scrambled to make sure that all kitchen galleys were properly stocked, all passengers and crew fed, and all rooms and cabins spotlessly clean. Everyone in the victualling crew was new to his or her job on the *Titanic.* The ship had never sailed before. There were rules to learn and procedures to follow, and no one had come before to explain how to do it all.

Throughout, in coal bunkers in the lower decks, trimmers shoveled coal down chutes to the boiler rooms below, where stokers (also called *firemen*) in turn fed the coal to the enormous furnaces, 159 in all, that provided the steamship with its power. These boiler rooms sometimes reached 120 degrees and were so hot that stokers worked only four-hour shifts.

Day 5: An Icy Chill in the Air

Until the moment the *Titanic* struck the iceberg, on the fifth day of her maiden voyage, the ship's last full day was much like her previous days except for the weather. After lunch, passengers noticed a sudden chill in the air. Wrote Lawrence Beesley in *The Loss of the S. S. Titanic:*

> The library was crowded that afternoon, owing to the cold on the deck: but through the windows we could see the clear sky with brilliant sunlight that seemed to augur a fine night and clear day to-morrow, and the prospect of landing in two days, with calm weather all the way to New York, was a matter of general satisfaction to all of us.

Passengers going to bed on Sunday, April 14, before the *Titanic* struck the iceberg could count the number of days remaining in the voyage on one hand. Monday, Tuesday, and maybe Wednesday remained. The ship, they were told, would arrive in New York on Tuesday evening or Wednesday morning.

Chapter 6

The Collision and Sinking

On the evening of April 14, 1912, the *Titanic* was in the waters of the North Atlantic, south of the Grand Banks of Newfoundland. It was a Sunday. The ship was five days into her maiden voyage and three to four days away from her destination, New York. She traveled at about 21 knots (about 24 miles per hour), a reasonable rate of speed for a ship of her size and capabilities. Her captain and crew had received warnings of a large ice field ahead; they had taken what they considered adequate precautions.

Then, at 11:40 p.m., the unthinkable happened. Lookout Frederick Fleet, stationed in the crow's nest of the *Titanic,* saw what he knew immediately was a large, menacing iceberg. The words "Iceberg right ahead" began the drama, and 37 seconds later, the *Titanic* struck the iceberg. Two hours and 40 minutes after that, the *Titanic* sank.

This chapter delves into the horrible events of the night of April 14–15, 1912, when the *Titanic* sank to the bottom of the North Atlantic. It examines whether the crew of the *Titanic* correctly heeded the iceberg warnings from other ships and whether excessive speed was to blame for the disaster. It describes the actions of the crew, heroic and otherwise, to evacuate the ship, and presents some firsthand accounts from survivors.

Heeding Iceberg Warnings

Captain Edward J. Smith and the officers on the *Titanic* were well aware that they might encounter icebergs in the North Atlantic. Knowing about icebergs was part of their training. This passage comes from a 1909 pilot book printed by the Hydrographic Office of the British Admiralty:

[O]ne of the chief dangers in crossing the Atlantic lies in the probability of encountering masses of ice, both in the form of bergs and of extensive fields of solid compact ice, released at the breaking up of winter in Arctic regions and drifted down by the Labrador Current across their direct route. Ice is more likely to be encountered in this route between April and August, both months inclusive.

On April 14 alone, six wireless messages were sent to the *Titanic* about icebergs in her path. This section looks at these wireless messages and explains the precautions that Captain Smith and his crew took — in vain, as it turned out — to prevent their ship from striking an iceberg.

Getting the wireless messages

On the day the *Titanic* struck the iceberg, she received or was forwarded six iceberg warnings. The warnings came by wireless from other ships or from the Hydrographic Office in Washington, D.C. Table 6-1 describes these wireless messages. Of the six messages, Marconi operators delivered two or perhaps three to officers on the bridge. The operators were too busy transmitting passenger messages to deliver the remaining messages to the *Titanic*'s commanding officers.

Table 6-1	April 14, 1912, Wireless Messages Regarding Icebergs	
Sender	*Time/Message*	*Response*
Caronia	9 a.m.: Captain, *Titanic* — West-bound steamers report bergs, growlers and field ice in 42° N. from 49° to 51° W., 12th April. Compliments — Barr.	Captain Smith acknowledged receipt of the message.
Baltic	1:42 p.m.: Captain Smith, *Titanic* — Have had moderate, variable winds and clear, fine weather since leaving. Greek steamer *Athenai* [sic] reports passing icebergs and large quantities of field ice today in lat. 41° 51' N., long. 49° 52' W . . . Wish you and *Titanic* all success. — Commander	Captain Smith acknowledged receipt of the message.

Sender	Time/Message	Response
Hydrographic Office, Washington D.C.	1:45 p.m.: *Amerika* passed two large icebergs in 41° 27' N., 50° 8' W., on the 14th April.	The message was probably set aside until the *Titanic* was within sending distance of Cape Race and could receive the message (at around 8 or 8:30 p.m. that evening). No *Titanic* officer read this message.
Californian (to *Antillian*)	7:30 p.m.: To Captain, *Antillian*, 6:30 p.m. apparent ship's time; lat. 42° 3' N., long. 49° 9' W. Three large bergs five miles to southward of us. Regards. — Lord.	*Titanic* Marconi operator Harold Bride picked up this message and delivered it to the bridge. Later, Bride didn't remember to which officer he handed it.
Mesaba	9:40 p.m.: From Mesaba to Titanic and all east-bound ships. Ice report in lat. 42° N. to 41° 25' N., long. 49° to long. 50° 30' W. Saw much heavy pack ice and great number large icebergs. Also field ice. Weather good, clear.	This message was set aside so that Marconi operators Jack Phillips and Harold Bride could continue sending passengers' messages. It was not delivered to the bridge. No officer read it.
Californian	Approximately 11:05 p.m.: Say old man, we are stopped and surrounded by ice.	Wireless operator Phillips was working a backlog of messages from earlier in the day. He replied, "Shut up, shut up, I am busy; I am working Cape Race" (the wireless station in Newfoundland where wireless messages were relayed). The message was not delivered to an officer.

Taking precautions against icebergs

The wireless messages tell of a huge ice field in the *Titanic*'s path. Did the crew of the *Titanic* heed these messages and take the proper precautions? Here is what the *Titanic* crewmen did on the night of April 14:

- **5:20 p.m.:** Captain Smith set the *Titanic* on a course slightly to the south and west of the route he would normally take his ship.

- **7:15 p.m.:** First Officer William Murdoch ordered the fore-scuttle hatch closed so that no light emanated from the hatch and they could see forward of the ship without any light interfering — "As we are in the vicinity of ice and there is a glow coming from that, and I want everything dark before the bridge," he said.

- **9:30 p.m.:** Second Officer Charles Lightoller sent a message to the crow's nest to "keep a sharp lookout for ice, particularly small ice and growlers." (A *growler* is an iceberg of small mass.)

- **10 p.m.:** Lookouts Frederick Fleet and Reginald Lee, when they relieved Archibald "Archie" Jewell and George Symons in the crow's nest, also received Lightoller's order to watch out for small ice and growlers.

What the crew of the *Titanic* didn't do in the way of precautions was slow the ship or post extra lookouts. In a situation like this, lookouts would often be posted on the bow of the ship, in addition to in the crow's nest. Especially in the case when there was no moon, the bow lookouts had a better chance of seeing any large mass devoid of stars where an iceberg would be silhouetted against the sky, as their field of vision would have been straight on rather than angled down from the crow's nest. Captain Stanley Lord of the *Californian,* the ship nearest to the *Titanic,* took these precautions (and had his wireless operator tell the *Titanic* "we are stopped and surrounded by ice"). Captain Lord slowed his ship to a crawl before the ice field to wait for daybreak, when icebergs would be easier to see.

In its "Report on the Loss of the *Titanic,*" the British Commission of Inquiry (see Chapter 10) offered a simple explanation why Captain Smith didn't halt his ship or steer it even further south to avoid the ice field:

> It was shown that for many years past, indeed, for a quarter of a century or more, the practice of liners using this track when in the vicinity of ice at night had been in clear weather to keep the course, to maintain the speed and to trust to a sharp look-out to enable them to avoid the danger. This practice, it was said, had been justified by experience, no casualties having resulted from it.

So Captain Smith was following precedent when he didn't change course to avoid the ice field. He was, however, deeply concerned for his ship's safety. Lightoller described a conversation he had with Captain Smith about the calm water and lack of wind making it difficult to spot icebergs. "There is not much wind," Captain Smith remarked to Lightoller. "No, it is a flat calm," Lightoller replied. Wind-blown or choppy water ripples against the base of icebergs and exposes them more readily, but on the night the *Titanic* sank, the wind was "flat calm," making icebergs harder to see.

Was speed to blame?

After the sinking, there was immediate speculation that reckless, excessive speed caused the *Titanic* to strike the iceberg. One survivor was certain that excessive speed was to blame. In the April 24, 1912, edition of the *Chicago American,* survivor Charles Dahl said:

> No ship could have driven a straight course through that field of ice. If the *Titanic* had missed one floe she would have struck another. At the high speed of the boat, the disaster was inevitable. In the morning I counted nineteen icebergs within a radius of ten miles. One of them was five miles long.

The British Commission of Inquiry agreed with Dahl, stating, "[T]he loss of the said ship was due to collision with an iceberg, brought about by the excessive speed at which the ship was being navigated."

The story was that J. Bruce Ismay, chairman and managing director of the White Star Line, encouraged Captain Smith to push the great liner to higher speeds. If she arrived in New York on Tuesday night rather than Wednesday morning, her arrival would make headlines in the Wednesday-morning newspapers and give the White Start Line many pages of free publicity.

But no evidence suggests that Ismay asked Captain Smith to push the *Titanic* to greater speeds. Moreover, the *Titanic* was not built for speed but for luxury. Ismay's purported hope to get into New York a day early was simply not realistic. The story of his wanting the ship to go faster has survived the decades probably due to Ismay's actions on the night of the sinking. Ismay survived the sinking aboard Collapsible Lifeboat C when many women and children didn't survive. Ismay's survival cast negative connotations on everything he supposedly did and said on the truncated voyage. Ismay resigned his position with the White Star Line a year after the *Titanic* sank.

Before retiring to his captain's quarters at 9:30 p.m., Captain Smith told Lightoller, "If it [navigating the ship through ice fields] becomes at all doubtful let me know at once; I will be just inside."

At 10 p.m., First Officer Murdoch relieved Second Officer Lightoller on the bridge of the *Titanic.*

Colliding with the Iceberg

At 11:40 p.m., lookouts Frederick Fleet and Reginald Lee shivered at their posts in the crow's nest, 50 feet above the forecastle deck. It was a clear night with no moon. When their watch began, they were told to keep a sharp eye for icebergs. They squinted into the thin mist ahead of the ship. Neither had binoculars (Chapter 11 explains why). Twenty minutes remained on their watch. They looked forward to retiring to their warm berths below decks.

Suddenly, Fleet saw the outlines of a large dark object looming in the mist, and he rang the 16-inch brass bell in the crow's nest three times to signal "object directly ahead." He rang the telephone connecting the crow's nest to the bridge, and when Sixth Officer James Moody answered, he shouted into the phone, "Iceberg right ahead."

Moody relayed the order to First Officer Murdoch in the wheelhouse, who did the following in quick succession:

1. Ordered a *port around,* a maneuver to avoid the iceberg by swinging her bow hard to the left and then hard to the right.

2. Ordered (by way of the engine-room telegraph, a communication device that sent bell signals from the bridge to the engine room) the ship's engines to stop and then reverse.

3. Sounded a bell alarm to give ten seconds' warning to stokers and trimmers in the hull that the watertight-compartment doors were about to be closed. As I explain in Chapter 2, the *Titanic*'s hull was divided into 16 compartments that could be made watertight (or near watertight) by closing their doors. This safety measure was designed to prevent the entire hull of the ship from being flooded, and the ship from sinking, in the event of an emergency.

4. Pulled the switch to slam down the 15 watertight-compartment doors in the hull.

The iceberg was about 500 yards away when Fleet sighted it. In the following 37 seconds, thanks to actions taken by the *Titanic*'s crew, the ship's bow moved slightly to port (to the left) and did not strike the iceberg head on. But a ship the size of the *Titanic* at full steam can't be stopped or even slowed significantly in 500 yards, and the ship struck the iceberg on her starboard (right) side.

The iceberg was enormous. Newspaper accounts said it was 50 to 100 feet high and 200 to 400 feet long. Passengers stirred from their beds by the rough shudder of the collision could see through portholes the iceberg scrape the starboard side of the *Titanic.* As the ship and iceberg collided, chunks of ice ripped from the iceberg flooded the starboard decks.

Captain Smith rushed onto the bridge. He asked Murdoch what happened. "An iceberg, sir," Murdoch answered. "I hard-starboarded and reversed the engines, and I was going to hard-a-port around it, but she was too close. I could not do any more. I have closed the watertight doors."

To the layperson, Murdoch's actions would seem to be contradictory to the actual movement of the ship, as it sounds like he ordered the ship to turn starboard or right. In 1912, however, this command was actually the correct command to turn the ship *port* or *left.* The order "hard-a-starboard" was an antiquated holdover from the days when a ship's tiller controlled its rudder. Hence, pushing the tiller to the right (starboard) would actually turn a ship left (port), and vice versa. (Think of circle bisected by a vertical line. If you take the top of the line [the tiller] and move it right, the bottom of the line [the rudder] moves to the left.) So when Quartermaster Robert Hichens turned the wheel counterclockwise (left or port), he was correctly following the order "hard-a-starboard."

In an interview on CBS shortly before her death, first-class passenger Edith (Rosenbaum) Russell explained what she saw as she watched the iceberg pass from a promenade deck:

> Just before going to my state room, A11, there was a bump. As I turned the handle of my room there was another bump. As I got into my room, there was a third bump. . . . I slipped on a coat over my white satin evening dress and went right out from my own state room because my state room had a door leading to the promenade deck. As I got out onto the promenade deck, I saw a large grey, what looked to me like a build-ing, floating by. But that building kept bumping along the rail, and as it bumped it sliced off bits of ice and that ice fell all over the deck. We just picked up the ice and started playing snow balls. We thought it was fun. We asked the officers if there was any danger, and they said, "Oh, no, nothing at all, nothing at all, nothing at all. Just a mere nothing. We just hit an iceberg."

Few passengers had any idea that the ship was less than three hours from sinking. Passengers came out of staterooms and cabins to inquire why the engines had stopped. The porters assured them that nothing was the matter. Men playing cards in the first-class dining saloon continued their games. Some crew members who felt the disturbance of the collision thought the *Titanic* had broken a propeller blade.

Below decks, in Boiler Rooms 5 and 6, the stokers and trimmers knew better than anybody that the ship was in danger. The side of Boiler Room 6 ripped open, sending a cold, violent flood of water into the room; seawater was also pouring into Boiler Room 5. The stokers and trimmers fled for their lives.

Assessing the Damage

Immediately, Captain Smith and Thomas Andrews, the chief designer of the *Titanic,* went below decks to inspect the damage. The iceberg had pierced the hull, buckling the hull plates and popping rivets as it scraped the ship. Five of the watertight compartments in the hull were flooding, and worse yet, the five were next to one another at the front of the ship where the iceberg did its damage. The watertight compartments were devised so that the ship would remain afloat if any two were flooded, but when the five compartments at the front of the ship filled with water, their combined weight would sink the ship.

Andrews figured that the *Titanic* had two hours left before the frontmost compartments flooded entirely with water and the ship sank.

By the way, Andrews and Smith didn't see the break in the hull themselves. By the time they arrived at the Tank Top deck, the lowest deck on the ship, the so-called watertight compartments where the damage was done were already flooded. No one knew how large a hole the iceberg rent in the hull of the *Titanic* until 1996, when an undersea expedition sponsored by RMS Titanic, Inc., actually inspected the damage. It was only about 12 square feet, significantly smaller than most people thought. (You can read about expeditions to the *Titanic* wreck in Chapter 15.)

Sending Out Distress Signals

When Captain Smith returned to the bridge, he ordered Fourth Officer Joseph Boxhall to calculate the *Titanic*'s position. Then he had the *Titanic*'s Marconi operators send out distress signals. The first one, tapped at 12:15 a.m., was

CQD – MGY

followed by the *Titanic*'s position. MGY were the *Titanic*'s call letters. The message translates to

All stations: distress – RMS Titanic

The British inquiry into the *Titanic* sinking (discussed in Chapter 10) compiled a list of wireless messages pertaining to the *Titanic* that were transmitted in the North Atlantic on April 15, 1912. Seventy messages were sent in all. Ships of all nationalities rallied to the aid of the *Titanic,* relaying messages, making inquiries, and trading information. *La Provence,* a French steamship, and the *Mount Temple,* a Canadian ship, picked up the first distress message at 12:15 a.m. The *Titanic*'s last message, picked up by the *Carpathia* at between 2:15 and 2:25 a.m., was "We are sinking fast. Passengers being put into boats."

The *Carpathia,* a Cunard Line steamship, hearing the *Titanic*'s distress messages, raced to the *Titanic*'s aid. (The *Carpathia* would succeed in rescuing more than 700 survivors from lifeboats later in the morning on April 15.) The closest ship to the *Titanic,* the *Californian,* a cargo ship, did not receive messages from the *Titanic* because her Marconi operator was asleep. (Chapter 7 explains the role of the *Carpathia* and *Californian* in rescue efforts.)

Besides the wireless messages, the *Titanic* sent out two types of distress messages:

✔ **Rockets:** Starting at 12:45 a.m. and continuing for an hour, Fourth Officer Boxhall fired off signal rockets from the Boat deck. He fired eight rockets in all. Crewmen on the *Californian* about 15 miles away saw the flashing white lights from the rockets but weren't sure what to make of them.

✔ **Morse lamp:** Boxhall tried to signal a ship he saw in the distance — generally believed to be the *Californian* — by Morse lamp, but he got no response. (A *Morse lamp* is a hand lantern with a shutter that can be opened and closed to transmit Morse code.)

Boarding and Launching the Lifeboats

Captain Smith and his crew had done everything in their power to summon another ship to their aid, but the nearest ship to receive her distress signals, the *Carpathia,* would not arrive for four hours, and at best the *Titanic* had only two hours remaining. In two hours, the frontmost compartments of her hull would flood, weighing down the front of the ship and causing the ship to sink. Thomas Andrews, the chief designer of the *Titanic,* said that sinking was inevitable.

At 12:05 a.m., water was already flooding the firemen's quarters and mail room on the Lower deck, the deck above the Tank Top (the lowest part of the ship) where the hull had been breached. Captain Smith gave the order to uncover the lifeboats and begin evacuating the ship. But the deck crew wasn't trained to load or launch the lifeboats, and there weren't enough lifeboats for all the passengers and crew.

Looking at the lifeboat scandal

After the *Titanic* sank and the U.S. and British governments conducted their investigations of the disaster, the lifeboats became the subject of a scandal. As I explain in Chapter 11, the *Titanic* carried 20 lifeboats with a capacity to rescue a total of 1,178 people. But to rescue all her passengers and crew, the *Titanic* required enough lifeboats for more than 2,200 people. Moreover, the lifeboats the *Titanic* did have were not filled to capacity when they were launched into the ocean. Between 705 and 713 people were rescued on the lifeboats, but if the lifeboats had been full when they launched, 1,178 people (an additional 467 to 473 people) would have been saved.

The *Titanic* didn't carry enough lifeboats because British Board of Trade laws regarding lifeboats were out of date. The Board of Trade required ships over 10,000 tons to carry at least 16 lifeboats. The *Titanic* exceeded this requirement. But at 46,000 tons, she needed many more lifeboats than the 16 she was required to have by law.

Examining whether the deck crew was prepared

The deck crew — the members of the *Titanic*'s crew responsible for seeing passengers into the lifeboats — was not prepared for the chaos and confusion of April 15. Here's why:

- ✔ The ship had not conducted a lifeboat drill. Crew members were not instructed how to safely board passengers into lifeboats, how to launch lifeboats using the *davits* (the apparatuses that hung over the side of the ship and were used to swing the lifeboats over the water and lower them down), or how to manage the lifeboats after they reached the water.

- ✔ Each lifeboat was assigned deck-crew members, but some crew members weren't clear about which lifeboat they were assigned.

- ✔ Each lifeboat had oars and a supply of water, but lamps, compasses, and food were not stored in the lifeboats. They were kept in lockers on the Boat deck. In the scramble to launch the lifeboats, many put to sea without lamps, a compass, or food for their passengers.

Launching the lifeboats

Lifeboats were kept on the Boat deck, the uppermost deck of the ship. Stewards ran through the decks below banging on doors and instructing passengers to put on their life jackets and assemble on the Boat deck.

The first lifeboat was launched at 12:45 a.m. and the last at 2:05 a.m. Lifeboats were launched from the port and starboard sides of the ship under the supervision of officers Harold Lowe, William Murdoch, James Moody, Charles Lightoller, and Henry Wilde. (Chapter 11 looks in detail at when each lifeboat was launched and how many passengers each lifeboat carried.)

As inconceivable as it sounds, passengers at first were reluctant to board the lifeboats. Some were not convinced that that the ship was sinking — or they refused to believe that the ship was sinking. They had been assured that the shuddering noise heard earlier was of no consequence. The thought of being lowered overboard in a little boat to the dark, foreboding ocean 65 feet below terrified them. Staying aboard a sturdy ocean liner was preferable to capsizing in a little boat in the middle of the ocean at night, they thought. Besides, wasn't the *Carpathia* on her way to rescue everybody?

On the Boat deck, as they loaded passengers into the lifeboats, officers had to shout orders and instructions over the loud racket made by steam being released through the ship's valves and whistles. When the *Titanic* cut her engines, it caused excess steam pressure to build up in the ship's boilers. Now this steam was being released to keep the boilers from exploding.

Until now, third-class passengers had been confined to lower decks of the ship. Trying to get to the lifeboats on the Boat deck, they got lost in the unfamiliar passages and stairways of the upper decks. Immigrants who didn't speak English couldn't find out from the stewards where they were supposed to go or what they were supposed to do.

Titanic officers observed the "women and children first" rule when loading the lifeboats, but if a lifeboat wasn't full when the time came to launch it, men were invited to board. Some women, like Ida Straus (see Chapter 3), couldn't bear to leave their husbands behind on the *Titanic,* and they chose not to leave the ship. In some instances, officers thought a lifeboat needed a strong man to row or an experienced sailor, and they asked a man on the Boat deck to board a lifeboat along with the women and children.

One man unable to board a lifeboat asked first-class passenger Constance Willard, 21, to take his child to safety. In the Sunday, April 21, 1912, edition of the *Chicago Tribune,* Willard talks about the incident:

> I never will forget an incident that occurred just as we were about to be lowered into the water. I had just been lifted into the boat and was still standing, when a foreigner rushed up to the side of the vessel and holding out a bundle in his arms cried with tears running down his face: "O, please, kind lady, won't you save my little girl, my baby. For myself it is no difference, but please, please take the little one." Of course, I took the child.

By 1:30 a.m., panic began to break out among the passengers and crew still on the *Titanic.* The ship now slanted forward such that standing on the Boat deck was difficult. Fifth Officer Lowe had to fire three warning shots with his pistol, a Browning automatic, when passengers tried to jump into Lifeboat 14 as it was being lowered over the Boat deck.

In Archibald Gracie's 1913 book, *The Truth About the Titanic,* first-class passenger Elizabeth Shutes, a governess, said:

> Our lifeboat, with thirty-six in it, began lowering to the sea. This was done amid the greatest confusion. Rough seamen all giving different orders. No officer aboard. As only one side of the ropes worked, the lifeboat at one time was in such a position that it seemed we must capsize in mid-air. At last the ropes worked together, and we drew nearer and nearer the black, oily water. The first touch of our lifeboat on that black sea came to me as a last good-bye to life, and so we put off — a tiny boat on a great sea — rowed away from what had been a safe home for five days.

By the time the last lifeboat was launched at 2:05 a.m., Promenade (A) deck — with the Verandah Café, first-class smoking room, Lounge, and Reading and Writing Room (see Chapter 4) — was flooded. There wasn't enough time to launch two of the Englehardt collapsible lifeboats, so these two boats were cut loose and fell overboard. (Later, at sea, passengers from Lifeboat 14 transferred into one of the collapsible boats. The other, though overturned, served as a life raft for 30 people, including the *Titanic*'s wireless operators and Second Officer Lightoller.)

Also at 2:05 a.m., Captain Smith relieved Marconi operators McBride and Phillips of their duty. In Walter Lord's book *A Night to Remember,* we learn that Smith said, "Men, you have done your duty. . . .You can do no more. Abandon your cabin now. It's every man for himself. You look out for yourselves. I release you — that's the way it is at this kind of time, every man for himself."

At 2:18 a.m., the ship's electrical system failed. All lights aboard the ship went out.

Sinking into the North Atlantic

By now the bow of the ship was submerged, and the stern reared high in the night air. It happened exactly as Thomas Andrews predicted. The chief designer of the *Titanic* said the bow, or front, of the ship would sink as the forward compartments — where the ship struck the iceberg — filled with water. As the *Titanic*'s bow sank, her stern rose, and those still on the Boat deck scrambled to the stern to stay clear of the water, or they took their chances and jumped into the frigid Atlantic.

In her 1912 essay "The *Titanic*: From a Lifeboat," 19-year-old Helen Bishop described the scene from her vantage point in Lifeboat 7, a mile away:

> We did not begin to understand the situation till we were perhaps a mile or more away from the *Titanic.* Then we could see the rows of lights along the decks begin to slant gradually upward from the bow. Very slowly the lines of light began to point downwards at a greater and greater angle. The sinking was so slow that you could not perceive the lights of the deck changing their position. The slant seemed to be greater about every quarter of an hour. That was the only difference.

> In a couple of hours, though, she began to go down more rapidly. Then the fearful sight began. The people in the ship were just beginning to realize how great their danger was. When the forward part of the ship dropped suddenly at a faster rate, so that the upward slope became marked, there was a sudden rush of passengers on all the decks towards the stern. It was like a wave. We could see the great black mass of people in the steerage sweeping to the rear part of the boat and breaking through into the upper decks.

Astonishingly, the ship's three enormous propellers now appeared above the water. The giant ship was nearly perpendicular to the surface of the ocean. It could no longer bear the strain of carrying so much seawater or being in a position — nose down — for which it wasn't constructed. At 2:20 a.m., people in the lifeboats and those in the ocean still capable of hearing heard a terrible, destructive noise — the sound of a steamship cracking in two.

The *Titanic*'s bow sank first. As it plunged to the ocean floor, it sent giant bubbles of trapped air to the surface. Her stern fell backward to the surface of the ocean, rested there a moment as if nothing had happened, and then sank too while people in the lifeboats watched in abject horror.

In the Friday, April 19, 1912, edition of the *Newark Evening News,* first-class passenger Henry Blank recalled seeing the *Titanic* sink:

> After we were some distance from the ship, I heard revolver shots on board, but I don't know what part of the ship they came from. I was under the impressions, as were many in my boat, that everyone had escaped. When there arose a roar from the vessel herself and the screams of those passengers and crew still, I was almost overcome by the horror of the situation. Realizing that many were still aboard and left to perish has left a permanent scar. We saw the *Titanic* plunge forward and then down out of sight but not before we heard the explosions of her boilers. The sea was very calm and there was floating ice everywhere. The women in our boat began to get chilled and we men took off our coats and wrapped them about them.

Seaman Edward John Buley testified at the U.S. Senate Subcommittee *Titanic* Hearing (see Chapter 10):

> She went down as far as the after funnel, and then there was a little roar, as though the engines had rushed forward, and she snapped in two, and the bow part went down and the afterpart came up and stayed up five minutes before it went down. . . . It was horizontal at first, and then went down.

In Jay Henry Mowbray's 1912 book *Sinking Of The Titanic, Eyewitness Accounts* (Courier Dover Publications), Lady Lucy Christiana Duff-Gordon described the sinking this way:

> Suddenly I had seen the *Titanic* give a curious shiver. The night was perfectly clear. There was no fog, and I think we were a thousand feet away. Everything could be clearly seen. There were no lights on the boats except a few lanterns which had been lighted by those on board.

> Almost immediately after the boat gave this shiver we heard several pistol shots and a great screaming arose from the decks.

> Then the boat's stern lifted in the air and there was a tremendous explosion. Then the *Titanic* dropped back again. The awful screaming continued. Ten minutes after this there was another explosion. The whole forward part of the great liner dropped down under the waves. The stern rose a hundred feet, almost perpendicularly. The boat stood up like an

enormous black finger against the sky. The screaming was agonizing. I never heard such a continued chorus of utter despair and agony.

Then there was another great explosion and the great stern of the *Titanic* sank as though a great hand was pushing it gently down under the waves. As it went, the screaming of the poor souls left on board seemed to grow louder. It took the *Titanic* but a short time to sink after that last explosion. It went down slowly without a ripple.

Waiting in the Lifeboats to Be Rescued

In the lifeboats (see Figure 6-1), survivors listened to the agonizing cries of their fellow passengers and crew dying in the ice-cold waters of the North Atlantic. They wondered whether the cries they heard came from loved ones and friends. They wondered whether the story they heard, of a ship called the *Carpathia* coming to their rescue, was true, and if it were true, whether the *Carpathia* would be able to find them.

Figure 6-1:
A *Titanic* lifeboat holding some of the lucky few survivors.

© Everett Collection

Meanwhile, passengers in some of the lifeboats undertook rescue efforts of their own:

- Lifeboat 4, one of the last lifeboats to launch, rescued seven men from the water (one died in the lifeboat, and another died on the *Carpathia*).

- In Lifeboat 14, Officer Lowe decided to conduct a search for survivors in the water. He moved passengers from his lifeboat into other lifeboats and, along with some volunteers, rowed toward the cries of the dying. He was able to rescue four swimmers.

- In Lifeboat 6, Margaret Tobin Brown, later known as "the unsinkable Molly Brown," insisted (against the objections of Quartermaster Robert Hichens) on turning back. If they returned, Hichens said, they would be swamped by desperate people seeking a place on a lifeboat. But Brown persuaded the women in the lifeboat to take the oars and row back, and if Hichens didn't like it, Brown said she would throw him overboard.

In the lifeboats, the survivors shivered and huddled together for warmth. Most lifeboats did not have lamps or a compass. Occasionally someone would light a piece of paper to signal their lifeboat's position to the other lifeboats. All eyes scoured the horizon for the *Carpathia* or another ship.

Mary Eloise Hughes Smith, whose husband died on the *Titanic* (and who would remarry another *Titanic* survivor), testified at the U.S. Senate Subcommittee *Titanic* Hearing as to what the ice field looked like:

> The night was beautiful; everything seemed to be with us in that respect, and a very calm sea. The icebergs on the horizon were all watched with interest; some seemed to be as tall as mountains, and reminded me of the pictures I had studied in geography. Then there were flat ones, round ones also.

To Elizabeth Shutes in Lifeboat 3, the arrival of the *Carpathia* was like "a living painting." In Lawrence Beesley's 1912 book, *The Story of the Titanic: As Told by Its Survivors,* she described what she saw:

> The stars slowly disappeared, and in their place came the faint pink glow of another day. Then I heard, "A light, a ship." I could not, would not, look while there was a bit of doubt, but kept my eyes away. All night long I had heard, "A light!" Each time it proved to be one of our other lifeboats, someone lighting a piece of paper, anything they could find to burn, and now I could not believe. Someone found a newspaper; it was lighted and held up. Then I looked and saw a ship. A ship bright with lights; strong and steady she waited, and we were to be saved. . . . That same ship that had come to save us might run us down. But no; she is still. The two, the ship and the dawn, came together, a living painting.

The *Carpathia* arrived at dawn and rescued more than 700 *Titanic* passengers by 8:30 a.m. Chapter 7 describes the efforts of the *Carpathia* and her crew to come to the aid of the *Titanic*.

Chapter 7

Surviving the Sinking of the Titanic

In This Chapter

▶ Surveying survival rates among passengers and crew

▶ Discovering who came to the aid of the *Titanic*

▶ Remembering the survivors of the disaster

*I*n the aftermath of any disaster — natural or manmade — the goal is always to maximize the number of survivors. The perfect disaster, if any disaster can be called perfect, is one in which only property damage and material losses occur and no lives are lost.

The moment that Thomas Andrews — the manager of construction at Harland and Wolff, the chief designer of the *Titanic,* and a passenger on the maiden voyage — confirmed that the ship would go down, the sinking of the *Titanic* became the furthest thing imaginable from a perfect disaster. Not enough lifeboats were aboard to carry all the passengers to safety. Even worse, the loss of life could have been averted if ships had arrived in time to transfer passengers from the *Titanic.*

This chapter is all about the *Titanic*'s survivors and their rescue. First, I show you the survival rates among the passengers and crew, and then I chronicle the efforts to rescue them and get them to New York. Next, I examine the heroic actions of the *Carpathia*'s Captain Arthur Henry Rostron to rescue *Titanic* survivors. Finally, I show you the not-so-heroic actions of Captain Stanley Lord of the *Californian* and introduce you to some famous *Titanic* survivors.

Examining Survival Rates

If you were aboard the *Titanic* when the ship sank, what would be your chances of surviving? The answer to this question depends a lot on whether you were a passenger or an employee (a *nonpassenger*) on the ships. Tables 7-1 and 7-2 show the disparity between survival rates of passengers and nonpassengers. (The numbers come from the U.S. and British inquiries into the disaster, which I discuss in Chapter 10.)

Table 7-1	*Titanic* Survival Rates		
	Total	*Deceased*	*Survived*
Passengers	1,316	818 (62%)	498 (38%)
Nonpassengers	908	696 (77%)	212 (23%)
Totals	**2,224**	**1,514 (68%)**	**710 (32%)**

What's particularly tragic about the numbers reported here is that human error caused many of the deaths. Not only was the number of lifeboats inadequate, but also, the lifeboats were only partially filled (see Chapter 11). More than 1,100 people could have been saved if the lifeboats had been filled to capacity.

Despite the specific numbers that appear in Table 7-1, the exact number of survivors and people who died when the *Titanic* sank is difficult to reckon. The number of people on board when the ship sank and whether to classify some people as passengers or crew are both debatable points. Moreover, what constitutes a survivor is an open question. If someone survived for two days after the ordeal, should he or she be considered a survivor? What if he or she survived a week? Thus, these numbers should be looked at as illustrative — not definitive.

Passenger survival rates

If you were a passenger, your chances of surviving depended greatly on the type of ticket you bought — a first-class, second-class, or third-class ticket. As Table 7-2 shows, first-class passengers survived at a rate of 62 percent, which is more than twice the rate of third-class passengers.

Table 7-2	Passenger Survival Rates by Class	
Passengers	*Total*	*Survived*
First class	325	202 (62%)
Second class	285	118 (41%)
Third class	706	178 (25%)
Totals	**1,316**	**498 (38%)**

In 1912, Lord Mersey issued a report titled *British Parliamentary Papers, Shipping Casualties (Loss of the Steamship "Titanic"),* which published findings from the British Commission of Inquiry (see Chapter 10). In it, Mersey addressed the disparity in class survival rates and the accusations of preference in who was allowed into the lifeboats. Consider his words:

> It has been suggested before the Enquiry that the third-class passengers had been unfairly treated; that their access to the boat deck had been impeded; and that when at last they reached that deck the first and second-class passengers were given precedence in getting places in the boats. There appears to have been no truth in these suggestions. It is no doubt true that the proportion of third-class passengers saved falls far short of the proportion of the first and second class, but this is accounted for by the greater reluctance of the third-class passengers to leave the ship, by their unwillingness to part with their baggage, by the difficulty in getting them up from their quarters, which were at the extreme ends of the ship, and by other similar causes.

Even if you were a first-class passenger with a higher likelihood of getting a seat in a lifeboat, your chances of getting that seat increased if you were a woman or child. The "women and children first" rule applied when loading the lifeboats, although the rule wasn't strictly or equally enforced. If a lifeboat was about to be launched on the starboard side, and empty seats were available, men could take the seats if no women or children were at hand to take them. On the port side, however, it was more apt to be "women and children *only*" — very few men escaped the ship from this side. So if you were a man, your chances of survival were greatly increased by going starboard as opposed to going port.

Nonpassenger survival rates

Whether nonpassengers (those who were employed on the ship) survived depended greatly on their occupations. For example, because they manned the lifeboats, deck crew members survived at a high rate — a whopping 68 percent. Not all crew members were so lucky.

The nonpassengers consisted of the officers, the deck and engineering crews, the victuallers, the restaurant staff, the guarantee group, the musicians, and the postal clerks. The engineering crew and the victuallers were the largest nonpassengers contingents. Table 7-3 provides an overview of the occupations of each group of nonpassengers and their estimated survival rates.

Table 7-3	Nonpassenger Survival Rates by Occupation Type	
Type	**Occupations**	**Survived**
Deck crew	Able seaman, lookout, quartermaster, trimmer	68%
Officers	Captain, officer	57%
Engineering crew	Electrician, engineer, fireman/stoker, greaser, mess steward, trimmer	22%
Victuallers	Baker, chef, cook, pantryman, scullion, steward/stewardess, storekeeper, Turkish bath attendant	19%
Restaurant staff	Cook, waiter	4%
Guarantee group	Draughtsman, electrician, electrician's apprentice, fitter, joiner, plumber, shipbuilder	0%
Musicians	Bandmaster, bassist, cellist, pianist, violinist	0%
Postal clerks	Postal clerk	0%

The *guarantee group* consisted of employees of Harland and Wolff who went on the *Titanic*'s maiden voyage to complete unfinished work and troubleshoot mechanical errors.

Seeing Which Ships Aided in the Titanic Rescue and Recovery Efforts

It's an unwritten rule that when a ship at sea sends an SOS or any other type of distress call, ships that receive the message are supposed to head immediately for the vessel in trouble. It's a sailor's code. It's a sacred duty. It's the right and honorable thing to do. Nothing else takes priority over helping that ship and its passengers and crew.

About three dozen ships were in the North Atlantic when the *Titanic* sank. Of the three dozen, the following ships were near enough to the *Titanic* to potentially come to the rescue of her passengers and crew:

✔ **The *Californian*:** This ship was between 14.7 and 16.7 miles from the *Titanic*. However, Captain Stanley Lord of the *Californian* didn't come to the aid of the *Titanic*. (For more information, see "Reviewing the role of the Californian" later in this chapter. You can also read more in Chapter 10.)

✔ **The *Carpathia*:** This ship, which was on its way from New York to the Mediterranean, was 58 miles away from the *Titanic*. Under orders from its captain, Arthur Henry Rostron, the *Carpathia* raced to the *Titanic* and succeeded in rescuing more than 700 survivors. (For more information, see "Going to the rescue with the *Carpathia* and her crew" later in this chapter.)

- The *Baltic:* This ship, a liner in the White Star Line along with the *Titanic,* was en route from New York to Liverpool. The *Baltic* traveled some 130 miles toward the site of the sinking but was later advised by the *Carpathia* that her rescue services were not needed.

- The *Olympic:* Learning of the disaster, this ship headed toward the *Titanic* but was informed by the *Carpathia* when 100 miles away from the site of the sinking that there was no hope of finding any more passengers alive. Whatever passengers had survived were aboard the *Carpathia.* The *Olympic,* which was built for the White Star Line, was a sister ship of the *Titanic* (see Chapter 2).

In the following sections, I discuss the two ships that were the closest to the *Titanic* and could feasibly help: the *Carpathia* and the *Californian.*

Going to the rescue with the Carpathia and her crew

Even though the *Titanic* never made it to New York, some of her passengers did. They arrived there, devastated and traumatized, aboard the *Carpathia.* The *Carpathia* carried more than 700 survivors into New York Harbor on April 18, 1912, three days after the *Titanic* sank. And boy, did those survivors have a story to tell!

This section looks at the good service the *Caparthia* did for the *Titanic* survivors, starting with the moment her Marconi operator heard the distress call and ending with the arrival of the *Carpathia* in New York Harbor.

Hearing the distress call

The *Carpathia* was a passenger steamship in the Cunard Line. As the *Titanic* foundered, the *Carpathia* was sailing eastward from New York City to the Mediterranean. The ship was 58 miles from the *Titanic* when she received the distress call from the foundering ship.

The *Carpathia* Marconi operator, Harold Thomas Cottam, received the distress message from the *Titanic* at 11:20 p.m. Here's how Cottam described it in the April 19, 1912, edition of *The New York Times:*

> It was only a streak of luck that I got the message at all, for on the previous night I had been up until 2:30 o'clock in the morning, and the night before that until 3 o'clock, and I had planned to get to bed early that night. I thought I'd take some general news, as I didn't know how the coal strike in England was going, and I was interested in it. When I had been taking this some time, there was a batch of messages coming through for the *Titanic* from the long-distance Marconi wireless station at Cape Cod, which transmits the day's news at 10:30 New York time every evening.

> When Cape Cod had been going some time, he starting sending a batch of messages for the *Titanic,* and, having heard the *Titanic* man being pushed with work during the afternoon, I thought I'd give him a hand by taking them and retransmiting them the following morning as I had nothing much to work on. . . .
>
> I put the telephones on and called the *Titanic* and asked him if he was aware that a batch of messages was being transmitted for him via Cape Cod. And his answer was: "Come at once. We have struck a berg."

Immediately, Cottam went to the bridge to alert First Officer H. V. Dean of the *Titanic*'s plight. Dean in turn went below decks to alert Arthur Henry Rostron, the captain of the *Carpathia.*

Captain Rostron would later tell the members of the U.S. Senate Subcommittee *Titanic* Hearing the following information:

> The whole thing was absolutely providential. I will tell you this, that the wireless operator was in his cabin, at the time, not on official business at all, but just simply listening as he was undressing. He was unlacing his boots at the time. He had this apparatus on his ear, and the message came. That was the whole thing. In 10 minutes maybe he would have been in bed, and we would not have heard the message.

Check out Chapter 10 to read more about the *Titanic* hearing.

Preparing for rescue: Captain Rostron takes charge

The code of conduct of commanders of ships at sea embodies a standard of behavior and selflessness that is incredibly impressive. To the captain, safeguarding the passengers, crew, and ship comes above everything else, and all orders given are to serve that tenet — with no exceptions. Ship commanders are totally in charge and answer to no one, not even the company that owns the ship.

After Captain Rostron learned that the *Titanic* had struck an iceberg and was requesting assistance, he immediately ordered his ship turned around and then — after the order was given — turned to Cottam and asked, "Are you sure?" His goal was to pick up survivors. Captain Rostron warned his crew that they would possibly have to take more than 2,000 survivors from the *Titanic.* His leisurely cruise to the Mediterranean was over.

Captain Rostron realized that he needed to put more men on lookout duty; otherwise, his ship would possibly suffer the same fate as the *Titanic.* With all the free-floating ice in the area, the *Carpathia* could easily hit an iceberg. Rostron added a man to the crow's nest, stationed two men on the bow of the ship, and placed a man on each wing of the bridge. He also assigned his second officer, James Bisset, to stand sentinel on the starboard bridge wing. The captain selected men with excellent eyesight. What's more, he personally served as a lookout from his vantage point on the bridge.

During the U.S. Senate Subcommittee *Titanic* Hearing, Captain Rostron wrote out the orders he gave to prepare his ship for the *Titanic* survivors. The following meticulously conceived and remembered list is what Captain Rostron detailed for the Senate subcommittee:

- English doctor, with assistants, to remain in first-class dining room.
- Italian doctor, with assistants, to remain in second-class dining room.
- Hungarian doctor, with assistants, to remain in third-class dining room.
- Each doctor to have supplies of restoratives, stimulants, and everything to hand for immediate needs of probable wounded or sick.
- Purser, with assistant purser and chief steward, to receive the passengers, etc., at different gangways, controlling our own stewards in assisting *Titanic* passengers to the dining rooms, etc.; also to get Christian and surnames of all survivors as soon as possible to send by wireless.
- Inspector, steerage stewards, and master at arms to control our own steerage passengers and keep them out of the third-class dining hall, and also to keep them out of the way and off the deck to prevent confusion.
- Chief steward: That all hands would be called and to have coffee, etc., ready to serve out to all our crew.
- Have coffee, tea, soup, etc., in each saloon, blankets in saloons, at the gangways, and some for the boats.
- To see all rescued cared for and immediate wants attended to.
- My cabin and all officers' cabins to be given up. Smoke rooms, library, etc., dining rooms, would be utilized to accommodate the survivors.
- All spare berths in steerage to be utilized for *Titanic*'s passengers, and get all our own steerage passengers grouped together.
- Stewards to be placed in each alleyway to reassure our own passengers, should they inquire about noise in getting our boats out, etc., or the working of engines.
- To all I strictly enjoined the necessity for order, discipline, and quietness to avoid all confusion.
- Chief and first officers: All the hands to be called; get coffee, etc. Prepare and swing out all boats.
- All gangway doors to be opened.
- Electric sprays in each gangway and over side.
- A block with line rove hooked in each gangway.
- A chair sling at each gangway, for getting up sick or wounded.
- Boatswains' chairs. Pilot ladders and canvas ash bags to be at each gangway, the canvas ash bags for children.

✔ Cargo falls with both ends clear; bowlines in the ends, and bights secured along ship's sides, for boats ropes or to help the people up.

✔ Heaving lines distributed along the ship's side, and gaskets handy near gangways for lashing people in chairs, etc.

✔ Forward derricks; topped and rigged, and steam on winches; also told off officers for different stations and for certain eventualities.

✔ Ordered company's rockets to be fired at 2:45 A.M. and every quarter of an hour after to reassure *Titanic.*

✔ As each official saw everything in readiness, he reported to me personally on the bridge that all my orders were carried out, enumerating the same, and that everything was in readiness.

Captain Rostron also ordered his crew to have oil ready in case the sea was choppy around where the *Titanic* foundered. If necessary, the oil could be poured down the *Carpathia*'s sinks and toilets to calm the water immediately surrounding the *Carpathia.* According to reports, Captain Rostron prayed silently as the *Carpathia* steamed toward the *Titanic.*

The *Titanic* was 58 miles to the northwest of the *Carpathia. Carpathia*'s usual speed was 14 knots, so Captain Rostron estimated that he could make the trip in about four hours. Under Rostron's orders, all power on the ship was diverted to the boilers for extra steam. The *Carpathia* made its journey to the *Titanic* in only three-and-a-half hours. The *Carpathia* traveled at an astonishing 17½ knots — a speed the *Carpathia* would never again achieve.

Years after his rescue of the *Titanic* survivors, Captain Rostron told Captain Barr of the *Caronia,* "When day broke, I saw the ice I had steamed through during the night, I shuddered, and could only think that some other Hand than mine was on that helm during the night."

Arriving at the scene of the disaster

The *Carpathia* arrived at the scene of the foundered *Titanic* before dawn on April 15, 1912.

In the April 19, 1912, edition of *The New York Times,* Marconi operator Harold Thomas Cottam of the *Carpathia* described his first view of the disaster:

> The first sign we got shortly before dawn, was a green light off the port bow of the *Carpathia.* It was a beacon on one of the small boats, and we knew then that the *Titanic* had gone but that there were survivors for us to pick up.
>
> I was kept busy in the wireless room for the next few minutes, and the first of the rescue I saw was a boat alongside and the passengers being hauled aboard. Most of them were woman and children. Some were crying, and they seemed overcome by the calamity. As they were raised to the deck several of them collapsed.

I saw wood and debris from the sunken *Titanic* when dawn came, but I did not see a body in the water. Daylight showed that [we] were right on the scene of the disaster, for there were ten or a dozen boats around us when it became light enough to see and as rapidly as possible their occupants were taken aboard. We remained near the spot, looking for additional survivors for about three hours, and then, convinced that there was no human being alive in the sea of ice in which we floated, we started for New York. As soon as *Carpathia* arrived on the scene, her crew began bringing *Titanic*'s passengers aboard, taking their names and class designations, and attending to their needs. Many of the *Carpathia*'s first-class passengers gave up their quarters to the *Titanic* passengers who seemed most in need. Captain Rostron gave up his quarters as well.

Ruth Becker, a *Titanic* survivor who was 12 years old when the *Titanic* sank, recalled the following in *Titanic: Destination Disaster: The Legends and the Reality,* by John P. Eaton and Charles A. Haas (W. W. Norton & Company):

The *Carpathia* was on its way to Europe when it picked up our distress call and came to our rescue, so it was [partly] full of its own passengers. Therefore the 705 extra survivors had no place to sit except in the dining saloons and [on] the decks. The children sat on the floor. I remember we children ate sugar lumps off the dining room table. At night our family slept in the officers' quarters, which were in the bottom of the ship. I didn't like that at all. It scared me to be way down there. There was really nothing to do. Everybody just sat around talking, telling about their experience, and crying. The *Carpathia* passengers were wonderful. They couldn't do enough for us. One lady gave Mother a dress. We wore our coats over our night clothes.

The last *Titanic* passenger was aboard the *Carpathia* by 8:30 a.m., and by this time the *Californian* was also on site. Before leaving the area, Captain Rostron convened a memorial service for the *Titanic*'s victims as the *Carpathia* passed over the spot where the *Titanic* went down.

Docking in New York Harbor

A reported 40,000 people crowded the docks of New York Harbor waiting for the *Carpathia* to arrive with survivors of the *Titanic*. She arrived on Thursday, April 18, 1912, three days after the *Titanic* sank. The *Carpathia* docked in New York at Little West 12th Street at 4 a.m.

The *Carpathia* eventually docked at Pier 54 for passengers and the *Titanic* survivors to disembark, but that wasn't the ship's first stop. Upon arriving in New York, she first stopped at Pier 59 to unload all the *Titanic* lifeboats that the *Carpathia* had taken onboard. Captain Rostron knew that the lifeboats belonged to the White Star Line and, being the consummate professional that he was, knew that his responsibility was to return them to the company. (No *Carpathia* passengers or *Titanic* survivors were allowed to leave the ship at Pier 59.)

The sinking of the *Carpathia*

Like the *Titanic,* the *Carpathia* lies at the bottom of the ocean. During World War I, the *Carpathia* was commissioned as a troop transport ship. On July 15, 1918, the *Carpathia* left Liverpool as part of a convoy bound for the United States. Two days later, shortly after midnight on July 17, in the Celtic Sea south of Ireland, a German submarine fired upon her, landing one torpedo in the engine room and another in the port side.

After Captain William Prothero gave orders to abandon the ship, her 57 passengers boarded lifeboats. The German submarine then surfaced and fired a third torpedo at the *Carpathia,* whereupon the *HMS Snowdrop,* a Royal Navy sloop, fired on the submarine and succeeded in driving it away. All passengers and crew of the torpedoed *Carpathia* were rescued aboard the *Snowdrop.*

In 2000, American author Clive Cussler of the National Underwater and Marine Agency announced that he had discovered the wreck of the *Carpathia* in the Celtic Sea.

By the time the *Carpathia* arrived in New York, the whole world knew what had happened to the *Titanic.* The White Star Line's offices were besieged by relatives of passengers and by the media. Some of the White Star Line's news updates were, by necessity, delivered from a fourth-floor balcony of its offices. Apparently, no executives wanted to wade into the teeming masses on the street demanding information.

Small boats loaded with reporters raced out to the *Carpathia* as it steamed into port. During the journey to New York, the *Carpathia* had transmitted nothing but survivors' names, deliberately omitting any other information about the *Titanic* and her sinking. New York newspapers were irate. They reacted with what Daniel Allen Butler in *"Unsinkable": The Full Story of RMS Titanic* (Stackpole Press) describes as "calculated petulance." They "pouted" and blared headlines like "Watchers Angered by *Carpathia*'s Silence" and "*Carpathia* Lets No Secrets of *Titanic*'s Loss Escape by Wireless."

Reviewing the role of the Californian

In contrast to the heroic efforts of the *Carpathia* to save the *Titanic*'s passengers and crew, the actions of the crew of the *Californian* were muddled at best and contemptible at worst. The *Californian* was a cargo steamship of the Leland Line. On the night the *Titanic* sank, she was on her way from London, England, to Boston, Massachusetts. She carried no passengers.

Hearing reports of icebergs in the part of the North Atlantic through which his ship traveled, Captain Stanley Lord of the *Californian* halted his ship for the night. It was too dark to voyage safely, and the captain believed his ship had encountered a large ice field. "We were surrounded by a lot of loose ice, and we were about a quarter of a mile off the edge of the field," he later told the members of the U.S. Senate Subcommittee *Titanic* Hearing. The time was 10:21 p.m., about an hour and 20 minutes before the *Titanic* struck the iceberg. Later inquiries would put the *Californian* 14.7 to 16.7 miles from the *Titanic.*

Before he retired for the night, Captain Lord had his wireless operator send a message to the *Titanic* about the ice field his ship had encountered. The wireless operator duly tapped this message: "I say old man, we are stopped and surrounded by ice." The wireless operators of the *Titanic,* however, didn't heed the message. Their wireless equipment had broken down earlier in the day. They had recently repaired the equipment and were busy catching up to the backlog of messages that had been sent earlier. Wireless operator Jack Phillips of the *Titanic* replied, "Shut up, shut up, I am busy; I am working Cape Race." (Cape Race was the wireless station in Newfoundland where wireless messages were relayed.)

What happened on the *Californian* in the next several hours while the *Titanic* sank and Captain Lord slept in his quarters below decks is a subject of debate.

At about 12:45 a.m. on April 15, Apprentice James Gibson and Second Officer Herbert Stone, who was in charge of the bridge, noticed first one and then another flash of white light on the horizon. Were these rockets fired as distress signals from the large ship that Stone had noticed on the horizon earlier that night? Stone called down the speaking tube to Captain Lord to alert him to the strange light flashes. Captain Lord thought perhaps they were company rockets that ships used to identify themselves to other ships in the same company. He told Stone to try signaling the ship by Morse lamp, which Stone did but to no avail. Lord didn't instruct Stone to wake the wireless operator and try to contact the ship by wireless.

At the British Board of Trade Commission of Inquiry into the *Titanic* sinking, Second Officer Stone reported telling Gibson, "A ship is not going to fire rockets at sea for nothing" and "Look at her now; she looks very queer out of the water; her lights look queer."

At 2 a.m., about 20 minutes before the *Titanic* sank, Stone and Gibson watched the lights from the distant ship slowly fade.

The crew of the *Californian* didn't learn about the *Titanic*'s demise until its wireless operator received the news about 5 a.m. At 6 a.m., Captain Lord ordered his ship to steam toward the *Titanic*'s last known position. The ship reached the disaster site at 7:45 a.m., but it was too late. The *Carpathia* was already on the scene and had succeeded in rescuing all passengers and crew from the lifeboats.

Senator William Alden Smith, one of the members of the U.S. Senate Subcommittee *Titanic* Hearing, condemned Captain Lord in his final report. He wrote

The failure of Captain Lord to arouse the wireless operator on his ship, who could have easily ascertained the name of the vessel in distress and reached her in time to avert loss of life, places a tremendous responsibility upon this officer from which it will be very difficult for him to escape. Had he been as vigilant in the movement of his vessel as he was active in displaying his own signal lamp, there is a very strong probability that every human life that was sacrificed through this disaster could have been saved.

Meeting Some Titanic Survivors

The 700 or so *Titanic* survivors were an elite group. They were in that lucky third of people aboard the ship who didn't end up dying in subfreezing water. (Hypothermia was the dominant cause of death for those who ended up in the water. Many were found afloat still wearing their life jackets.)

For many, being a *Titanic* survivor ultimately defined their lives — and not as positively as you may expect. The fact that they survived a horrendous tragedy was with them every day. When being introduced to others, they often were introduced as *Titanic* survivors.

An early — and erroneous — account

As soon as the *Titanic* survivors landed in New York, the media clamor began. The press sought out anyone and everyone who was on the ship and who would agree to talk to them.

An early account of the sinking, including survivors' stories, was published in the Plymouth, England, *Witney Gazette* on Saturday, May 4, 1912. The arrival in Plymouth of the *Red Laplander* was met with great interest because the ship carried 167 survivors, all of them members of the *Titanic*'s crew. The article brought to light several fascinating details about the disaster, some of which were later refuted. For example, crew members interviewed by the *Witney Gazette* reported the following erroneous information:

✔ Officer Murdoch shot himself.

✔ *Titanic* Captain Edward J. Smith was seen swimming in the water carrying a child.

✔ The violinist played "Nearer, My God, To Thee" solo until he went under with the ship.

To its credit, the article mentioned what perhaps was the first description of the ship breaking in half:

The *Titanic* broke in two between the funnels. There were explosions. The men believe that the machinery fell out of the hull when she split and the bow went down. The stern rose straight up in the air before the final plunge.

The article also talked about crew members' remarks regarding the admirable strict discipline during the sinking and loading of lifeboats and that no one in the hold moved from their posts until they heard the order "Every man for himself."

This section looks at several groups of survivors: a couple of notorious members of the deck crew who survived, passengers who became famous because of their survival, survivors (many of them also famous) who lived to old ages, and those who committed suicide.

Many *Titanic* survivors refused to talk about their experiences on the *Titanic.* They shunned interview requests, refused to attend *Titanic* conventions, avoided talking to reporters, and even steered clear of discussing what happened with their own families.

Hearing the stories of two notorious deck crewmen who survived

The *Titanic* had 59 members on her deck crew. The crew, led by 20 able seamen, was responsible for the efficient and proper operation of the ship on a daily basis. In addition to being responsible for everything on deck, these able seamen were the go-to lifeboat guys. They had been trained in the operation of the davits and the ropes, and knew how to lower the lifeboats in case of an accident.

In the case of the *Titanic,* however, some deck crew members ended up in lifeboats ahead of passengers. In fact, 40 deck crew members survived the sinking. As a result, other, less-qualified people had to be in charge of lowering and operating the lifeboats.

In the following sections, I discuss two of the more notable crew members who survived the sinking.

Lookout Frederick Fleet

Lookout Frederick Fleet was on duty in the crow's nest the night the *Titanic* struck the iceberg. His "Iceberg right ahead" call has become an iconic symbol of the great ship's fate. Fleet, who had also served four years as a lookout on the *Oceanic,* was to receive an extra five shillings for lookout duty. Fleet survived the sinking by hopping in Lifeboat 6.

In the British Commission of Inquiry hearings, Fleet asserted that if he would have had binoculars the night the *Titanic* sunk, he might have been able to see the iceberg earlier. Fleet took lookout duty at 10 p.m. on the night of April 14, 1912, and he spotted the iceberg just before 11:40 p.m. After the ship struck the iceberg and its fate was sealed, Fleet was assigned to help load the lifeboats.

Interestingly, after the *Titanic* tragedy, from June 1912 to August 1912, Fleet continued to work for the White Star Line, serving as a seaman briefly on the *Olympic.* However, he was considered not only an embarrassment to the company, but also a token of bad luck and a jinx. He left the company and worked for other ship lines; built ships for Harland and Wolff; and even, in his later years, sold newspapers on street corners. Later in this chapter, I explain the circumstances surrounding Fleet's 1965 suicide.

Quartermaster Robert Hichens

Quartermaster Robert Hichens is best known for arguing with Margaret (Molly) Brown. This description of him is a bit of a simplification, but his quarrel with Ms. Unsinkable in Lifeboat 6 has become the stuff of legend.

A couple of incidents in Lifeboat 6 involving Quartermaster Hichens stand out as memorable. Most notable was his refusal to go back to pick up passengers in the water. When asked at the British Commission of Inquiry whether he could hear cries of distress from people in the water and whether he headed toward them, he responded, "We had no compass in the boat and I did not know what direction to take. If I had a compass to know what course I could take from the ship, I should know what course to take, but I did not know what course to go upon." A commissioner retorted, "You had your ears. Could not you hear where these cries came from?" Hichens replied, "Your Lordship, in the meantime, the boats were yelling one to another as well as showing their lights to try and let each other know whereabouts they were."

As officer in charge of the lifeboat, Hichens did not want the passengers to row toward the cries. Brown was the one who took it upon herself to order the people in the boat to row. When Hichens protested, she threatened to throw him overboard. Hichens told members of the U.S. Senate Subcommittee *Titanic* Hearing that he was fearful of the *Titanic*'s suction when she went down. His reputation has suffered over the past 100 years for supercilious behavior and what some call bad decisions as officer in charge of Lifeboat 6.

Charles Joughin: Surviving by intoxication

Charles Joughin, one of the *Titanic*'s bakers, allegedly survived several hours in the icy water around the ship after she sank by being seriously intoxicated. His blood alcohol was so high, it essentially worked as a "biological antifreeze," so to speak. Joughin remained on the ship until the very last moment, and then he simply stepped off into the water. He reported feeling no suction whatsoever. He said that he paddled around for around three hours until he was rescued. He didn't even get his hair wet.

Later in life, in a letter to author Walter Lord, Joughin was blunt in his assignment of blame: "My conclusions of cause: Grave error on part of Captain Smith [who] kept course in spite of ice warnings and severe drop in temperature from 5 P.M. Loss of life: life boat shortage, for the number of passengers and crew, but many more could have been saved, had the women obeyed orders. In those circumstances the crew are helpless."

Joughin died in 1956 at the age of 78 in Patterson, New Jersey.

After the sinking, Hichens continued to serve on steamships. He died of heart failure in 1940 aboard the *English Trader* off the coast of Hong Kong at the age of 58. He was buried at sea.

Note: If you choose to do further research on Quartermaster Robert Hichens, be on the lookout for alternative spellings of his name. In this book, I use the commonly accepted spelling Hichens. However, his name also appears on websites and in books as Hichins, Hitchins, and Hitchens.

Becoming famous for surviving

A number of people became famous for having survived the *Titanic,* some for only a few hours and some for many decades. This section presents some of the people who became well known after surviving the sinking of the *Titanic.*

Rosa Abbott

Rosa Abbott (real name Rhoda Abbott) was the only female *Titanic* passenger who actually went down with the ship and survived. Abbott, a third-class passenger, was on the stern when the ship went under. She was swept away from the ship and, when she surfaced, was able to make it to the Collapsible A lifeboat. Her two young sons, however, were lost to the sea.

Abbott remarried in 1914 and moved to Florida. She ultimately returned to London with plans of moving back permanently to the United States, but that never happened. She died of heart failure in 1946 at the age of 73.

Lawrence Beesley

Lawrence Beesley was a second-class passenger and *Titanic* survivor who went on to write a bestselling account of the sinking called *The Loss of the S.S. Titanic: Its Story and Its Lessons.* Beesley had been on his way to the United States for a vacation when the *Titanic* sank. He began jotting down details of that night while still on the *Carpathia* after being rescued.

Beesley, a Christian Scientist, remembered tucking a blanket under the feet of a cold baby in Lifeboat 13. He also remembered two perilous moments in the lifeboat: one as they were descending into the ocean and he saw water gushing from the *Titanic*'s hull (which probably could have capsized them), and another as his lifeboat almost got stuck beneath the descending Lifeboat 15.

Helen Candee

Helen Candee was a writer known for the books *Susan Truslow* (1900); *How Women May Earn a Living* (1900); *An Oklahoma Romance* (1901); *Decorative Styles and Periods* (1906); *The Tapestry Book* (1912); *Angkor, the Magnificent* (1924); *New Journeys in Old Asia* (1927); and *Weaves and Draperies* (1931).

She was a first-class passenger on the *Titanic* and was rescued in Lifeboat 6. After her rescue, Candee wrote about visiting the bow of the *Titanic* before sunrise; it is said that her visit to the bow inspired Cameron's "I'm flying!" scene (with Jack and Rose) in the 1997 movie.

Candee broke her ankle falling into the lifeboat, and the delay in getting it treated resulted in her needing a cane to walk for almost a year.

Candee was an early feminist. In March 1913 she participated in a rally called Votes for Women in Washington, D.C.

Winnifred Vera Quick Van Tongerloo

Winnifred Vera Quick Van Tongerloo was one of just five remaining *Titanic* survivors when she died on July 4, 2002. Van Tongerloo was born on January 23, 1904, and was 8 years and 3 months old when the *Titanic* sailed. She was a second-class passenger and was rescued in Lifeboat 11. She resided in Michigan.

Does Winnifred Vera Quick Van Tongerloo have the most unusual name among survivors? If she doesn't, she's high in the running.

Meeting some of the last survivors

In the 50 or 60 years after the sinking, a vast number of the *Titanic* survivors died. By September 1973, only 100 *Titanic* survivors were still living. Here's a look at a few of the more famous of the last 100 survivors.

Washington Dodge, Jr., died 1974

Washington Dodge, Jr., was 4 years old when he was rescued from the *Titanic* in Lifeboat 5. His father's account of the sinking made the newspapers (see Chapter 8), and the whole family became quite well known for their survival. Dodge, Jr., was married twice; became an investment banker; and died at the age of 67.

Edith (Rosenbaum) Russell, died 1975

After surviving the sinking of the *Titanic* at age 34, Edith Russell tried unsuccessfully to find a publisher for her account of the sinking. She served during World War I as perhaps the first female war correspondent. (*Russell* was her professional name.) She never married, and her final years were spent as a recluse living in a hotel in London. She was 98 when she died.

Frank Prentice, died 1982

Frank Prentice was a 22-year-old storekeeper on the *Titanic* victualling crew. As the ship was foundering, he talked about jumping overboard and swimming to Lifeboat 4. He ultimately did end up in the freezing water and was rescued by Lifeboat 4. Shortly before he died at the age of 92 in May 1982, Prentice appeared in the documentary *Titanic: A Question of Murder* in that same year.

Edwina Troutt, died 1984

Edwina Troutt, who was 27 years old when she survived the *Titanic* sinking, was a beloved guest at *Titanic* conventions and continued to attend even into her late 90s. She died in California at the age of 100. Edwina never let the *Titanic* sinking spook her: She made several Atlantic crossings throughout her life.

Ruth Becker, died 1990

When the *Carpathia* docked in New York with Ruth Becker, age 12, and her mother, Nellie, her mother told the gathered reporters, "Don't ask me anything. Ask Ruth. She'll tell you everything." Ruth was at first a reluctant survivor. She didn't want to talk about the *Titanic* for the decades during which she worked as a teacher. But after she retired, she began attending *Titanic* conventions and willingly discussing the sinking. She died in 1990 at the age of 90. Her ashes were scattered over the *Titanic*'s resting place.

Eva Hart, died 1996

Eva Hart was one of the most outspoken of all the *Titanic* survivors. She routinely talked about the negligence of having too few lifeboats, and she went on record as being an avid antisalvage advocate. She felt the *Titanic* was a gravesite, and she didn't believe anything should be taken from the ship or the debris field. Hart wrote an autobiography in 1994 called *Shadow of the Titanic — A Survivor's Story* (New York University Press). She also dedicated a memorial to the *Titanic* on the grounds of the National Maritime Museum in London. She died in 1996 at the age of 91. The Eva Hart pub in Essex, England, is named in her honor.

Edith Brown, died 1997

Edith Brown, who was 15 years old when she survived the *Titanic*'s sinking, was best known for appearing at a ceremony in 1993 during which she was presented with her father's pocket watch that had been recovered from the *Titanic* wreckage. RMS Titanic, Inc., found the watch; identified it with certainty as belonging to Thomas Brown; and then saw to it that it was returned to Edith, the rightful owner's daughter. Edith Brown Haisman died in Southampton in 1997 at the age of 100.

Eleanor Johnson Shuman, died 2008

Eleanor Shuman was less than 2 years old when the *Titanic* went down in 1912. Shuman was returning to the United States on the *Titanic* after visiting her family in Europe. Her mother and brother also survived. Shuman died in Illinois on March 7, 1998.

In late 1997, at the premiere of the movie *Titanic*, Shuman met director James Cameron. She told the press that Cameron said that she, Shuman, reminded him of his character Rose from the movie. "So when you see Rose," she later told reporters, "think of me."

Shuman also said that the movie revived memories of the sinking, even though she was just an infant when the *Titanic* foundered. "I can still see all the hands reaching up to me from below," she told the media after seeing the movie. "I didn't want to go. And I remember the noise. Everybody was yelling and crying and screaming." She also said that the movie's realism made it difficult for her to watch. "I did a lot of crying," she admitted.

Lillian Asplund, died 2006

Lillian Asplund was the last *Titanic* survivor with actual memories of the sinking. She remembered being passed through a window of the Promenade deck to a lifeboat and looking up and seeing the faces of her father and her three brothers. She was 5 years old at the time. She said that memory haunted her for her entire life. This recollection may have been the only time Asplund ever talked about the *Titanic*. She died in Massachusetts in 2006 at the age of 100.

Barbara Joyce West Dainton, died 2007

Barbara Dainton was the second-to-last remaining survivor of the sinking of the *Titanic* when she died at the age of 96 on October 16, 2007. Dainton was born in May 1911 and was 11 months old when the *Titanic* sailed. She was a second-class passenger and was rescued in Lifeboat 10. Dainton resided in England, one of only two British *Titanic* passengers to survive, and throughout her life, she steadfastly refused to discuss the *Titanic* with anyone. In her obituary in the *UK Telegraph* on November 9, 2007, it was reported that at one point she had said she "wanted nothing to do with the *Titanic* people."

Elizabeth Gladys Millvina Dean, died 2009

Millvina Dean was the last *Titanic* survivor to die, and she was certainly one of the most beloved of all the survivors. She died in 2009 at the age of 97. She was only 10 weeks old when she sailed on the *Titanic,* and she didn't learn that she had been on the ship until she was 8 years old. She attended many *Titanic* society conventions until poor health prevented her from traveling. She spent her final years in a nursing home in Southampton, England. Reportedly, Kate Winslet, Leonardo DiCaprio, and James Cameron donated approximately $35,000 to pay her nursing home fees.

Considering Titanic survivor suicides

For some, the traumatic memories of the *Titanic* disaster may have been too much to bear. Several *Titanic* survivors ended up in mental institutions, and others committed suicide. Did they kill themselves because of the *Titanic* disaster? Some almost certainly did, but others ended their lives after seemingly less significant events.

The following sections look at people who ended their own lives after surviving the disaster.

Annie Robinson

Six months after the *Titanic* sank, on October 10, 1912, Annie Robinson, who had been a stewardess on the *Titanic,* threw herself overboard from the steamship *Devonian* after hearing its foghorn blow in Boston Harbor. Did the foghorn trigger an uncontrollable panic due to her memory of the *Titanic*'s whistles blowing after the ship collided with the iceberg?

Dr. Washington Dodge

Dr. Washington Dodge shot himself in the head on June 30, 1919. Dr. Dodge was reportedly under investigation in a Watergate-type corruption probe, and it's not likely that traumatic memories of the *Titanic* disaster had much to do with his decision to commit suicide. (See Chapter 8 for Dr. Dodge's account of the sinking.)

Dr. Henry William Frauenthal

On March 11, 1927, Dr. Henry William Frauenthal jumped from the seventh-floor window of a hospital, killing himself. Here's a brief bit of background: Frauenthal was a big guy, and when he jumped into a *Titanic* lifeboat, he broke the ribs of the woman passenger he landed on. Did his memories of hurting the woman on the lifeboat have anything to do with his decision to kill himself and how he chose to do it?

Juha Niskanen

Juha Niskanen was a third-class survivor on his way from Finland to Boston when the *Titanic* sank. He eventually moved to California to pan for gold. After failing to find gold, on August 13, 1927, he set his cabin on fire and then killed himself.

John B. (Jack) Thayer

A September 23, 1945, *Philadelphia Inquirer* article reported, "John B. Thayer, 3d, financial vice president of the University of Pennsylvania and a member of an old Philadelphia family, who had been reported missing since Wednesday, was found dead, his wrists and throat cut, in a parked automobile . . . at 48th St. and Parkside Ave. yesterday morning."

Thayer survived the sinking of the *Titanic* on an overturned lifeboat. His mother also survived, but his father died in the sinking. Was Thayer's suicide related to his experiences on the *Titanic,* which had occurred when he was 17 years old? Not according to his longtime friend Governor John C. Bell, Jr., who told the *Inquirer,* "Mr. Thayer had been suffering from a nervous breakdown during the last two weeks. 'The breakdown,' Mr. Bell explained, 'was due, I believe, to worrying about the death of his son, Edward C. Thayer, who was killed in the service.'"

Jack Thayer's account of the sinking

In Logan Marshall's 1912 book, *Sinking of the Titanic and Great Sea Disasters* (General Books LLC), John B. (Jack) Thayer described what he saw as the *Titanic* went down:

> Her deck was turned slightly toward us. We could see groups of the almost fifteen hundred people aboard, clinging in clusters or bunches, like swarming bees; only to fall in masses, pairs or singly, as the great part of the ship, two hundred and fifty feet of it, rose into the sky, till it reached a sixty-five or seventy degree angle. Here it seemed to pause, and just hung, for what felt like minutes. Gradually she turned her deck away from us, as though to hide from our sight the awful spectacle.

John Morgan Davies, Jr.

The death of John Morgan Davies, Jr., by deliberate barbiturate overdose was reported in the December 17, 1951, *Daily Mining Gazette.* The paper stated that he "died suddenly in Detroit Sunday morning." In the article, they acknowledged his experience in surviving the *Titanic* disaster. Many reports of his death claim he was despondent over a divorce.

Phyllis Jane Quick

When 3-year-old Phyllis Jane Quick arrived home in Detroit after surviving the sinking of the *Titanic* in Lifeboat 11, the April 20, 1912, *Detroit Journal* reported that Phyllis's mother, Jane, told her husband, "Oh Fred, it was terrible. I never expected to see my loved ones again!" Jane Quick went on to travel the country and tell audiences of her and her children's experiences aboard the *Titanic.*

Phyllis grew up and went to work for the phone company. She married, had four children, and lived in the same place for 40 years. On March 15, 1954, at the age of 45, she shot herself in the head. Did her suicide have anything to do with her experiences on the *Titanic?* Or a better question may be, could her mother's lifelong obsession with reliving the *Titanic* tragedy and constantly talking about it have depressed Phyllis? Her mother lived another 20 years and died in 1965 of a heart attack.

Frederick Fleet

Frederick Fleet's suicide is one of the saddest stories related to the *Titanic* disaster. (See the earlier section "Lookout Frederick Fleet" for more on Fleet's role on the *Titanic.*) His childhood was horrible; he never knew his father; and his mother abandoned him as a child to live with a boyfriend in Springfield, Massachusetts.

At age 16, he began his career at sea. Nine years later, he was the lookout the night the *Titanic* struck the iceberg and was the one who shouted, "Iceberg right ahead." During testimony, he asserted that if he would have had binoculars, he would have seen the iceberg earlier. Later, he claimed he felt personally responsible for the deaths of the more than 1,500 passengers lost. (See Chapter 11 for more info on the missing crow's-nest binoculars.)

Fleet returned to the sea and served briefly on the *Olympic* and other ships before retiring in 1936 at the age of 49. All his life, he saved his Seaman's Discharge Book, of which his time on the *Titanic* took up only two lines: "Discharged at sea. Destination intended for New York." After working a variety of menial jobs, Fleet ultimately sold newspapers on a corner in Southampton, England, and drank alone in pubs. On December 28, 1964, Fleet's wife died, and her brother, with whom they lived, told Fleet he had to leave the house. Fleet hanged himself in the garden two days later.

Masabumi Hosono lived . . . and lived to regret it

Masabumi Hosono was the only Japanese passenger on the *Titanic*. He survived by taking a spot in the almost-full Lifeboat 13. His survival, as wonderful an event as any survival of a sinking ship could be, wasn't cheered upon his return to his native Japan. Instead, it was considered a disgrace to Japanese notions of honor. He was fired from his job, trashed in the newspapers, described in school textbooks as an example of how to be dishonorable, and ultimately perceived as immoral and cowardly.

He died in 1939, 27 years after the sinking. According to some accounts, he was encouraged to commit suicide as retribution for his "cowardice," but he died of natural causes, albeit a depressed and disgraced man. After his death, his granddaughter found and released his diary, in which he wrote about not wanting to do anything "disgraceful as a Japanese." His writings are perceived today as his redemption.

Chapter 8

"I Was There": Firsthand Accounts of the Sinking

The *Titanic* struck the iceberg at 11:40 p.m.; it sank at 2:20 a.m. It took the *Titanic* 2 hours and 40 minutes to sink. Many survivors were able to observe and recall what happened during that time.

In all, approximately 710 people survived the sinking of the *Titanic*. (The reported number of survivors ranges from 705 to 712.) Their accounts were published in newspapers; journals; and, later, in the transcripts of the British Commission of Inquiry and the U.S. Senate Subcommittee *Titanic* Hearing, among other places. (I present some additional transcripts from the British and U.S. hearings in Chapter 10.) All the accounts are moving and revealing. For this chapter, I chose the most dramatic, detailed, and emotional narratives about what it was like to be aboard a sinking ship in the middle of the North Atlantic in the darkness of a frigid, moonless night.

Watching the Ship's Final Moments from a Lifeboat

Here are the gripping accounts of three first-class women passengers who survived the *Titanic* sinking, including silent-film star Dorothy Gibson. Their stories take us back in time and allow us to experience the terrible final moments of the great ship *Titanic* in a way that no clinical, historical account of the events of that night can possibly do. These accounts truly tell us what it was like to be on the RMS *Titanic* on the night of April 14–15, 1912. The immediacy of these accounts will take your breath away.

Emily Maria Borie Ryerson: "She seemed to break in half as if cut with a knife"

Emily Maria Borie Ryerson was 48 years old when she gave this testimony to the U.S. Senate. Along with her husband, Arthur, and children Suzette, Emily, and John, she boarded the *Titanic* at Cherbourg, France. Her husband perished with the ship. Ironically, the Ryerson family was returning to their home in Pennsylvania aboard the *Titanic* to attend the funeral of son Arthur Jr., a Yale University student who had recently died in an automobile accident.

From the 1912 U.S. Senate Subcommittee *Titanic* Hearing:

> I was a passenger on the steamship *Titanic* on April 14, 1912. At the time of collision I was awake and heard the engines stop, but felt no jar. My husband was asleep, so I rang and asked the steward, Bishop, what was the matter. He said, "There is talk of an iceberg, ma'am, and they have stopped, not to run into it." I told him to keep me informed if there were any orders. It was bitterly cold, so I put on a warm wrapper and looked out the window (we were in the large cabins on the B deck, very far aft) and saw the stars shining and a calm sea, but heard no noise. It was 12 o'clock. After about 10 minutes I went out in the corridor, and saw far off people hurrying on deck. A passenger ran by and called out, "Put on your life belts and come up on the boat deck." I said, "Where did you get those orders?" He said, "From the captain." I went back then and told Miss Bowen and my daughter, who were in the next room, to dress immediately, roused my husband and the two younger children, who were in a room on the other side, and then remembered my maid, who had a room near us. Her door was locked and I had some difficulty in waking her. By this time my husband was fully dressed, and we could hear the noise of feet tramping on the deck overhead. He was quite calm and cheerful and helped me put the life belts on the children and on my maid. I was paralyzed with fear of not all getting on deck together in time, as there were seven of us. I would not let my younger daughter dress, but she only put on a fur coat, as I did over her nightgown. My husband cautioned us all to keep together, and we went up to A deck, where we found quite a group of people we knew. Everyone had on a life belt, and they all were very quiet and self-possessed.

We could hear the rockets . . .

We stood about there for quite a long time — fully half an hour, I should say. I know my maid ran down to the cabin and got some of my clothes. Then we were ordered to the boat deck. I only remember the second steward at the head of the stairs, who told us where to go. My chief thought and that of everyone else was, I know, not to make a fuss and to do as we were told. My husband joked with some of the women he knew, and I heard him say, "Don't you hear the band playing?" I begged him to let me stay with him, but he said, "You must obey orders. When they say, 'Women and children to the boats,' you must go when your turn comes.

I'll stay with John Thayer. We will be all right. You take a boat going to New York." This referred to the belief that there was a circle of ships around waiting. The *Olympic,* the *Baltic,* were some of the names I heard. All this time we could hear the rockets going up — signals of distress. Again, we were ordered down to A deck, which was partly enclosed.

No more boys

We saw people getting into boats, but waited our turn. There was a rough sort of steps constructed to get up to the window. My boy, Jack, was with me. An officer at the window said, "That boy can't go." My husband stepped forward and said, "Of course, that boy goes with his mother; he is only 13." So they let him pass. They also said, "No more boys." I turned and kissed my husband, and as we left he and the other men I knew — Mr. Thayer, Mr. Widener, and others — were all standing there together very quietly. The decks were lighted, and as you went through the window it was as if you stepped out into the dark. We were flung into the boats. There were two men — an officer inside and a sailor outside — to help us. I fell on top of the women who were already in the boat, and scrambled to the bow with my eldest daughter. Miss Bowen and my boy were in the stern and my second daughter was in the middle of the boat with my maid. Mrs. Thayer, Mrs. Widener, Mrs. Astor, and Miss Eustis were the only others I knew in our boat.

Presently an officer called out from the upper deck, "How many women are there in that boat?" Someone answered, "Twenty-four." "That's enough; lower away."

Confusion

The ropes seemed to stick at one end and the boat tipped, someone called for a knife, but it was not needed until we got into the water, as it was but a short distance, and I then realized for the first time how far the ship had sunk. The deck we left was only about 20 feet from the sea. I could see all the portholes open and water washing in, and the decks still lighted. Then they called out, "How many seaman have you," and they answered one. "That is not enough," said the officer. "I will send you another," and he sent a sailor down the rope. In a few minutes after several other men not sailors came down the ropes over the davits and dropped into our boat. The order was given to pull away. Then they rowed off — the sailors, the women, anyone — but made little progress; there was a confusion of orders; we rowed toward the stern, someone shouted something about a gangway, and no one seemed to know what to do. Barrels and chairs were being thrown overboard.

Then suddenly, when we still seemed very near, we saw the ship was sinking rapidly. I was in the bow of the boat with my daughter and turned to see the great ship take a plunge toward the bow, the two forward funnels seemed to lean and then she seemed to break in half as if cut with a knife, and as the bow went under the lights went out; the stern stood up for several minutes, black against the stars, and then that, too, plunged down, and there was no sound for what seemed like hours, and then began the cries for help of people drowning all around us, which seemed to go on forever. Someone called out, "Pull for your lives, or you'll be sucked under," and everyone that could rowed like mad. I could see my younger daughter and Mrs. Thayer and Mrs. Astor rowing, but there seemed to be no suction. Then we turned to pick up some of those in the water. Some of the women protested, but others persisted, and we dragged in six or seven men; the men we rescued were principally stokers, stewards, sailors, etc., and were so chilled and frozen already they could hardly move. Two of them died in the stern later and many were raving and moaning and delirious most of the time. We had no lights or compass. There were several babies in the boat, but there was no milk or water. (I believe these were all stowed away somewhere, but no one knew where, and as the bottom of the boat was full of water and the boat full of people it was very difficult to find anything).

No lights

After the *Titanic* sank we saw no lights, and no one seemed to know what direction to take. Lowe, the officer in charge of the boat, had called out earlier for all to tie together, so we now heard his whistle, and as soon as we could make out the other boats in the dark, five of us were tied together, and we drifted about without rowing, as the sea was calm, waiting for the dawn. It was very cold, and soon a breeze sprang up, and it was hard to keep our heavy boat bow on; but as the cries died down we could see dimly what seemed to be a raft with about 20 men standing on it, back to back. It was the overturned boat; and as the sailors on our boat said we could still carry 8 or 10 more people, we called for another boat to volunteer and go to rescue them. So we two cut loose our painters and between us got all the men off. They were nearly gone and could not have held out much longer. Then, when the sun rose we saw them standing about 5 miles away, and for the first time saw the icebergs all around us. The *Carpathia* steamed toward us until it was full daylight; then she stopped and began picking up boats, and we got on board about 8 o'clock. Very soon after we got on board they took a complete list of the names of all survivors. The kindness and the efficiency of all the arrangements on the *Carpathia* for our comfort can never be too highly praised.

Daisy Minahan: "The cries were horrible"

Daisy Minahan, a schoolteacher from Wisconsin, the daughter of Irish immigrants, was 33 years old on the night the *Titanic* sank. After visiting relatives in Ireland, she boarded the ship at Queenstown with her older brother William, a doctor; and his wife, Lillian. Her brother died aboard the *Titanic*.

From the 1912 U.S. Senate Subcommittee *Titanic* Hearing:

I was asleep in stateroom C-78; I was awakened by the crying of a woman in the passageway. I roused my brother and his wife, and we began at once to dress. No one came to give us warning. We spent five minutes in dressing and went on deck to the port side. The frightful slant of the deck toward the bow of the boat gave us our first thought of danger.

An officer came and commanded all women to follow, and he led us to the boat deck on the starboard side. He told us there was no danger, but to get into a lifeboat as a precaution only. After making three attempts to get into boats, we succeeded in getting into lifeboat No. 14. The crowd surging around the boats was getting unruly.

Officers were yelling and cursing at men to stand back and let the women get into the boats. In going from one lifeboat to another we stumbled over huge piles of bread lying on the deck.

No seamen to man it . . .

When the lifeboat was filled there were no seamen to man it. The officer in command of No. 14 called for volunteers in the crowd who could row. Six men offered to go. At times when we were being lowered we were at an angle of 45° and expected to be thrown into the sea. As we reached the level of each deck men jumped into the boat until the officer threatened to shoot the next man who jumped. We landed in the sea and rowed to a safe distance from the sinking ship. The officer counted our number and found us to be 48. The officer commanded everyone to feel in the bottom of the boat for a light. We found none. Nor was there bread or water in the boat. The officer, whose name I learned afterwards to be Lowe, was continually making remarks such as, "A good song to sing would be, 'Throw Out the Life Line,' and "I think the best thing for you women to do is to take a nap."

Was Lowe drunk?

The *Titanic* was fast sinking. After she went down the cries were horrible. This was at 2:20 A.M. by a man's watch who stood next to me. At this time three other boats and ours kept together by being tied to each other. The cries continued to come over the water. Some of the women implored Officer Lowe, of No. 14, to divide his passengers among the three other boats and go back to rescue. His first answer to those requests was, "You ought to be damn glad you are here and have got your own life." After some time he was persuaded to do as he was asked. As I came up to him to be transferred to the other boat he said, "Jump, God damn you, jump." I had showed no hesitancy and was waiting only my turn. He had been so blasphemous during the two hours we were in his boat that the women at my end of the boat all thought he was under the influence of liquor. Then he took all of the men who had rowed No. 14, together with the men from the other boats, and went back to the scene of the wreck. We were left with a steward and a stoker to row our boat, which was crowded. The steward did his best, but the stoker refused at first to row, but finally helped two women, who were the only ones pulling on that side. It was just 4 o'clock when we sighted the *Carpathia,* and we were three hours getting to her. On the *Carpathia,* we were treated with every kindness and given every comfort possible.

A stewardess who had been saved told me that after they left Southampton that there were a number of carpenters working to put the doors of the airtight compartments in working order. They had great difficulty in making them respond, and one of them remarked that they would be of little use in case of accident, because it took so long to make them work.

Daisy Minahan's personal letter to Senator William Alden Smith

Daisy Minahan gave her official testimony for the U.S. Senate Subcommittee *Titanic* Hearing to a notary public in Wisconsin. Apparently, she couldn't (or chose not to) travel to the actual hearing location. Her testimony was admitted into the record. She also then chose to write a personal letter to Senator Smith, who chaired the hearing, in which she told him that Captain Smith had been with her and her party during the time someone else had testified he had been seen talking to an officer. Here's what she wrote:

Dear Sir:

I have given you my observations and experiences after the disaster, but want to tell you of what occurred on Sunday night, April 14.

My brother, his wife, and myself went to the café for dinner at about 7:15 P.M. (ship's time). When we entered there was a dinner party already dining, consisting of perhaps a dozen men and three women. Capt. Smith was a guest, as also were Mr. and Mrs.

Widener, Mr. and Mrs. Blair, and Maj. Butt. Capt. Smith was continuously with his party from the time we entered until between 9:25 and 9:45, when he bid the women good night and left. I know this time positively, for at 9:25 my brother suggested my going to bed. We waited for one more piece of the orchestra, and it was between 9:25 and 9:45 (the time we departed), that Capt. Smith left.

Sitting within a few feet of this party were also Sir Cosmo and Lady Duff-Gordon, a Mrs. Meyers, of New York, and Mrs. Smith, of Virginia. Mr. and Mrs. Harris also were dining in the café at the same time.

I had read testimony before your committee stating that Capt. Smith had talked to an officer on the bridge from 8:45 to 9:25. This is positively untrue, as he was having coffee with these people during this time. I was seated so close to them that I could hear bits of their conversation.

Dorothy Gibson: "A sense of desolation never to be forgotten"

Dorothy Gibson was a silent-film actress, Broadway singer, and model. She was 22 years old and returning from a vacation in Italy with her mother aboard the *Titanic* when the great ship sank. Soon after arriving in New York aboard *Carpathia,* Gibson starred in the first movie about the *Titanic,* a silent one-reeler called *Saved from the Titanic* (1912). According to the movie's publicists, Gibson wore the same clothing in the movie that she wore when the *Titanic* sank: a white silk evening dress, cardigan, and polo coat. (For more about this and other *Titanic* movies, see Chapter 17.)

From the April 21, 1912, *New York Morning Telegraph:*

> On the night of the disaster there had been a great deal of merriment on board, the prospect of reaching the American shore having the effect of making everyone happy. After a stroll about the ship in company with my mother, I was invited by several friends to take part in a game of bridge, and I joined them after my mother had retired to her room on Deck E. The salon in which I joined my friends was on Deck A, and we played until 10 p.m. We remained in the salon. About half an hour later we felt a slight jar. No one in the party thought anything of it and we continued to laugh and converse for fully fifteen minutes. Then it was that I noticed considerable nervousness on the part of the stewards and such of the officers as came within range of my vision, but nothing was said by them to give the passengers an inkling of what had happened.

> ### Ship was listing

> Good nights having been said, I stepped out upon deck with the intention of taking a short stroll before retiring, when I noticed that the great ship was leaning heavily on one side. I am not enough of a sailor to know whether it was port or starboard, but the fact remains she was lopsided. On my way below to Deck E I encountered a steward and asked him if there was anything wrong. He tried to push me aside, but I stood resolutely and then he snapped out "Nothing wrong!" and disappeared to the deck above.

> It was at this stage of the proceedings that I became somewhat uneasy and made haste to arouse my mother. There was little or no excitement on board the ship, and in many of the salons that I passed I saw the passengers engaged in card playing and other forms of divertissement. The night was as clear as crystal. The moon was shining brilliantly and the stars twinkled without being obscured by a single cloud. [*Note:* There was no moon the night *Titanic* sank.] Even at a glance I could see icebergs around us and the water seemed filled with the shattered remains of others.

When my mother and myself started to go to the side of the ship that was highest out of the water, we were obliged to climb a veritable hill. By this time the officers had aroused the passengers and they were besieging the bulwarks and asking more questions than any one man could answer in a week. In the meantime the big steamship kept sagging down and when I asked one of the officers what significance the water on one of the stairways carried he replied with a smile that there was no cause for alarm. "One of the compartments has been punctured," he said with a faint smile, "but the ship is sturdy enough to weather a little thing like that."

Lifeboats are lowered

A few minutes later the order came to lower the lifeboats and then for the first time I realized we were in great peril. I clung to my mother and pressed my way down toward the railing. We were badly jostled and pushed about, but that mattered not, so long as I found that I was being pushed nearer the lifeboats that were being lowered. My mother remained wonderfully calm throughout the ordeal and when the crew prepared to lower the first lifeboats we were among the first to enter. The designer of the steamship, who was aboard in company with Mr. Ismay of the White Star Line, ran to and fro with a face of greenish paleness and declined to answer any of the questions hurled at him from the panic-stricken passengers crowding the rail.

When our boat pulled away there were 26 persons aboard and four of those were men. No sooner had we started for the open sea than we discovered to our dismay that the lifeboat was without a plug. This was remedied by volunteer contributions from the lingerie of the women and garments from the men. Then the third officer, who was in charge of the boat, announced that he was without lights or compass. He asked for matches, and happily I was able to supply him. During the bridge game I had picked up from the table a box of French matches which one of the gentlemen had been using, and after toying with it at intervals placed it in my belt intending to preserve it as a souvenir of the trip. To what use the third officer expected putting these matches I do not know, because the morning was clear and we were able to see many miles in all directions.

Cries of anguish

Suddenly there was a wild coming together of voices from the direction of the ship and we noticed an unusual commotion among the people huddled about the railing. Then the awful thing happened, the thing that will remain in my memory until the day I die.

The *Titanic* seemed to lurch slightly more to the side and then the fore. A minute, or probably two minutes, later she sank her nose into the ocean, swayed for a few minutes and disappeared, leaving nothing behind her on the face of the sea but a swirl of water, bobbing heads and lifeboats that were threatened by the suction of the waters. After the vessel had disappeared, the officer in command of our boat wanted to return, saying that there was room for several more passengers and pointing out the possibility of being able to rescue some of those who might be swimming. But immediately behind us was another lifeboat carrying forty people and as no one could be seen in the water some of the passengers in the other boat were transferred to ours.

It was a sense of desolation never to be forgotten. To make matters worse the weather became bitterly cold, and many of the women in the boat were clad in the lightest of evening gowns and some more scantily. The men behaved like heroes, except one chap, who calmly stretched himself in the forepart of the lifeboat and promptly fell asleep regardless of what might happen. There was a young Englishman who managed to wear his monocle throughout the excitement and proved himself a much better man than he looked. He divested himself of what clothing he could spare for the shelter of the women and cheered us with his drawing dialect and his words of hope.

Carpathia is sighted

It was shortly after 5 o'clock when the frozen and benumbed sufferers in our boat were aroused into activity by the announcement that a string of black smoke on the horizon told the approach of a steamship. Up to this time we had been wondering whether the operator of the wireless on the *Titanic* had been able to send out his signal of distress. This thought bothers us greatly. To drift about aimlessly in the open sea with the assurance that the wireless had communicated with a vessel, no matter how far distant, would be a consolation, but to drift in the hope that we might encounter a vessel accidentally was different.

Warming ourselves as best we could in the cramped quarters of a lifeboat, we watched that streak of black smoke grow larger and larger, and then we were able to discern the hull of a steamship heading in our direction. But, thank God, the volume of smoke grew and one of the men, who seemed to know the way of the sea, remarked that the vessel was crowding on all steam. This, of course, cheered us, because we knew that crowding on all steam meant haste.

It seemed ages to me, but as a matter of fact it was shortly after 6 o'clock when we found ourselves alongside the *Carpathia,* with its rails swarming with kindly faces, and men and women crowding about in the anxiety to render help. Captain Rostron of the *Carpathia* had caused everything to be placed in readiness, and as the accommodations were limited, the passengers opened their staterooms and did everything in their power to allay our suffering. I was a guest in the room of Mr. and Mrs. James Russell Lowell, and my mother was looked after by kind people whose names I neglected to learn.

Lack of discipline

Once aboard the *Carpathia* it became evident to me that there had been a deplorable lack of discipline on board the *Titanic.* Comparison of the two crews brought this truth home to me. In the exciting moments before the sinking of the *Titanic,* there appeared no concerted action among the officers and crew. Everything was confusion, and it was the men among the passengers who enforced the orders of Captain Smith that the women and children be the first to enter the lifeboats. As a matter of fact, Captain Smith and Mr. Ismay dined from 6 o'clock until 10, and during that time we had learned that four steamships had warned the *Titanic* of the presence of icebergs and large masses of floating ice in our course.

Many of the collapsible lifeboats collapsed in reality when the passengers attempted to enter them, and the manner in which the life buoys were distributed was slipshod in the extreme. I am thankful that my mother and myself as well as the others were rescued, and that we are back in New York, but it is my sincere wish that the officials of the White Star Line be made to answer for the negligence which caused this disaster and the pain and sorrow they have brought upon the survivors. The "unsinkable" *Titanic* might still be the monarch of the sea had ordinary precaution been used in charting her course and providing a sufficient number of lifeboats.

Thrown into the Sea: The Barber's Tale

Charles Weikman, of Palmyra, New Jersey, the chief barber on the *Titanic,* survived the sinking. Although he swore after his *Titanic* ordeal that he would never go to sea again, Weikman later became chief barber of *Lusitania,* another ship with a storied history.

Weikman is unusual among survivors in that he stayed with the ship until the last moments and was then fortunate enough to be rescued. In the following passage, Weikman starts by describing his ordeal after the ship sank. Then he backs up and describes what happened after the *Titanic* struck the iceberg.

From the April 20, 1912, issue of *The North American:*

He clung to wreckage

After all the boats had left the ship . . . every one gathered on the top deck. As I bent over, throwing a lifebelt around my shoulders, I heard a terrible cry go up from those left on the vessel, and I turned around to see the stern of the ship disappearing under the waves. The stern rose out of the water to an almost perpendicular position and, with hundreds of others, I was thrown out into the sea. As I hit the chilly water I was stunned for a second, and then struck out for a pile of wreckage that was drifting about fifty feet away.

Then one of those unaccountable acts of providence helped me, and I was able to be saved. One of the boilers in the ship, which still had fires under it, exploded. This created a large wave, which came rapidly toward me, and on the crest of the wave I was dashed within reaching distance of the wreckage. I clung desperately. The *Titanic* had disappeared. Then I must have become unconscious, for the next thing I knew I had been picked up by a lifeboat.

Barber will quit the sea

I had closed my shop and was taking a turn on the promenade. Looking through the windows I could see the passengers in the main saloon playing cards and reading. Suddenly, I was startled to hear the hoarse voice of a lookout command "Port your helm!"

There was a dead silence for a moment and then I felt the vessel lurch slightly and heard the side plates of the ship wrench and scrape. The bell in the engine room then clanged out the signal for reversing the engine, and I knew that we had struck something. Passengers by this time had become alarmed and were pouring from the doorways of the saloons and rushing up the companionways. Everyone had a question on his or her lips, and for a moment the vessel was in a state of great excitement and disorder.

Talked to Mr. Widener

I remember distinctly Mr. Widener coming up to me as I stood in the bow and asking me quietly what the trouble was. He left me without awaiting my answer. The hands of my watch at this time told me that it was just 12 o'clock. Not a soul on board knew that the ship had been rent and strained almost one-third of its length on the starboard side. Neither did a soul on board know that at that very moment water was pouring through the rent plates and that the ship was slowly on its way to the bottom.

I was one of those sent to release the boats from the davits, and upon reaching the upper deck I found that a long, orderly line of passengers had been formed. The passengers were filed into the boats, four at a time — three women and one man. In a secluded corner of the deck I made out the forms of Colonel John Astor and his wife. I called to them to come over and get in one of the boats. I saw them clasp each other in a final embrace, and then they approached me.

Mrs. Astor took her seat in the boat first and the colonel hesitated for a moment. I told him to hurry, but he only smiled and shook his head. He then walked to the rail and looked down at the nearing waterline. I saw him once more a little while later standing with Mr. Widener and his son Harry at the rail. They were all aiding and giving words of cheer to the heart-broken women, whose sobs and pleadings rose above the noise of the screeching davits as the boats were being lowered.

During all this time the vessel had been settling slowly and now it was noticed that it had commenced to sink faster. Those of us who remained on board must die. The parting of the last two boats from the ship's side caused all those on board to rush to the rail. Here I found Mr. and Mrs. Isadore Straus, their arms enfolding one another. Mrs. Straus clambered out of a lifeboat when she learned that her husband would be unable to accompany her to safety. She remarked that she would rather stay on board with her husband than leave the ship without him. They went down to their death in the sea locked in each other's arms.

Signaling Distress: A Telegraph Operator's Rescue

Junior Marconi operator Harold Sydney Bride was only 22 when he signed on to the *Titanic*. He was one of the lucky crew members to survive the sinking.

Bride's remembrance of the *Titanic*'s final hours is one of the most powerful archival records of the disaster. Bride (shown in Figure 8-1) dictated his story to a *New York Times* reporter a few minutes after 9 p.m. on Thursday, April 18, 1912, in the Marconi room of the *Carpathia,* immediately after the *Carpathia* docked in New York. "Thrilling Story by *Titanic*'s Surviving Wireless Man" first appeared in the following day's edition and was reprinted in the Sunday, April 28, 1912, special *"Titanic"* edition of *The New York Times,* where "Story" was replaced by "Tale" in the title. Bride was paid $1,000 by *The New York Times* for his story. (As I show in Chapter 10, this payment became a focal point of questioning during testimony to the U.S. Senate Subcommittee *Titanic* Hearing by Guglielmo Marconi, the inventor of the Marconi radio telegraph system.)

Figure 8-1:
Harold Bride being helped off the *Carpathia.*

© Time Life Pictures/Mansell/Time Life Pictures/Getty Images

From the April 19, 1912, issue of *The New York Times:*

Asleep when crash came

I didn't have much to do aboard the *Titanic* except to relieve [Marconi operator Jack] Phillips from midnight until some time in the morning, when he should be through sleeping. On the night of the accident I was not sending, but was asleep. I was due to be up and relieve Phillips earlier than usual. And that reminds me — if it hadn't been for a lucky thing, we never could have sent any call for help.

The lucky thing was that the wireless broke down early enough for us to fix it before the accident. We noticed something wrong on Sunday, and Phillips and I worked seven hours to find it. We found a "secretary" burned out, at last, and repaired it just a few hours before the iceberg was struck.

Phillips said to me as he took the night shift, "You turn in, boy, and get some sleep, and go up as soon as you can and give me a chance. I'm all done for with this work of making repairs."

There were three rooms in the wireless cabin. One was a sleeping room, one was a dynamo room, and one an operating room. I took off my clothes and went to sleep in bed. Then I was conscious of waking up and hearing Phillips sending to Cape Race. I read what he was sending. It was traffic matter.

I remembered how tired he was, and I got out of bed without my clothes on to relieve him. I didn't even feel the shock. I hardly knew it had happened after the Captain had come to us. There was no jolt whatever. I was standing by Phillips telling him to go to bed when the Captain put his head in the cabin.

"We've struck an iceberg," the Captain said, "and I'm having an inspection made to tell what it has done to us. You better get ready to send out a call for assistance. But don't send it until I tell you."

The Captain went away and in ten minutes, I should estimate the time, he came back. We could hear a terrible confusion outside, but there was not the least thing to indicate that there was any trouble. The wireless was working perfectly.

"Send in the call for assistance," ordered the Captain, barely putting his head in the door.

"What call should I send?" Phillips asked.

"The regulation international call for help. Just that."

Then the Captain was gone. Phillips began to send "C. Q. D." ["All stations: distress"]. He flashed away at it and we joked while he did so. All of us made light of the disaster.

Men joked about the distress call

We joked that way while he flashed signals for about five minutes. Then the Captain came back.

"What are you sending?" he asked.

"C. Q. D.," Phillips replied.

The humor of the situation appealed to me. I cut in with a little remark that made us all laugh, including the Captain.

"Send 'S. O. S.,'" I said. "It's the new call, and it may be your last chance to send it."

Phillips with a laugh changed the signal to "S. O. S." The Captain told us we had been struck amidships, or just back of amidships. It was ten minutes, Phillips told me, after he had noticed the iceberg that the slight jolt that was the collision's only signal to us occurred. We thought we were a good distance away.

We said lots of funny things to each other in the next few minutes. We picked up first the steamship *Frankfurd*. We gave her our position and said we had struck an iceberg and needed assistance. The *Frankfurd* operator went away to tell his Captain. He came back, and we told him we were sinking by the head. By that time we could observe a distinct list forward.

The *Carpathia* answered our signal. We told her our position and said we were sinking by the head. The operator went to tell the Captain, and in five minutes returned and told us that the Captain of the *Carpathia* was putting about and heading for us.

Great scramble on deck

Our Captain had left us at this time and Phillips told me to run and tell him what the *Carpathia* had answered. I did so, and I went through an awful mass of people to his cabin. The decks were full of scrambling men and women. I saw no fighting, but I heard tell of it.

I came back and heard Phillips giving the *Carpathia* fuller directions. Phillips told me to put on my clothes. Until that moment I forgot that I was not dressed. I brought an overcoat to Phillips. It was very cold. I slipped the overcoat upon him while he worked.

Every few minutes Phillips would send me to the Captain with little messages. They were merely telling how the *Carpathia* was coming our way and gave her speed. I noticed as I came back from one trip that they were putting off women and children in lifeboats, I noticed that the list forward was increasing. Phillips told me the wireless was growing weaker. The Captain came and told us our engine rooms were taking water and that the dynamos might not last much longer. We sent that word to the *Carpathia*.

I went out on deck and looked around. The water was pretty close up to the boat deck. There was a great scramble aft, and how poor Phillips worked through it I don't know. He was a brave man. I learned to love him that night, and I suddenly felt for him a great reverence to see him standing there sticking to his work while everybody else was raging about. I will never live to forget the work of Phillips for the last awful fifteen minutes.

I thought it was about time to look about and see if there was anything detached that would float. I remembered that every member of the crew had a special lifebelt and ought to know where it was. I remembered mine under my bunk. I went and got it, then I thought how cold the water was. I remembered I had some boots, and I put those on, and an extra jacket and I put that on. I saw Phillips standing out there still sending away, giving the *Carpathia* details of just how we were doing.

We picked up the *Olympic* and told her we were sinking by the head and were about all down. As Phillips was sending the message I strapped his lifebelt to his back. I had already put on his overcoat. I wondered if I could get him into his boots. He suggested with a sort of laugh that I look out and see if all the people were off in the boats, or if any boats were left, or how things were.

I saw a collapsible boat near a funnel and went over to it. Twelve men were trying to boost it down to the boat deck. They were having an awful time. It was the last boat left. I looked at it longingly a few minutes. Then I gave them a hand, and over she went. They all started to scramble in on the boat deck, and I walked back to Phillips. I said the last raft had gone.

Then came the Captain's voice: "Men, you have done your full duty. You can do no more. Abandon your cabin. Now it's every man for himself. You look out for yourselves. I release you. That's the way of it at this kind of time. Every man for himself." I looked out. The boat deck was awash. Phillips clung on sending and sending. He clung on for about ten minutes, or maybe fifteen minutes, after the Captain had released him. The water was then coming into our cabin.

When he worked something happened I hate to tell about. I was back in my room getting Phillips's money for him, and as I looked out the door I saw a stoker, or somebody from below decks, leaning over Phillips from behind. He was too busy to notice what the man was doing. The man was slipping the lifebelt off Phillips's back. He was a big man, too. As you can see, I am very small. I don't know what it was I got hold of. I remembered in a flash the way Phillips had clung on — how I had to fix that lifebelt in place because he was too busy to do it.

I knew that man from below decks had his own lifebelt and should have known where to get it. I suddenly felt a passion not to let that man die a decent sailors' death. I wished he might have stretched rope or walked a plank. I did my duty. I hope I finished him. I don't know. We left him on the cabin floor of the wireless room, and he was not moving.

Band plays in ragtime

From aft came the tunes of the band. It was a ragtime tune, I don't know what. Then there was "Autumn." Phillips ran aft, and that was the last I ever saw of him alive.

I went to the place I had seen the collapsible boat on the boat deck, and to my surprise I saw the boat and the men still trying to push it off. I guess there wasn't a sailor in the crowd. They couldn't do it. I went up to them and was just lending a hand when a large wave came awash of the deck. The big wave carried the boat off. I had hold of an oarlock, and I went off with it. The next I knew I was in the boat. But that was not all. I was in the boat, and the boat was upside down, and I was under it. And I remember realizing that I was wet through, and that whatever happened I must not breathe, for I was under water. I know I had to fight for it, and I did. How I got out from under the boat I do not know, but I felt a breath of air at last.

There were men all around me — hundreds of them. The sea was dotted with them, all depending on their lifebelts. I felt I simply had to get away from the ship. She was a beautiful sight then. Smoke and sparks were rushing out of her funnel. There must have been an explosion, but we had heard none. We only saw the big stream of sparks. The ship was gradually turning on her nose — just like a duck that goes down for a dive. I had only one thing on my mind — to get away from the suction. The band was still playing. I guess all of the band went down.

They were playing "Autumn" then. I swam with all my might. I suppose I was 150 feet away when the *Titanic* on her nose, with her afterquarter sticking straight up in the air, began to settle — slowly.

Pulled into a boat

When at last the waves washed over her rudder there wasn't the least bit of suction I could feel. She must have been going just so slowly as she had been.

I forgot to mention that, besides the *Olympic* and *Carpathia,* we spoke to some German boat, I don't know which, and told them how we were. We also spoke to the *Baltic.* I remembered those things as I began to figure what ships would be coming towards us.

I felt, after a little while, like sinking. I was very cold. I saw a boat of some kind near me and put all my strength into an effort to swim to it. It was hard work. I was all done when a hand reached out from the boat and pulled me aboard. It was our same collapsible. The same crowd was on it. There was just room for me to roll on the edge. I lay there, not caring what happened. Somebody sat on my legs. They were wedged in between slats and were being wrenched. I had not the heart left to ask the man to move. It was a terrible sight all around — men swimming and sinking.

I lay where I was, letting the man wrench my feet out of shape. Others came near. Nobody gave them a hand. The bottomup boat already had more men than it would hold and it was sinking. At first the larger waves splashed over my clothing. Then they began to splash over my head, and I had to breathe when I could.

As we floated around on our capsized boat, and I kept straining my eyes for a ship's lights, somebody said, "Don't the rest of you think we ought to pray?" The man who made the suggestion asked what the religion of the others was. Each man called out his religion. One was a Catholic, one a Methodist, one a Presbyterian. It was decided the most appropriate prayer for all was the Lord's Prayer. We spoke it over in chorus with the man who first suggested that we pray as the leader.

Some splendid people saved us. They had a rightsideup boat, and it was full to its capacity. Yet they came to us and loaded us all into it. I saw some lights off in the distance and I knew a steamship was coming to our aid. I didn't care what happened. I just lay and gasped when I could and felt the pain in my feet. At last the *Carpathia* was alongside and the people were being taken up a rope ladder. Our boat drew near and one by one the men were taken off of it.

On the raft with survivors and a dead man

One man was dead. I passed him and went to the ladder, although my feet pained terribly. The dead man was Phillips. He had died on the raft from exposure and cold, I guess. He had been all in from work before the wreck came. He stood his ground until the crisis had passed, and then he had collapsed, I guess.

But I hardly thought then. I didn't think much of anything. I tried the rope ladder. My feet pained terribly, but I got to the top and felt hands reaching out to me. The next I knew a woman was leaning over me in a cabin, and I felt her hand waving back my hair and rubbing my face. I felt somebody at my feet and felt the warmth of a jolt of liquor. Somebody got me under the arms. Then I was hustled down below to the hospital. That was early in the day, I guess. I lay in the hospital until near night, and they told me the *Carpathia*'s wireless man was getting "queer," and would I help.

After that I never was out of the wireless room, so I don't know what happened among the passengers. I saw nothing of Mrs. Astor or any of them. I just worked wireless. The splutter never died down. I knew it soothed the hurt and felt like a tie to the world of friends and home.

How could I, then, take news queries? Sometimes I let a newspaper ask a question and get a long string of stuff asking for full particulars about everything. Whenever I started to take such a message I thought of the poor people waiting for their messages to go — hoping for answers to them. I shut off the inquirers, and sent my personal messages. And I feel I did the right thing.

The newly published Francatelli account

Laura Francatelli, secretary to Sir Cosmo Duff-Gordon and his wife, Lady Lucy Christiana, traveled with them in first class. She was the one who awakened her employers after she saw water seeping into her cabin.

Francatelli did not testify before either the British or U.S. boards of inquiry, but her affidavit describing her experiences onboard the *Titanic* and then in the lifeboats was entered into evidence at the UK hearings.

In her account, she talks about feeling an "awful rumbling" when the ship hit the iceberg. She recounts how she and Mrs. Duff-Gordon refused to get on the last lifeboat because Sir Cosmo wasn't allowed to accompany them. The three of them ultimately ended up on a rowboat along with nine other passengers and crew members. She wrote, "The boat was not a lifeboat, but quite a small ordinary rowing boat and not too safe. It could not have lived in high waves for five minutes, in fact it was of so little use that when the *Carpathia* picked us up they let our boat go and did not trouble to take it aboard the *Carpathia*." (*Note:* The boat Francatelli was referring to was one of the emergency cutters, more substantial than an ordinary rowboat but not as large as the standard wooden lifeboats.)

Many *Titanic* aficionados believe that Sir Cosmo bought passage in the rowboat for himself, his wife, and Miss Francatelli by paying off crew members. *Titanic* survivor C. E. Henry Stengel vehemently disagreed with that report, and Francatelli confirmed Stengel's account in her written statement. She wrote, "Later on I heard the men speaking about losing their kits. Sir C Duff-Gordon said he would make it all right for them . . . he would give them £5 each. A day or two after we had got on board *Carpathia* Sir Cosmo told me to write out cheques for £5 each for the seven men in the boat." (*Note:* To Francatelli, the money was clearly intended to help the crew members get back on their feet and replace their missing kits — *not* the payoff of a favoritism bribe.)

The typed account by Francatelli was put up for auction on October 16, 2010, with the expectation that it would sell for £15,000. It ultimately sold to a Middle Eastern collector for £20,000 (just over $32,000).

. . . I was still sending my personal messages when Mr. Marconi and *The Times* reporter arrived to ask that I prepare this statement.

There were, maybe, 100 left. I would like to send them all, because I could rest easier if I knew all those messages had gone to the friends waiting for them. But an ambulance man is waiting with a stretcher, and I guess I have got to go with him. I hope my legs get better soon.

The way the band kept playing was a noble thing. I heard it first while we were still working wireless, when there was a ragtime tune for us, and the last I saw of the band, when I was floating out in the sea with my lifebelt on, it was still on deck playing "Autumn." How they ever did it I cannot imagine.

That and the way Phillips kept sending after the Captain told him his life was his own, and to look out for himself, are two things that stand out in my mind over all the rest.

Reading the Powerful Accounts of Dr. and Mrs. Dodge

As the *Titanic* foundered, Dr. Washington Dodge, a millionaire financier and the City of San Francisco's assessor, saw his wife, Ruth, and son, Washington, safely into Lifeboat 7. He then managed to make it himself into Lifeboat 13.

Lifeboat 7, with a capacity of 65 passengers, was launched from the starboard side of the *Titanic* at 12:45 a.m. It was the first lifeboat to leave the ship. It carried only 27 people, 38 short of capacity.

Lifeboat 13, also with a capacity of 65 passengers, was launched from the starboard side of the *Titanic* at 1:40 a.m. Lifeboat 13, the 13th lifeboat to leave the ship, carried only 54 people, 11 short of capacity. It arrived at the *Carpathia* at 4:45 a.m.

After his arrival in New York, Dr. Dodge and his family checked into the Hotel Wolcott. Over the next few days, he told his story to reporters from all over the world. The first two newspaper stories reprinted here, both from Dr. Dodge, were reported from New York. Mrs. Dodge's account, the third story, was given to a reporter in San Francisco after the family returned home.

These three firsthand accounts of the wreck of the *Titanic* are breathtaking. They are three of the most compelling and horrifying stories to come out of that terrible night.

In these accounts, Dr. and Mrs. Dodge describe seeing steerage passengers shot and their bodies falling into the water. Dr. Dodge relates hearing Captain Smith exclaim "My God!" upon being told that the ship was listing. He remembers seeing disgraced White Star Line Chairman J. Bruce Ismay fleeing the ship in a lifeboat.

Mrs. Dodge tells of facing the bitter cold with her 4-year-old son wearing only a pair of pajamas and a life belt. She describes how passengers in her lifeboat argued about whether to go back for people in the water and how some passengers threatened to overpower the crew if such an attempt was made.

These historical reports are powerful and thrilling. They reaffirm that even though the *Titanic* story has evolved into almost-mythical status, the nightmare happened to real people, cowards and heroes among them. The actions of the victims and survivors cannot help but make us wonder how we would conduct ourselves in such surreal and dreadful circumstances.

From the April 19, 1912, *San Francisco Bulletin:*

SAN FRANCISCO'S ASSESSOR TELLS STORY OF THE WRECK OF THE TITANIC FROM WHICH HE ESCAPES AFTER THRILLING EXPERIENCE

NEW YORK, April 19. — Dr. Washington Dodge of San Francisco, at the Hotel Wolcott here, gave the following account of the wreck:

"We had retired to our stateroom, and the noise of the collision was not at all alarming. We had just fallen asleep. My wife awakened me and said that something had happened to the ship. We went on deck and everything seemed quiet and orderly.

"The orchestra was playing a lively tune. They started to lower the lifeboats after a lapse of some minutes. There was little excitement.

Ship seemed safer

"As the lifeboats were being launched, many of the first-cabin passengers expressed their preference of staying on the ship. The passengers were constantly being assured that there was no danger, but that as a matter of extra precaution the women and children should be placed in the lifeboats.

"Everything was still quiet and orderly when I placed Mrs. Dodge and the boy in the fourth or fifth boat. I believe there were 20 boats lowered away altogether. I did what I could to help in keeping order, as after the sixth or seventh boat was launched the excitement began.

"Some of the passengers fought with such desperation to get into the lifeboats that the officers shot them, and their bodies fell into the ocean. . . .

The ship seemed calm

"I saw Colonel Astor, Major Butt and Captain Smith standing together . . . There was absolutely no excitement among them. Captain Smith said there was no danger.

"The starboard side of the *Titanic* struck the big berg and the ice was piled up on the deck. None of us had the slightest realization that the ship had received its death wound.

"Mrs. [Isidor] Straus showed most admirable heroism. She refused in a very determined manner to leave her husband, although she was twice entreated to get into the boats. Straus declined with great fervor to get in the boat while any women were left.

"I wish you would say for me that Colonel Astor, Major Butt, Captain Smith and every man in the cabins acted the part of a hero in that awful night.

"As the excitement began I saw an officer of the *Titanic* shoot down two steerage passengers who were endeavoring to rush the lifeboats. I have learned since that twelve of the steerage passengers were shot altogether, one officer shooting down six. The first-cabin men and women behaved with great heroism."

Owes life to steward

One of the stewards of the *Titanic,* with whom Dr. and Mrs. Dodge had crossed the Atlantic before on the *Olympic,* knew them well. He recognized Dodge as the thirteenth boat was being filled. The steerage passengers were being shot down and some of the steerage passengers were stabbing right and left in an endeavor to reach the boat.

The thirteenth boat was filled on one side with children, fully 20 or 30 of them, and a few women. All in the boat were panicstricken and screaming. The steward had been ordered to take charge of the thirteenth, and, seizing Dodge, pushed him into the boat, exclaiming that he needed his help in caring for his helpless charges.

Dodge said that when the boats were drawing away from the ship they could hear the orchestra playing "Lead, Kindly Light," and rockets were going up from the *Titanic* in the wonderfully clear night. "We could see from the distance that two boats were being made ready to be lowered. The panic was in the steerage, and it was that portion of the ship that the shooting was made necessary."

"I will never forget," Mrs. Dodge said, "the awful scene of the great steamer as we drew away. From the upper rails heroic husbands and fathers were waving and throwing kisses to their womenfolk in the receding lifeboats."

From the April 20, 1912, *San Francisco Bulletin:*

DR. DODGE GIVES STORY OF RESCUE

Several Boats Lowered Only Half Filled; "Tumbled In" When Told to

NEW YORK, April 20. — "At 10 p.m. Sunday while my wife and I went out for a stroll along the *Titanic*'s promenade deck we found the air icy cold — so cold, in fact, that we were driven inside although we had on heavy wraps. This change of temperature had occurred in the previous two hours. We went to bed and were awakened about 11:40 by a jar which gave me the impression that a blow on the side had moved the entire vessel laterally to a considerable angle. With only my overcoat and slippers, I went through the companion way, but, to my surprise, found no one seriously considering the shock.

"Men in evening clothes stood about chatting and laughing, and when an officer — I did not know his name — hurried by I asked, 'What is the trouble?' He replied:

"'Something wrong; something is wrong with the propeller; nothing serious.'

"I went back to my stateroom, where my wife had already arisen to dress herself and I dissuaded her from dressing herself or our four-year-old son.

"A little while later, still feeling nervous, I went up to the promenade deck and there saw a great mass of ice close to the starboard rail. Going back to my cabin again, I met my bedroom steward, with whom I had crossed the ocean before, who whispered to me that 'Word has come from down below for everyone to put on life preservers.'

"I rushed back to my stateroom and told my wife the news and made her come up on deck with the baby, even half clothed. The boats on the starboard side were then suspended from the davits, but no passengers wanted to get in.

Room in the boat

"It was a drop of fifty feet to the surface of the sea, and, apparently everybody considered that they were safer on the 'unsinkable *Titanic*' than in a small boat whose only propelling power was four oars. The first boat was only half filled, for the simple reason that no one would get aboard.

"Personally, I waited for the lifeboat to become filled, and then saw there was plenty of room. I asked the officer at the rail, whose name I do not know, why I also could not get in, as there was plenty of room. His only reply was, 'Women and children first,' and the half-filled boat sheared off.

"Before the next boats were lowered passengers who had become excited were calmed by the utterances of the officers that the injury was trivial and that in case it proved serious at least four steamships had been summoned by wireless and would be on hand within an hour.

Saw wife in boat

"I watched the lowering of the boat in which my wife and child were until it was safely launched on an even keel, and then I went to the starboard side of the ship, where the boats with the odd numbers from one to fifteen were being prepared for dropping over the side.

"The thing that impressed me was that there was not sufficient men to launch the boats, and, as a matter of fact, when the ship went down there was still one boat on the davits and one on the deck.

"The peculiar part of the whole rescue question was that the first boats had no more than thirty passengers, with four seamen to row, while the latter boats averaged from forty to fifty, with hardly one person aboard who knew how to move an oar.

"All this time the *Titanic* had a slight list to port, but just after the collision Captain Smith, coming hurriedly up and inquiring what the list was and finding it eighteen degrees to starboard, said 'My God!' "

Sailor offers stockings

As there is always a touch of humor in the most gruesome of happenings, it is told by Mrs. Dodge that one of the sailors in the boat in which she embarked insisted on taking off his shoes and giving her his stockings, saying: "I assure you, ma'm, that they are perfectly clean. I just put them on this morning."

"I waited until what I thought was the end," continued Dr. Dodge. "I certainly saw no signs of any women or children on deck when I was told to take a seat in boat number thirteen. When lowered we nearly came abreast of the three-foot stream that the condenser pumps were still sending out from the ship's side. We cried out and the flow halted. I cannot imagine how that was done.

"Another danger to us was that the boat in which [Bruce] Ismay escaped was lowered, owing to the angle of the sinking ship, almost directly above us. If it had come ten feet farther both boats would have gone to the bottom, but our yells and cries stopped this catastrophe also.

"Tumbled in"

"When boat number [thirteen] was being lowered from the 'A' deck it stayed there for at least two minutes while the officers in charge were calling for more women and children. But as none responded the officers said (and I am sorry I do not know their names) 'some of you men tumble in,' and I 'tumbled.'

"In my boat when we found ourselves afloat we also found that the four oars were secured with strands of tarred rope. No man in the crowd had a pocket knife, but one had sufficient strength in his fingers to tear open one of the strands. That was the only way in which we got our boat far enough away from the *Titanic*'s side to escape the volume of the condenser pumps.

"Here is another thing that I want to emphasize; only one of all the boats set adrift from the vessel's side had a lantern. We had to follow the only boat that had one, and if it had not been for that solitary lantern possibly many of the other boats might have drifted away and gone down.

"To show how lightly even the executive officers of the ship took the matter of the collision is proven by the fact that the officer in charge of the boat in which my wife was saved refused to let his men row more than half a mile from the *Titanic* because that he would soon have orders to come back.

"We saw the sinking of the vessel. The lights continued burning all along its starboard side until the moment of its downward plunge. After that a series of terrific explosions occurred, I suppose either from the boilers or weakened bulkheads.

"And then we just rowed about until dawn when we caught sight of the port light of the *Carpathia,* and knew that we were saved.

Boats without passengers

"One curious point I noticed is that the first two boats launched held only their crews. Half an hour later I was told by an officer that they were launched in that shape to stand by in case of accident to her small boats.

"But there were no accidents and practically nothing for these boats to do, so many valuable lives were lost.

"If a sea had been running I do not see how many of the small boats would have lived. For instance, on my boat there were neither one officer or a seaman. The only men at the oars were stewards, who could no more row than I could serve a dinner.

"While order prevailed until the last lifeboat had been lowered, hell prevailed when the officers, who had kept the steerage passengers below, with their revolvers pointed at them to prevent them from making their way to the upper deck.

Steerage passenger shot

"When the steerage passengers came up many of them had knives, revolvers and clubs and sought to fight their way to the two unlaunched, collapsible boats. Many of these were shot by the officers.

"Only one of the rafts floated, and even that did not float above the water's edge. From 40 to 50 persons who had jumped overboard clambered aboard it and stood upon it, locked arm and arm together until it was submerged to a depth of at least 18 inches. They all tried to hold together, but when the *Carpathia*'s boat reached them there were only 16 left.

"The most horrible part of the story is that statement that several persons in the lifeboats saw, when the *Titanic* took her final plunge, that her four great smokestacks sucked up and carried down in their giant maws dozens of the third class passengers, then huddled together on the forward upper deck."

From the April 30, 1912, *San Francisco Bulletin:*

DR. DODGE'S WIFE TELLS STORY OF TITANIC WRECK

Reaches Home with Husband and Son after Terrible Experience at Sea

SAN FRANCISCO, APRIL 30. — Seated in the library of her home on Washington Street, amid a profusion of flowers sent by friends to express their welcome home, Mrs. Washington Dodge again told the story of her experiences on the night the ill-fated *Titanic* went down.

Dr. and Mrs. Dodge and their 5-year-old son, Washington Dodge Jr., arrived in the city yesterday afternoon, little the worse for their experience. [*Note:* Their son was actually 4 at the time.] The parents' one anxiety is for the boy, who is seriously ill from the effects of the exposure to the ice-chilled air on the night of the disaster.

"Was it cold?" said Mrs. Dodge. "You can imagine how cold it was when I tell you that we passed fifty-six miles of icebergs after we got on the *Carpathia*. The baby had nothing on but his pajamas and a life preserver.

"I think it is foolish to speak of the heroism displayed. There was none that I witnessed. It was merely a matter of waiting your turn for a lifeboat, and there was no keen anxiety to enter the boats because everybody had such confidence in that wretched ship. The officers told us that they had wireless communication with seven vessels, which were on the way to relieve us, and the men believed themselves as safe on board as in the boats. It seemed the vaguest possibility that the ship might sink before one of the seven vessels arrived.

"Of course, I left the *Titanic* before it began to settle into the water. The steerage passengers had not come on deck. In fact, there were few on the deck from which we left and more men than women.

Took second boat

"It happened this way. There seems to have been an order issued that all women should congregate on the port side of the vessel. The vessel was injured on the starboard side, and even when I left the ship there was a slight list to starboard. We did not hear this order. I was in my stateroom, had retired again after the accident when the doctor came saying he had met our steward and had been told to get into a life preserver. I slipped on my fur coat over my night robe and preserver, put on my shoes without stockings; I did not stop to button them.

"We had made a practice of sitting on the starboard side of the deck, the gymnasium was there, and naturally when we went above we turned to starboard. They were lowering boats. I entered the second boat with my baby. This boat had an officer in command, and enough officers to man the oars. Several women entered with me and as we commenced to lower the boat the women's husbands jumped in with them. I called to the doctor to come, but he refused because there were still a few women on deck. Every woman in that second boat with the exception of myself, had her husband with her.

Boats half-filled

"I supposed all the women were congregated on the port side because it would naturally be the highest side, and the safest because [it would be] the last to go down. We had no idea then that there would not be enough boats to go around. In fact, the first boats were only half filled.

"There must have been some confusion in orders, else I do not see why some of the women were not sent from port to starboard to enter those boats being lowered there. My husband got into the thirteenth boat. At that time there were no women on the starboard side. There was not one woman in the boat he entered, and no member of the crew.

"Bruce Ismay entered the fifteenth boat from starboard. It was being lowered at the same time, and the doctor says he remembers this because there was some fear that the boats might swing into each other as they were lowered down the side of the vessel.

Crying of the doomed

"The most terrible part of the experience was that awful crying after the ship went down. We were a mile away, but we heard it — oh, how we heard it. It seemed to last about an hour, although it may have been only a short time, for some say a man could not have lived in that water over fifteen minutes. At last it died down.

"Our officer and the members of the crew wanted to go back and pick up those whom they could, but the women in the boat would not let them. They told them if they attempted to turn back their husbands would take the oars from them, and the other men outnumbered the crew. I told them I could not see how they could forbid turning back in the face of those awful cries. I will remember it until I die, as it is. I told them: 'How do I know, you have your husbands with you, but my husband may be one of those who are crying.'

"They argued that if we got back where the people were struggling, some of the steerage passengers, crazed with fear and the cold, might capsize the boat struggling to get it, or might force the officers to overload so we would all go down.

Women hysterical

"After the crying died down, two or three of the women became hysterical — about what I don't know; they were missing none of their people. I was trying to keep baby from realization of what was happening, but when these women shrieked he would begin crying and asking, 'Where's papa?'

"Finally I did what everyone thinks a strange thing. I changed lifeboats in mid-ocean. We overtook the first boat. It was hardly half filled. They offered to take any of us aboard, and to get away from the hysteria of the others I changed.

On the Carpathia

"The most pathetic thing was the scene on board the *Carpathia* during the rescue. As each boat drew up the survivors would peer over, straining to see the face of someone they had left behind. They were the young brides — everybody on board, of course, had known they were brides, and they had watched them laughing and promenading with their husbands.

"The moans of anxiety and disappointment as each boat failed to bring up those that they were looking for were awful and finally that awful despair which fell over everyone when we knew there were no more boats to pick up.

"Still they would not give up hope.

"'Are you missing anyone?' the passengers would ask each other, never 'Have you lost anyone?'

Kindness of passengers

"Too much cannot be said of the kindness of the *Carpathia*'s passengers. They gave up staterooms, they took the very clothing off their bodies for us. I left the *Carpathia* wearing garments given me by a woman whose name I do not know and will never know."

She exhibited the bloomer trousers she had cut for Baby Dodge from a blanket given her by a sailor.

"I am sorry that I knew the names of so few passengers. There were two men aboard particularly, who every day used to come on the sun deck to play with the baby, and we often fell into conversation. Those men were not among the survivors. I do wish I had known their names that I might tell their wives some of the beautiful things they had said to me of their home life, casually, in these conversations."

Chapter 9

How the World Learned about the Titanic's Loss

*T*he nightmare of the *Titanic*'s sinking was made even more dramatic by the suspense of having to wait for news reports about the historic event. For the families and friends of the passengers and crew, the wait was especially hard. They waited with anxiety and anticipation to find out whether their friends and loved ones were among the survivors.

This chapter presents the first news reports about what really happened to the *Titanic* on that fateful night of Sunday, April 14, 1912. I show how the story first broke and how those newspapers that rushed to judgment ended up publishing erroneous stories. I also explain which papers stepped up to fill in the details, both about the disaster itself and the science behind the disaster.

As you read the dramatic reports in this chapter, keep in mind how different the world of news reporting was in 1912. In today's world of instantaneous communication, people take the news for granted. They can read about and watch the news almost as soon as events occur. But in 1912, satellite telephone communication wasn't available. And e-mail and the Internet weren't even in people's wildest dreams. Figure 9-1 offers a reminder of how people got their news in the early 1900s.

Figure 9-1:
Newsboy
Ned Parfett
outside
Oceanic
House In
London her-
alding the
disaster.

© Archive Holdings, Inc./Getty Images

Breaking the Story in The New York Times

The New York Times' managing editor Carr Van Anda first scooped the world on the *Titanic* story when he published the news of the ship's collision with the iceberg in the morning edition of the April 15, 1912, issue. He then announced in the afternoon edition — with certainty — that the ship had sunk.

Van Anda's instinct to publish was based on an unconfirmed Associated Press bulletin that had been issued as the result of an intercepted wireless message. His instinct proved sound, and *The New York Times* was the first newspaper in the country to break the news of the *Titanic* disaster.

In 1912, *The New York Times* wasn't the prestigious "newspaper of record" it is today. It was just one of several daily papers serving New York. Van Anda's story immediately boosted the paper's reputation and was a contributing factor in transforming the paper into the highly respected institution it is today. The story instantly gave the paper clout and an esteem it has retained for more than ten decades.

Here is the complete text of Van Anda's groundbreaking story as it appeared on the front page of the *Times* in the morning edition. Notice the many sub-headlines that announce the story.

From the April 15, 1912, edition of *The New York Times:*

NEW LINER TITANIC HITS AN ICEBERG;

SINKING BY THE BOW AT MIDNIGHT;

WOMEN PUT OFF IN LIFE BOATS;

LAST WIRELESS AT 12:27 A.M. BLURRED

Allan Liner Virginian Now Speeding Toward the Big Ship.

BALTIC TO THE RESCUE, TOO

The Olympic Also Rushing To Give Aid — Other Ships Within Call.

CARMANA DODGED BERGS

Reports French Liner Niagara Injured and Several Ships Caught

BIG TITANIC'S FIRST TRIP

Bringing Many Prominent Americans, and Was Due in New York Tomorrow.

MISHAP AT VERY START

Narrowly Escaped Collision with the American Liner New York When Leaving Port.

Reports of ships on their way to help

HALIFAX, N. S., April 14. — A wireless dispatch received tonight by the Allan line officials here from Capt. Gambell of the steamer Virginian, states that the White Star liner *Titanic* struck an iceberg off the Newfoundland Coast and flashed out wireless calls for immediate assistance.

The *Virginian* put on full speed and headed for the *Titanic.*

No particulars have been received as to the extent of the damage sustained by *Titanic.*

The *Virginian* sailed from Halifax at midnight on Saturday night, and would probably be 300 miles off this coast when she picked up the calls from the *Titanic* for assistance.

The Allan liner has only about 200 passengers on board and would have ample accommodations for a large number of persons in case a transfer from the *Titanic* was necessary. The *Virginian* is a mail steamer, and so she is not likely to take the *Titanic* in tow.

Other stories in the April 15, 1912, edition of *The New York Times* reported the following:

✔ *Titanic* sent a wire to Cape Race, Newfoundland, saying she had been struck by an iceberg. Another message, received a half hour later, reported that the ship was sinking and that women were being boarded onto lifeboats.

✔ The *Olympic* was in communication with the *Titanic* and was "making all possible speed toward her."

Exploring How a Rush to Publish Led to Erroneous Stories

Rushing to judgment on the part of news organizations is nothing new. Erroneous news articles have been published since the dawn of news coverage. The front-page stories I present in this section tell how the passengers and crew of the *Titanic* were saved.

Keep in mind as you read these articles that the *Titanic* was believed to be utterly unsinkable. Perhaps this belief is what made the New York *Evening Sun* and the *Christian Science Monitor* journalists willing to believe the erroneous reports that were published on the front pages of their newspapers.

The Evening Sun reports that all passengers are saved

From the April 15, 1912, edition of the New York *Evening Sun:*

ALL SAVED FROM TITANIC AFTER COLLISION

RESCUE BY CARPATHIA AND PARISIAN;

LINER IS BEING TOWED TO HALIFAX

AFTER SMASHING INTO ICEBERG

Baltic, Virginian, Olympic and Other Ships
Summoned by Urgent Wireless Calls
BIGGEST OF LINERS IN CRASH
She Carried Over 1,400 Passengers,
Many of Prominence — Message from
Telling of Rescue

CANSO, N. S., April 15 The White Star liner *Titanic,* having transferred her passengers to the *Parisian* and *Carpathia,* was at 2 o'clock this afternoon being towed to Halifax by the *Virginian* of the Allan line.

The Virginian passed a line to the *Titanic* as soon as the passengers had been transferred, and the latest word received by wireless was that there was no doubt that the new White Star liner would reach port.

Agents of the White Star line at Halifax have been ordered to have wrecking tugs sent out to aid the *Virginian* with her tow into port.

OLYMPIC SENDS FIRST WORD OF RESCUE

The first definite news received direct by the White Star line officers here about the accident to the *Titanic* came at 11:05 o'clock.

The message read:

"PARISIAN and CARPATHIA in attendance on TITANIC. CARPATHIA has taken twenty boatloads of passengers. BALTIC approaching. OLYMPIC 260 away." CAPT. HADDOCK

It was later reported that the *Virginian* had arrived at the scene, had passed a line to the *Titanic,* and would tow her to Halifax.

The April 15, 1912, edition of the New York *Evening Sun* also reported this erroneous information:

✔ The *Baltic* of the White Star Line took aboard 20 boatloads of passengers from the *Titanic.*

✔ The *Titanic* was still afloat and was making her way to Halifax.

The Christian Science Monitor claims that passengers are safe

From the April 15, 1912, edition of the *Christian Science Monitor:*

Passengers Safely Moved and Steamer Titanic Taken in Tow

Carpathia and Parisian Care for Those Aboard Disabled Liner While Virginian Lends Aid to Make Port

BULKHEADS HOLD

Officials of White Star Company Confident Steamer is Unsinkable and Will Float Until Halifax is Reached

FACTS REGARDING ACCIDENT TO THE WHITE STAR LINER TITANIC

White Star liner Titanic, greatest vessel afloat, strikes iceberg shortly before midnight.

Wireless despatches immediately sent out that vessel is sinking.

Women and children placed in life boats ready for release.

Steamers Virginian and Parisian of Allan line and Carpathia of Cunard line reach side of the Titanic, Baltic of White Star line sighted on the way.

Passengers transferred to the Parisian and Carpathia, while Virginian takes vessel in tow to Halifax.

Second transfer to be made to Baltic, which will take passengers to New York, arriving on Thursday.

BULLETIN

The New Haven railroad will send a special Pullman train to Halifax to accommodate the passengers of the *Titanic.*

CANSO, N.S. The White Star liner *Titanic,* having transferred her passengers to the *Parisian* and *Carpathia,* was, at 2 o'clock this afternoon, being towed to Halifax by the *Virginian* of the Allan line.

The *Virginian* passed a line to the *Titanic* as soon as the passengers had been transferred, and the latest word received by wireless was that there was no doubt that the new White Star liner would reach port. Agents of the White Star line at Halifax have been ordered to have wrecking tugs sent out to aid the Virginian with her tow into port.

HALIFAX, N.S. Held afloat only by her watertight compartments, the great White Star liner *Titanic* is slowly crawling towards this harbor. Her passengers have been taken aboard the Cunard liner *Carpathia* and the *Parisian* of the Allan line only to have to face a second ordeal as they are to be again transferred to the *Baltic* of the White Star line this afternoon. The *Baltic* will take them to their journey's end in New York, where they are due on Thursday.

The disaster to the *Titanic* was unparalleled in the history of navigation. The largest, most luxurious and best appointed vessel ever laid down, she seemed proof against any disaster and it is to the very fact that she was a new steamer that the passengers on board, noted financiers and society leaders owe their lives.

Hardly another craft afloat could have withstood the terrific shock when the *Titanic* driving along at better than half speed, although in the midst of ice fields, crashed bow into a great, submerged mountain of ice which tore away her steel plates.

Only meager advices regarding the wreck have been received here by the wireless and these fail to clear up how the accident took place, or whether there was a panic among the passengers. That Capt. Smith, admiral of the White Star's fleet, and in command of this latest ocean creation, realized the danger was shown by an appeal for aid. The wireless of the *Titanic* picked up the Cape Race station and immediate aid was demanded.

The Allan liner Virginian was the first to be reached but almost before she had turned her prow toward the wounded ship, another craft had started on the same errand.

Then came a cruel waiting time, punctuated with brief wireless messages that caused the utmost alarm. "Hurry! Hurry!" was the burden of every word that came flashing through the air, but it was plain from the start that the badly needed aid must come from the steamers that were in the immediate vicinity.

Fleshing Out the Details of the Disaster

The *Boston Daily Globe* was the first newspaper to comprehend the enormity of the disaster. "The disaster is the greatest in the modern marine history of the world," the newspaper reported. The *Globe* was also one of the first newspapers to give precise details about the tragedy.

For instance, the newspaper revealed that male passengers had sacrificed the opportunity to save themselves in favor of women and children. It also reported that "wealth rubbed elbows with poverty" when citizens of New

York came in large numbers to the downtown offices of the White Star Line to find out whether friends and relatives were among the living.

The *Globe* articles also touch on some interesting *Titanic* minutia. For example, it provided that the ship carried 3,423 bags of mail, diamonds of great value, and large amounts of bonds. (That a newspaper would report the loss of mail illustrates how important shipping was in those days to transatlantic mail services.)

From the April 16, 1912, edition of the *Boston Daily Globe:*

Early mention of 1,500 dead

TITANIC SINKS, 1500 DIE

Carpathia Picks Up 675 Out of 2200 — Races for New York — Survivors Mostly Women and Children

Giant Steamer Goes Down Before Help Arrives

Virginian or Parisian May Have Some Survivors

White Star Officials Admit "Horrible Loss of Life"

Greatest Sea Tragedy in History Off Newfoundland Coast

The White Star Line steamer *Titanic,* the largest vessel in the world, sank at 2:20 yesterday morning at almost the exact spot at which she crashed into an iceberg less than four hours before she went to the bottom.

Out of about 2200 souls on board the steamer but 675 are known to have been saved. These, according to wireless dispatches, are on board the Cunard Liner *Carpathia* bound for New York.

This is believed to mean almost beyond doubt that more than 1500 people went down with the mammoth liner.

The only hope that more than 675 of the 1300 passengers and crew of 860 survive lies in the chance that the Allan liners *Virginian* or *Parisian,* which are known to have been in the vicinity of the *Titanic,* reached the scene in time to make some rescues.

The *Carpathia* is expected to reach New York Friday morning with the refugees.

Meager reports available indicate that when the *Carpathia* reached the scene of the disaster the *Titanic* was already beneath the waves and that the rescued were picked up from lifeboats and rafts as had been successfully cleared away on the *Titanic* before she went down.

Another article from the April 16, 1912, edition of the *Boston Daily Globe,* "Greatest of sea tragedies," noted with sadness that news of the loss of life reached Americans "with a much greater shock because hope had been buoyed up all day by reports that the steamship, although badly damaged, was not in a sinking condition and that all her passengers had been safely taken off."

Because the *Titanic* carried many wealthy titans of American industry whose names were known to the general public either from the Business pages or Society pages of the newspaper, the *Globe* listed in the April 16, 1912, article the "notable persons" who were believed to have perished. These people (whom you can read about in Chapter 3) were mentioned in the article:

- **John Jacob and Madeleine Astor:** The Astor family was one of the wealthiest in turn-of-the-twentieth-century America. John Jacob Astor IV was an investor and real estate developer. The Astors were returning from a European honeymoon aboard the *Titanic.* Madeleine, 29 years younger than her husband, was John Jacob's second wife. She survived, but he did not.

- **Benjamin Guggenheim:** Son of the mining magnate Meyer Guggenheim, Benjamin was 46 when he died aboard the *Titanic.*

- **Isidor and Ida Straus:** Isidor was cofounder of the Macy's department store. He was 67 and his wife 63 when they died. Although an officer told Isidor he could board a lifeboat, he refused, offering the seat instead to his wife's maid. Ida also turned down the offer to board a lifeboat. She reportedly said, "I will not be separated from my husband. As we have lived, so will we die together."

The *Boston Daily Globe* of April 16, 1912, was the first to deliver news about women and children being boarded first on the *Titanic*'s lifeboats. It also was the first to inquire whether the "women and children first" rule applied to women and children in both steerage as well as first class. The newspaper quoted Vice President Philip Franklin of the White Star Line as saying, "There is no rule of the sea which requires such a sacrifice. It is a rule of courtesy on land, as well as sea, that gallant men have often observed in time of disaster." The newspaper further reported, "It was generally true, [Franklin] added, that men made this vital sacrifice at sea to the women of the steerage as well as those of wealthier class in the first and second saloons."

Also interesting in the *Globe* articles is a section titled "Capt Inman Sealby's Views." Sealby, who survived the sinking of the *Republic* in 1909, had spent 25 years at sea. He was the first to suggest that the *Titanic* didn't strike an iceberg head on but that it instead glanced off one.

From the April 16, 1912, edition of the *Boston Daily Globe:*

CAPT INMAN SEALBY'S VIEWS
Commander of Ill-Fated Republic
Believes the Side Was Torn out of the Titanic

ANN ARBOR, Mich. April 16 — Capt. Inman Sealby, in charge of the ill-fated *Republic* at the time she sank, now a senior law student in the University of Michigan, is most interested in the news of the sinking of the *Titanic.* He expressed no surprise that a collision with an iceberg would cause such a vessel, supposed to be absolutely safe, to sink.

Capt. Sealby has had 25 years' experience on the Atlantic and knows the grave danger of icebergs. He called attention to the fact that the *Titanic* struck the berg on the eve of the day when the transAtlantic liners change from the north to the south track because of danger from ice.

His opinion is that the *Titanic* did not strike the berg head on, as that would have only damaged her bow and could hardly have caused her to sink. He figures from his experience that a glancing blow was struck and that the berg scraped down one side, tearing holes through a large number of bulkheads. The *Republic* and the *Titanic* were both White Star liners.

Figure 9-2 shows another front-page article from April 16, 1912 — this one from *The* [New York] *World.* While not every detail is correct (the number of survivors is high, for example), you can see that the reporting improved greatly from some of the early erroneous stories.

Figure 9-2:
The April 16, 1912, edition of *The World* reporting the sinking.

Offering the First Scientific View of the Tragedy

Scientific American was the first journal to offer a comprehensive and authoritative article about the sinking of the *Titanic*. The article, "Wreck of the White

Star Liner Titanic: How the World's Greatest Steamship Went Down with 1,600 Souls," looks at the disaster from an almost purely scientific point of view and comes to some well-founded conclusions. For example, the journal was first to suggest that excessive speed and a shortage of lifeboats contributed to the tragedy.

The conclusions that this article reaches were confirmed as investigations were carried out in the months and years after the disaster. What is most impressive about this thorough article is that it appeared a mere two weeks after the *Titanic* went down, on April 27, 1912.

The article begins like this:

> In the long list of maritime disasters there is none to compare with that which, on Sunday, April 14th, overwhelmed the latest and most magnificent of the ocean liners on her maiden voyage across the Western Ocean. Look at the disaster from whatever point we may, it stands out stupefying in its horror and prodigious in its many-sided significance.

After describing how the *Titanic* was constructed, the article made this assertion, which was remarkable for its accuracy and succinctness:

> But there was just one peril of the deep against which this mighty ship was as helpless as the smallest of coasting steamers: the long glancing blow below the waterline, due to the projecting shelf of an iceberg. It was this that sent the *Titanic* to the bottom in the brief space of 2½ hours, and it was her very size and the fatal speed at which she was driven, which made the blow so terrible.

Next, the article discusses why the *Titanic* was traveling at dangerous speeds when it struck the iceberg:

> How such [an] experienced commander as Captain Smith should have driven his ship at high speed, and in the night, when he knew he was in the proximity of heavy ice fields is a mystery, which may never be cleared up. The night, it is true, was clear and starlit, and the sea perfectly smooth. Probably the fact that conditions were favorable for a good lookout, coupled with the desire to maintain a high average speed on the maiden trip of the vessel, decided the captain to "take a chance." Whatever the motive, it seems to be well established that the ship was not slowed down; and to this fact and no other must the loss of the *Titanic* be set down.
>
> Had the *Titanic* been running under a slow bell, she would probably have been afloat to-day.

Scientific American also took the British Board of Trade to task for failing to require the *Titanic* to carry enough lifeboats for all her passengers. (See Chapter 10 for a discussion of the British Board of Trade's role in the *Titanic* story.) Here's what it said:

Scientific American's tribute to Titanic's engineers

We can only imagine the furious panic that would have occurred had the *Titanic*'s lights not stayed on until she went down at 2:20 a.m. on Monday, April 15, 1912. The great ship was afloat on a jet-black sea in moonless darkness, yet it was an oasis of light in that blackness. For almost three hours, from the time the *Titanic* collided with the iceberg until her stern reared up and plunged to the bottom of the sea, all her lights blazed thanks to the dedicated and selfless engineering crew, none of whom ever left their posts.

The editors and staff of the respected journal *Scientific American* knew that the *Titanic*'s engineers were heroes of the noblest breed, and yet none of these men was even acknowledged by the survivors in the days immediately following the sinking. The following editorial was the journal's attempt to honor the memory of the *Titanic*'s brave engineering crew and to right what it (correctly) saw as a grave injustice. It appeared in the April 27, 1912, edition of *Scientific American:*

> There is a world of heroic and tragic significance in the fact that the survivors' stories of the last hours of the *Titanic* make no reference whatever to the thirty-five officers of the engineer force. Of the officers of the deck there is frequent mention and many of them are among the survivors. This is natural and proper, for they were standing at their posts of duty. We read also of farewells between them and other officers whose duties were concerned with the welfare of the *Titanic*'s passengers; but in all the records of those final eventful hours there is not a mention of any one of the band of men whose duties called for their presence far down in the deepest recesses of the ship.
>
> In the roll of the saved there is not the name of a single certified engineer. Why this literal silence of the grave? There can be but one answer. Every man of the engineer watch stuck to his post to the very last and went down with the ship. Furthermore, this

devotion to duty leads us to believe that such engineers as were not on watch may have voluntarily gone below to render what assistance they could in the sudden and frightful emergency.

This heroic devotion on the part of a little recognized body of professional men, the importance of whose duties on board ship is overlooked by the average transAtlantic passenger, will make an even greater impression upon our minds if we remember that they, above everybody else on that ship, must have known that she had received her death wound and that the hour of her sinking might be delayed, but not by any possibility averted. While those above deck, conscious of the enormous magnitude of the *Titanic* were exclaiming, "You cannot sink her," these men standing on the double bottom of the ship may possibly have seen the submerged edge of the iceberg come ripping through the sides of the ship, opening up boiler room after boiler room to the savage inrush of the water!

The bunkers, we learn, were arranged transversely to the ship. Hence if the bilges of side plating were ruptured, the inrush of water must have occurred before the very eyes of the engineers; and to the seafaring man there is no sight before which his courage will quail so quickly as this. Nevertheless, there is every reason to believe that not a man flinched from his trial. Steam was maintained in such boiler rooms as were not invaded by the water; the powerful bilge pumps were kept going to the very last minute; and the electric lighting plant was watched over, evidently with most careful solicitude. It is certain the pumps alone must have very materially delayed the sinking of the ship; and the value, in that hour of terrible stress, of the work done by the electrical engineers in keeping the lights going until the last trace of the ship had disappeared, is impossible to overestimate.

For years the British Board of Trade, renowned the world over for the jealous care with which it safeguards the life of the individual, has been guilty of the amazing anomaly of permitting the passenger ships of the vast British merchant marine to put to sea carrying boat accommodation for only one out of every three persons on board. The penalty for such unspeakable folly, we had almost said criminal and brutal negligence, may have been long delayed; but it was to come this night in a wholesale flinging away of human life, which has left a blot upon this institution which can never be effaced! Had the regulations called for the boat accommodations demanded by the German or our own government, every soul on board the *Titanic* could have been transferred and picked up by the rescuing ship.

We can conceive of no other motive than that of commercial expediency, the desire to reserve valuable space for restaurants, sun parlors or other superfluous but attractive features of the advertising pamphlet and the placard, for this criminal reduction of the last recourse of the shipwrecked to so small a measure.

Chapter 10

Investigating the Titanic's Demise

. . . .

In This Chapter

▶ Looking at the U.S. Senate's investigation

▶ Studying the British commission's findings

▶ Reading Joseph Conrad's assessment of the disaster

. . . .

*I*nvestigations into the *Titanic*'s sinking began almost immediately after the disaster occurred. Both the British and U.S. governments had "skin in the game," so to speak, and inquiries were launched to uncover the cause of the sinking and, of course, to try to assign blame.

The reports issued by the British and American governments were valuable for two reasons:

✔ They inquired into what caused the *Titanic* to sink.

✔ They provided a treasure trove of information for historians and *Titanic* aficionados.

Altogether, some 180 people, many of them survivors, gave testimony to the British and U.S. government investigatory commissions. The reports preserved the voices of survivors down through the ages. (You can hear some of those voices in Chapter 8, where you find some of the survivors' testimonies.)

This chapter looks at findings of the British and American investigations into the *Titanic* disaster. You can read the final reports of the British inquiry and American inquiry, as well as testimony by all witnesses, at the *Titanic* Inquiry Project at this website: www.titanicinquiry.org.

At the end of this chapter, I also include some contemporary commentary on the *Titanic*'s demise written by novelist and experienced seaman Joseph Conrad.

The U.S. Senate Investigation: What Can Be Done Better?

The U.S. Senate Subcommittee *Titanic* Hearing began in New York City's Waldorf-Astoria Hotel on April 19, 1912, only four days after the disaster. (The hearings began in New York because there was some sense of urgency to get them under way immediately.) After a week, the hearings moved to the new caucus room in the Russell Senate Office Building in Washington, D.C. (They were the first hearings ever held in that office.) The hearings were chaired by Senator William Alden Smith, a Republican from Michigan. According to the U.S. Senate inquiry report (issued on May 28, 1912), 82 witnesses testified before the subcommittee. However, the *Titanic* Inquiry Project — probably the most accurate and complete report of both government inquiries — gives the verbatim testimony of *88* separate witnesses (15 of which were by affidavit or submission only).

Chairman Smith, the subcommittee's lead questioner, was ridiculed in England for his obvious dearth of seafaring knowledge. Smith's cluelessness notwithstanding, the hearings he chaired were most assuredly not the whitewash that the British Commission of Inquiry became (as I discuss later in the chapter). The findings of the U.S. subcommittee were of great importance and value.

As well as investigating who was to blame for the disaster, the U.S. Senate Subcommittee *Titanic* Hearing looked at how to prevent future ocean-liner disasters from occurring. The subcommittee sought to find out how enormous ships like the *Titanic* could be made safer for their passengers and crew. The report also attempted to show precisely what happened aboard the *Titanic* during the hours before it sank.

To give you a sense of what the U.S. Senate Subcommittee *Titanic* Hearing was all about, this section looks at important conclusions from the subcommittee's final report, the testimony of Guglielmo Marconi (the inventor of the wireless telegraph), and the testimony of Captain Stanley Lord of the steamship *Californian* (which failed to arrive at the scene of the disaster in time to rescue survivors; see Chapter 7). It also shows how White Star Line Chairman and Managing Director J. Bruce Ismay recounted the disaster to the media after having testified at both the U.S. and British inquiries into the disaster.

Reading the committee's report

After interviewing its witnesses, the U.S. Senate Subcommittee *Titanic* Hearing put forth a final report that explained its conclusions. The final report described the fatalities and doled out blame, among other things.

For instance, the final report noted that fatalities were much higher among the third-class passengers than among first- and second-class passengers, and it even broke down the fatalities by percentage:

> Including the crew, the *Titanic* sailed with 2,223 persons aboard, of whom 1,513 were lost and 711 were saved. It will be noted in this connection that 60 per cent of the first class passengers were saved, 42 per cent of the second class passengers were saved, 25 per cent of the third class passengers were saved, and 24 per cent of the crew were saved.

While this report offers definitive numbers of passengers, victims, and survivors, the statistics vary among sources, and we cannot know for certain what these numbers actually were. (I explain the ambiguity in this book's Introduction.)

The subcommittee faulted the White Star Line for not properly preparing the crew to load passengers in the lifeboats and for not loading the lifeboats in an orderly fashion:

> Many of the crew did not join the ship until a few hours before sailing, and the only drill while the vessel lay at Southampton or on the voyage consisted in lowering two lifeboats on the starboard side into the water, which boats were again hoisted to the boat deck within a half hour. No boat list designating the stations of members of the crew was posted until several days after sailing from Southampton, boatmen being left in ignorance of their proper stations until the following Friday morning.

> The lack of preparation at this time was most noticeable. There was no system adopted for loading the boats; there was great indecision as to the deck from which boats were to be loaded; there was wide diversity of opinion as to the number of the crew necessary to man each boat; there was no direction whatever as to the number of passengers to be carried by each boat, and no uniformity in loading them. On one side only women and children were put in the boats, while on the other side there was almost an equal proportion of men and women put into the boats, the women and children being given the preference in all cases. The failure to utilize all lifeboats in their recognized capacity for safety unquestionably resulted in the needless sacrifice of several hundred lives which might otherwise have been saved.

> The vessel was provided with lifeboats . . . for 1,176 persons, while but 706 were saved. Only a few of the ship's lifeboats were fully loaded, while others were but partially filled. Some were loaded at the boat deck, and some at the A deck, and there were successfully lowered to the water. The twentieth boat was washed overboard when the forward part of the ship was submerged, and in its overturned condition served as a life raft for about 30 people, including Second Officer Lightoller, Wireless Operators Bride and Phillips (the latter dying before rescue), passengers Col. Gracie and Mr. Jack Thayer, and others of the crew, who climbed upon it from the water at about the time the ship disappeared. . . .

Had the sea been rough it is questionable whether any of the lifeboats of the *Titanic* would have reached the water without being damaged or destroyed. The point of suspension of the *Titanic*'s boats was about 70 feet above the level of the sea. Had the ship been rolling heavily the lifeboats as they were lowered would have swung out from the side of the ship as it rolled toward them and on the return roll would have swung back and crashed against its side. It is evident from the testimony that as the list of the *Titanic* became noticeable the lifeboats scraped against the side as they were being lowered. Every effort should be made to improve boat handling devices, and to improve the control of boats while being lowered.

The subcommittee indicated that the disaster was caused by a combination of excessive speed on the part of the ship and a failure to heed iceberg warnings. Here's what it reported:

On the third day out ice warnings were received by the wireless operators on the *Titanic,* and the testimony is conclusive that at least three of these warnings came direct to the commander of the *Titanic* on the day of the accident, the first about noon, from the *Baltic* of the White Star Line. It will be noted that this message places icebergs within 5 miles of the track which the *Titanic* was following, and near the place where the accident occurred.

This enables the committee to say that the ice positions so definitely reported to the *Titanic* just preceding the accident located ice on both sides of the track or lane which the *Titanic* was following, and in her immediate vicinity. No general discussion took place among the officers; no conference was called to consider these warnings; no heed was given to them. The speed was not relaxed, the lookout was not increased, and the only vigilance displayed by the officer of the watch was by instructions to the lookouts to keep "a sharp lookout for ice." It should be said, however, that the testimony shows that Capt. Smith remarked to Officer Lightoller, who was the officer doing duty on the bridge until 10 o'clock ship's time, or 8:27 o'clock New York time, "If it was in a slight degree hazy there would be no doubt we should have to go very slowly" and "If in the slightest degree doubtful, let me know." The evidence is that it was exceptionally clear. There was no haze, and the ship's speed was not reduced.

The speed of the *Titanic* was gradually increased after leaving Queenstown. The first day's run was 464 miles, the second day's run was 519 miles, the third day's run was 546 miles. Just prior to the collision the ship was making her maximum speed of the voyage — not less than 21 knots, or 24½ miles per hour.

The subcommittee was the first of the two official inquiries to offer details about the sinking of the *Titanic* and the subsequent rescue efforts by nearby steamships. Like the British Committee of Inquiry (which I discuss later in the chapter), the American committee faulted the *Californian* for not aiding the *Titanic* sooner:

Under this added weight of water the bow of the ship sank deeper and deeper into the water, and through the open hatch leading from the mail room, and through other openings, water promptly overflowed E deck, below which deck the third, fourth, fifth, sixth, seventh, and eighth transverse bulkheads ended, and thus flooded the compartments abaft No. 3 hold.

Sixteen witnesses from the *Titanic,* including officers and experienced seaman, and passengers of sound judgment, testified to seeing the light of a ship in the distance, and some of the lifeboats were directed to pull for that light, to leave the passengers and to return to the side of the *Titanic.* The *Titanic* fired distress rockets and attempted to signal by electric lamp and Morse code to this vessel. At about the same time the officers of the *Californian* admit seeing rockets in the general direction of the *Titanic* and say that they immediately displayed a powerful Morse lamp, which could be easily seen a distance of 10 miles, while several of the crew of the *Californian* testify that the side lights of a large vessel going full speed were plainly visible from the lower deck of the *Californian* at 11:30 p.m., ship's time, just before the accident. There is no evidence that any rockets were fired by any vessel between the *Titanic* and the *Californian,* although every eye on the *Titanic* was searching the horizon for possible assistance.

The committee is forced to the inevitable conclusion that the *Californian,* controlled by the same company, was nearer the *Titanic* than the 19 miles reported by her captain, and that her officers and crew saw the distress signals of the *Titanic* and failed to respond to them in accordance with the dictates of humanity, international usage, and the requirements of law. The only reply to the distress signals was a counter signal from a large white light which was flashed for nearly two hours from the mast of the *Californian.* In our opinion such conduct, whether arising from indifference or gross carelessness, is most reprehensible, and places upon the commander of the *Californian* a grave responsibility. The wireless operator of the *Californian* was not aroused until 3:30 A.M., New York time, on the morning of the 15th, after considerable conversation between officers and members of the crew had taken place aboard that ship regarding these distress signals or rockets, and was directed by the chief officer to see if there was anything the matter, as a ship had been firing rockets during the night. The inquiry thus set on foot immediately disclosed the fact that the *Titanic* had sunk. Had assistance been promptly proffered, or had the wireless operator of the *Californian* remained a few minutes longer at his post on Sunday evening, that ship might have had the proud distinction of rescuing the lives of the passengers and crew of the *Titanic.*

Hearing the testimony of Guglielmo Marconi

The passage of time always helps us see people and events in their proper light and in their proper context (as opposed to the sometimes misleading or incomplete picture provided in the throes of a situation). A quintessential example of this truism is the ridiculous and shortsighted grilling on the part of the U.S. Senate subcommittee of the communications pioneer Guglielmo Marconi.

Was Marconi, the inventor of the wireless, queried about the role of his wondrous invention in the rescue of the *Titanic* passengers who were able to be saved? No. Was the groundbreaking Italian genius asked for his opinions on how sea travel could be made safer with more effective use of his invention? No.

Instead, the great Marconi was mercilessly questioned about whether he gave his blessing to the selling of the surviving wireless operators' stories to newspapers.

Marconi answered Senator Smith's questions with as much deference and respect as he could muster. To his credit, Marconi honestly admitted that he saw nothing wrong with the operators being paid to talk to the newspapers about their ordeal. Senator Smith tried to insinuate that Marconi urged the operators to withhold details about the disaster from the public in order to sell this information for personal gain. Marconi adamantly denied that this was the case, and he staunchly defended the right of the operators to be paid for their stories.

Following are excerpts from the transcript of Marconi's impassioned testimony before the subcommittee. These excerpts include dialogue regarding the following people:

- **Harold Bride,** the surviving *Titanic* wireless operator

- **Jack Phillips,** the *Titanic* wireless operator who perished

- **John Bottomley,** Marconi's American operations manager

- **Frederick Sammis,** Marconi's chief U.S. engineer

- **Harold Cottam,** the *Carpathia*'s wireless operator

- **Adolph S. Ochs,** the publisher of *The New York Times*

- **Carr Van Anda,** the managing editor of *The New York Times*

Here are excerpts from Marconi's testimony:

Smith: Where were you when the *Carpathia* landed at the Cunard dock with the survivors of the *Titanic* wreck?

Marconi: I was dining with Mr. Bottomley. I had the intention of going on board the *Carpathia* as soon as she reached dock, but she happened to get in sooner than we expected. I therefore left the house where I was dining and proceeded to the dock, and we got on board.

Smith: What did you do when you got on board?

Marconi: I went to the wireless operating room.

Smith: Did you find the operator there?

Marconi: I found the operator there.

Smith: What did you say to him?

Marconi: I said I was glad to see him, and congratulated him on what I had heard he had done. I inquired after his senior operator, Phillips.

Smith: Did you send a wireless to the operator on the *Carpathia* and ask him to meet you and Sammis at the Strand Hotel, 502 West Fourteenth Street, saying, "Keep your mouth shut"?

Marconi: No, sir; I did not.

Smith: If any message of that kind was sent in your name, you did not send it?

Marconi: I did not send it.

Smith: And you know nothing of it?

Marconi: I know nothing of it, except some statements or rumors I have heard of it in the press.

Smith: I am going to read to you the following, and ask whether you know anything about any fact or circumstance connected with it.

This is from the commanding officer of the *Florida* to the Secretary of the Navy, dated April 22, and reads as follows:

On the evening of the steamship Carpathia's arrival in New York, the four following radiograms were intercepted by the chief operator, J. R. Simpson, chief electrician, United States Navy. They appear to me to be significant enough to be brought to the attention of the department:

SEAGATE TO CARPATHIA 8:12 P.M. "Say, old man, Marconi Co. taking good care of you. Keep your mouth shut, and hold your story. It is fixed for you so you will get big money. Now, please do your best to clear."

That was 8:12 P.M. Then follows:

8:30 P.M. To Marconi officer, Carpathia and Titanic Arranged for your exclusive story for dollars in four figures, Mr. Marconi agreeing. Say nothing until you see me. Where are you now? J. M. SAMMIS, Opr. C

9:00 P.M. From Seagate to Carpathia operator: Go to Strand Hotel, 502 West Fourteenth Street. To meet Mr. Marconi. C.

9:33 P.M. From Seagate to Carpathia: A personal to operator Carpathia. Meet Mr. Marconi and Sammis at Strand Hotel, 502 West Fourteenth Street. Keep your mouth shut. MR. MARCONI

What can you say about that, Mr. Marconi?

Marconi: I do not know anything whatever about any of those messages. They are not in the phraseology which I would have approved of if I had passed them. I should, however, say that I told Mr. Sammis or Mr. Bottomley — I do not remember which — that I, as an officer of the

British company, would not prohibit or prevent these operators from making anything which they reasonably could make out of selling their story of the wreck. I was anxious that, if possible, they might make some small amount of money out of the information they had.

Smith: . . . Let me ask you this. With the right to exact compensation for an exclusive story detailing the horrors of the greatest sea disaster that ever occurred in the history of the world, do you mean that an operator under your company's direction shall have the right to prevent the public from knowing of that calamity —

Marconi (interrupting): No.

Smith: Mr. Marconi, did you expect the operator to syndicate this information, or to give it exclusively to one newspaper?

Marconi: I did not expect him to give it exclusively.

Smith: Did you expect him to put the story up to the highest bidder?

Marconi: No, sir.

Smith: If I understand you correctly, you did not seek to control the operator, at all, in what he would say or to whom he would say it?

Marconi: No; I did not.

Smith: Do you know what the use of the words, "Arranged for your exclusive story for dollars in four figures, Mr. Marconi agreeing. Say nothing until you see me. J. M. Sammis," would indicate? What did he mean by "four figures"?

Marconi: I suppose it was something over a thousand dollars; but if you will allow me to repeat again —

Smith: Please do. I wish you would say anything you want to about it.

Marconi (continuing): For the fourth or fifth or sixth time, I say that I know nothing whatever about those messages.

Smith: And you understand that I am not saying that you do.

Marconi: Thank you.

Weighing the words of Californian Captain Stanley Lord

Stanley Lord was the captain of the *Californian* on the night the *Titanic* sunk. Among *Titanic* aficionados, two schools of thought exist regarding Captain Lord's actions (or inactions) on the tragic evening:

✔ The Lordites (as they're often called) believe that Captain Lord's *Californian* was not the ship seen by the *Titanic* as she foundered and that Captain Lord wasn't negligent in coming to the aid of the *Titanic*.

✔ The anti-Lordites (as they're often called) believe that crew members on the *Californian* saw the *Titanic*'s eight distress rockets but that the captain refused to go to the aid of the stricken vessel.

In my opinion, the alleged evidence put forth by the Lordites supposedly exonerating Captain Lord doesn't stand up to scrutiny. Investigations over the years have shown that Captain Lord was autocratic. His own crew feared him such that they would go out of their way to avoid any hint of conflict with their captain. After decades of research and study, the anti-Lordites believe that

✔ The *Californian* was indeed the "mystery ship" seen by passengers of the *Titanic* on the night of April 14.

✔ The crew of the *Californian* did see *Titanic*'s eight distress rockets.

✔ Captain Lord consciously refused to go to the aid of *Titanic*.

✔ The *Californian*'s log may have been altered to reflect Lord's version of the story.

The debate over Captain Lord's role and culpability in the death of more than 1,500 souls will never end because too many people refuse to believe that Lord was capable of such coldhearted behavior.

Captain Lord defended himself and his actions at the U.S. Senate Subcommittee *Titanic* Hearing. Here's an excerpt from his testimony:

Senator Smith: Did you attempt to communicate with the vessel *Titanic* on Sunday?

Captain Lord: Yes, sir.

Smith: What was that communication?

Lord: We told them we were stopped and surrounded by ice.

Smith: Did the *Titanic* acknowledge that message?

Lord: Yes, sir; I believe he told the operator he had read it, and told him to shut up, to stand by, or something; that he was busy.

Smith: Did you have further communication with the *Titanic?*

Lord: Not at all, sir.

Smith: Did the *Titanic* have further communication with you?

Lord: No, sir.

Smith: When you notified the *Titanic* that you were in the ice, how much ice were you in?

Lord: Well, we were surrounded by a lot of loose ice, and we were about a quarter of a mile off the edge of the field.

Smith: How badly were you interfered with by the ice on Sunday evening?

Lord: We stopped altogether.

Smith: What did you stop for?

Lord: So we would not run over the top of it.

Smith: When did you notify the *Titanic* of your condition? What was your purpose?

Lord: It was just a matter of courtesy. I thought he would be a long way from where we were. I did not think he was anywhere near the ice. By rights, he ought to have been 18 or 19 miles to the southward of where I was. I never thought the ice was stretching that far down.

Smith: Do you know anything regarding the *Titanic* disaster, of your own knowledge? Did you see the ship on Sunday?

Lord: No, sir.

Smith: Or any signals from her?

Lord: Not from the *Titanic.*

Smith: Was the *Titanic* beyond your range of vision?

Lord: I should think so; 19½ or 20 miles away.

Smith: How long did it take you to reach the scene of the accident, from the time you steamed up and got under way Monday morning?

Lord: From the time we received the message of the *Titanic*'s position?

Smith: Yes.

Captain Lord (reading): "Six o'clock, proceeded slow, pushing through the thick ice." I will read this from the log book. "Six o'clock, proceeded slow, pushing through the thick ice. 6:30, clear of thickest of ice; proceeded full speed, pushing the ice. 8:30, stopped close to steamship *Carpathia.*"

Smith: Was the *Carpathia* at that time at the scene of the wreck?

Lord: Yes, sir; she was taking the last of the people out of the boats.

Smith: If you had received the C. Q. D. call of distress from the *Titanic* Sunday evening after your communication with the *Titanic,* how long, under the conditions which surrounded you, would it have taken you to have reached the scene of that catastrophe?

Lord: At the very least, two hours.

Smith: You were about 20 miles away?

Lord: Nineteen and one-half to twenty miles from the position given me by the *Titanic.*

Smith: And the *Carpathia* was 53 miles away?

Lord: Yes, sir.

Smith: How long after the *Carpathia* reached the scene of this accident did you reach the scene?

Lord: Well, I don't know what time we got there.

Smith: Had the lifeboats, with their passengers, been picked up and taken aboard the *Carpathia?*

Lord: I think he was taking the last boat up when I got there.

Smith: Did you see any of the wreckage when you got there?

Lord: Yes, sir.

Smith: Tell the committee what you saw?

Lord: I saw several empty boats, some floating planks, a few deck chairs, and cushions; but considering the size of the disaster, there was very little wreckage. It seemed more like an old fishing boat that had sunk.

Smith: Did you see any persons, dead or alive?

Lord: No, sir.

Smith: Would it not be well to have your wireless operator at his post on duty at night, when other eyes are closed, in order that any possible signal of distress might not escape your attention?

Lord: We have the officer on the bridge, who can see as far at night as in the daytime.

Smith: But the officer on the bridge could not see the *Titanic* even with glasses, you said, that night.

Lord: No.

Smith: The wireless operator could have heard the call from the *Titanic* if he had been at his post of duty?

Lord: Yes; he would have heard that.

Smith: Captain, did you see any distress signals on Sunday night, either rockets or the Morse signals?

Lord: No, sir; I did not. The officer on watch saw some signals, but he said they were not distress signals.

Smith: They were not distress signals?

Lord: Not distress signals.

Smith: But he reported them?

Lord: To me. I think you had better let me tell you that story.

Smith: I wish you would.

Lord: When I came off the bridge, at half past 10, I pointed out to the officer that I thought I saw a light coming along, and it was a most peculiar light, and we had been making mistakes all along with the stars, thinking they were signals. We could not distinguish where the sky ended and where the water commenced. You understand, it was a flat calm. He said he thought it was a star, and I did not say anything more. I went down below. I was talking with the engineer about keeping the steam ready, and we saw these signals coming along, and I said, "There is a steamer coming. Let us go to the wireless and see what the news is." But on our way down I met the operator coming, and I said, "Do you know anything?" He said, "The *Titanic*." So, then, I gave him instructions to let the *Titanic* know. I said, "This is not the *Titanic;* there is no doubt about it." She came and lay, at half past 11, alongside of us until, I suppose, a quarter past 1, within 4 miles of us. We could see everything on her quite distinctly; see her lights. We signaled her, at half past 11, with the Morse lamp. She did not take the slightest notice of it. That was between half past 11 and 20 minutes to 12. We signaled her again at 10 minutes past 12, half past 12, a quarter to 1, and 1 o'clock. We have a very powerful Morse lamp. I suppose you can see that about 10 miles, and she was about 4 miles off, and she did not take the slightest notice of it. When the second officer came on the bridge, at 12 o'clock, or 10 minutes past 12, I told him to watch that steamer, which was stopped, and I pointed out the ice to him; told him we were surrounded by ice; to watch the steamer that she did not get any closer to her. At 20 minutes to 1 I whistled up the speaking tube and asked him if she was getting any nearer. He said, "No; she is not taking any notice of us." So, I said, "I will go and lie down a bit." At a quarter past 1 he said, "I think she has fired a rocket." He said, "She did not answer the Morse lamp and she has commenced to go away from us." I said, "Call her up and let me know at once what her name is." So, he put the whistle back, and, apparently, he was calling. I could hear him ticking over my head. Then I went to sleep.

Smith: You heard nothing more about it?

Lord: Nothing more until about something between then and half past 4, I have a faint recollection of the apprentice opening my room door; opening it and shutting it. I said, "What is it?" He did not answer and I went to sleep again. I believe the boy came down to deliver me the message that this steamer had steamed away from us to the southwest, showing several of these flashes or white rockets; steamed away to the southwest.

Reading J. Bruce Ismay's statement to the media

J. Bruce Ismay was chairman and managing director of the White Star Line. The U.S. Senate subcommittee was interested in his words and actions prior to and on the night of the *Titanic* disaster. Ismay was under scrutiny for two acts that sullied his reputation:

✔ Encouraging Captain Smith to sail faster than was safe

✔ Getting in a lifeboat when women and children were still onboard the ship

Ismay, after appearing before both *Titanic* inquiries (the U.S. Senate sub-committee and the British Board of Inquiry), felt dishonored enough to issue a statement to the media in his own defense. Here's an abridged version of his statement:

"I was a passenger . . . "

During the voyage I was a passenger and exercised no greater right or privileges than any other passenger. I was not consulted by the commander about the ship, her course, speed, navigation, or her conduct at sea. All these matters were under the exclusive control of the captain.

I saw Capt. Smith casually, as other passengers did. I was never in his room; I was never on the bridge until after the accident. I did not sit at his table in the saloon. I had not visited the engine room, nor gone through the ship, and did not go, or attempt to go, to any part of the ship to which any other first-class passenger did not have access.

It is absolutely and unqualifiedly false that I ever said that I wished that the *Titanic* should make a speed record or should increase her daily runs. I deny absolutely having said to any person that we would increase our speed in order to get out of the ice zone, or words to that effect.

Didn't talk to Smith

I was never consulted by Capt. Smith, nor by any other person. Nor did I ever make any suggestion whatsoever to any human being about the course of the ship.

The only information I ever received in the ship that other vessels had sighted ice was by a wireless message received from the *Baltic* which I have already testified to. This was handed to me by Capt. Smith, without any remarks, as he was passing me on the passenger deck on the afternoon of Sunday, April 14. I read the telegram casually, and put it in my pocket. At about ten minutes past 7, while I was sitting in the smoking room, Captain Smith came in and asked me to give him the message received from the *Baltic* in order to post it for the information of the officers. I handed it to him, and nothing further was said by either of us. I did not speak to any of the other officers on the subject.

If the information I had received had aroused any apprehension in my mind — which it did not — I should not have ventured to make any suggestion to a commander of Captain Smith's experience and responsibility, for the navigation of the ship rested solely with him.

Didn't dine with Smith

It has been stated that Captain Smith and I were having a dinner party in one of the saloons from 7:30 to 10:30 on Sunday night, and that at the time of the collision Captain Smith was sitting with me in the saloon. Both of these statements are absolutely false. I did not dine with the Captain. Nor did I see him during the evening of April 14. The doctor dined with me in the restaurant at 7:30, and I went directly to my stateroom and went to bed at about 10:30.

I was asleep when the collision occurred . . . . I put on an overcoat over my pyjamas and went up on the bridge deck, and on the bridge I asked Captain Smith what was the matter, and he said we had struck ice. I asked him whether he thought it serious, and he said he did. I then returned to my room and put on a suit of clothes. I had been in my overcoat and pyjamas up to this time. I then went back to the boat deck and heard Captain Smith give the order to clear the boats. I helped in this work for nearly two hours as far as I can judge. I worked at the starboard boats, helping women and children into the boats and lowering them over the side. I did nothing with regard to the boats on the port side. By that time every wooden lifeboat on the starboard side had been lowered away, and I found that they were engaged in getting out the forward collapsible boat on the starboard side. I assisted in this work, and all the women that were on this deck were helped into the boat. They were all, I think third-class passengers.

As the boat was going over the side Mr. Carter, a passenger, and myself got in. At that time there was not a woman on the boat deck, nor any passengers of any class, as far as we could see or hear.

When the boat reached the water I helped to row it, pushing the oar from me as I sat. This is the explanation of the fact that my back was to the sinking steamer. The boat would have accommodated certainly six or more passengers in addition, if there had been any on the boat deck to go.

Would have stayed aboard

These facts can be substantiated by Mr. W. E. Carter of Philadelphia, who got in at the same time that I did, and was rowing the boat with me. I hope I need not say that neither Mr. Carter nor myself would, for one moment, have thought of getting into the boat if there had been any women there to go in it. Nor should I have done so if I had thought that by remaining on the ship I could have been the slightest further assistance.

It is impossible for me to answer every false statement, rumour, or invention that has appeared in the newspapers. . . . I deeply regret that I am compelled to make any personal statement when my whole thought is on the horror of the disaster. In building the *Titanic* it was the hope of my associates and myself that we had built a vessel which could not

The bow railing of the *Titanic* illuminated by a Mir 1 submersible behind the forward anchor crane. The 'usticles' slant shows the direction of the current.

A painting of the sunken *Titanic* with the submersible *Alvin* at the bow.

Robert D. Ballard (standing), Jean-Louis Michel (far right), and others of the research team survey video screens aboard the *Knorr* during a probing of the wreck by the search vehicle *Argo*.

A fragment of the *Titanic*'s hull.

Titanic survivors Bertram Dean and Eva Hart examine ship mementos at Merseyside Maritime Museum in Liverpool.

A hand mirror displayed at *Titanic: The Artifact Exhibition* in Los Angeles in 2003.

...layed at the Science Museum in London

A white china coffee cup (missing its handle) a... saucer. This artifact is notable for its perfect...

aud Record Office of Shipping and
Tower Hill, London, E.

DEATH OF A SEAMAN.

255 of the Mer~~~~~~~~ping Act, 1894, ~

~en depos~~~~~~~~~~~~~ Act, in respect of

~t ~~ 131428

.14 W

aged 25 is stated to

~ and is supposed to have been drowned.

A pocketwatch found on a floating body shows water stains indicating the watch stopped just short of two o'clock. The ship sank at 2:20 a.m. local time.

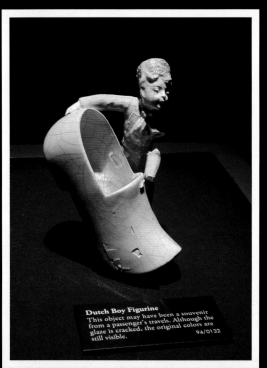

Dutch Boy Figurine
This object may have been a souvenir from a passenger's travels. Although the glaze is cracked, the original colors are still visible.   94/0132

A "Dutch boy and shoe" figurine that belonged to a passenger. The glazing is cracked, but the colors are still vivid.

A bowler hat displayed in *Titanic: The Artifact Exhibition* at the Metreon in 2006 in San Francisco.

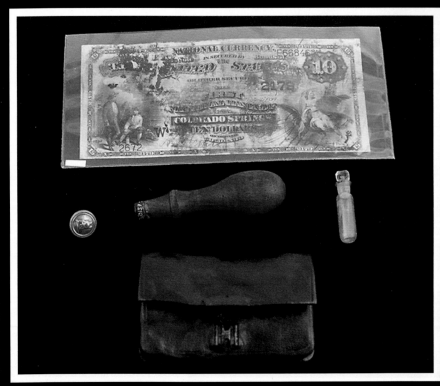

A ten-dollar bill printed in Colorado Springs, a button from a *Titanic* officer's uniform, a tool handle, a perfume vial, and a leather wallet.

be destroyed by the perils of the sea or the dangers of navigation. The event has proved the futility of that hope. Present legal requirements have proved inadequate. They must be changed, but whether they are changed or not, this awful experience has taught the steamship owners of the world that too much reliance has been placed on watertight compartments and on wireless telegraphy, and that they must equip every vessel with lifeboats and rafts sufficient to provide for every soul on board, and sufficient men to handle them.

The British Commission of Inquiry: Who's at Fault?

Along with the inconceivable loss of human life, the sinking of the *Titanic* had other potential far-reaching negative consequences for a great many people and companies, most notably the White Star Line and, by extension, the lucrative British shipping trade.

The British Board of Trade was responsible for establishing and enforcing shipbuilding regulations and shipping regulations in the United Kingdom. After the *Titanic* tragedy, the board moved quickly to start investigation hearings; it ordered a Commission of Inquiry. Members of the British Board of Trade were concerned that a different government agency would undertake an investigation and that its inquiry wouldn't be favorable to the board.

By 1912, when the British Board of Trade conducted its *Titanic* hearings, the organization was more than 200 years old. It started in 1696, when the British Parliament asked William III to establish a board to oversee commerce in the British Empire. As the years went by and the British Empire grew ever larger, the board's duties grew accordingly. By the late 19th century, the board was responsible for all matters relating to shipping and trade. Its Marine Department enforced shipbuilding regulations, inspected passenger ships, and investigated wrecks, among other duties. The British Board of Trade was, by 1912, a vast bureaucracy.

Clearly, an investigation into the *Titanic* disaster that was being led by the agency that made the shipping rules was rife with conflict of interest. For this reason, the public perceived (rightly) that the British inquiry was a bit of a farce. Instead of accepting responsibility for the role that lack of lifeboats played in the deaths of so many passengers, the inquiry (and the Board of Trade) focused its blame on the captain of the *Californian*. Read on to find out more about the findings of the British Commission of Inquiry.

Understanding the Board of Trade's lifeboat laws

After the *Titanic* disaster, critics of the British Board of Trade claimed that it was partly or wholly responsible for the inadequate number of lifeboats on board the *Titanic*. British Board of Trade laws required that ships weighing more than 10,000 tons carry at least 16 lifeboats. The *Titanic* was a 46,000-ton ship. When the board established its 16-lifeboat regulation, it didn't foresee the day when ships as large as the *Titanic* would be built; neither did it update its minimum lifeboat regulation after the *Titanic* was built.

The *Titanic* had deck space for 48 lifeboats, which would have been enough to rescue all passengers in the event of a disaster, but she carried only 20 when she set sail from Southampton. She was within Board of Trade requirements, but these requirements were tragically obsolete. I discuss the lifeboat issue in much more detail in Chapter 11.

Taking witness accounts

Beginning in May 1912, the British Commission of Inquiry conducted a hearing into the *Titanic* disaster. To accommodate the large number of people expected at the hearing, it was conducted at London Scottish Drill Hall, a cavernous glass-roofed building near Buckingham Palace where members of the London Scottish regiment drilled. On the dais sat Lord Mersey, Wreck Commissioner for the United Kingdom; behind him were a 20-foot-long replica of the *Titanic* and maps of the North Atlantic.

The hearing lasted for 36 days, concluding on July 3, 1912. In all, the commission heard 97 witnesses, including the following:

- Officials of the White Star Line, including its chairman and managing director, J. Bruce Ismay
- Sir Walter J. Howell, chief of the Board of Trade's Marine Department
- Guglielmo Marconi, inventor of the Marconi wireless telegraph
- *Titanic* crew members
- Officers from other ships, including the *Carpathia* and the *Californian*
- First-class passengers, including Sir Cosmo Duff-Gordon (who is testifying in Figure 10-1)

Conspicuously missing from the testimony were accounts by second- and third-class passengers.

Figure 10-1:
Sir Cosmo Duff-Gordon testifies at the British Commission of Inquiry.

Mary Evans/© Illustrated London News Ltd/Everett Collection

Issuing the final report

The British Commission of Inquiry issued its "Report on the Loss of the *Titanic*" on July 30, 1912. The report was generally considered a whitewash. It absolved Captain Smith and the White Star Line of any blame for the disaster. It completely overlooked the lack of lifeboats as a cause of the tragedy. The White Star Line, the Commission concluded, had complied with lifeboat regulations and other active requirements of seagoing vessels.

What Lord Mersey and the British Commission did was dump the responsibility for the more than 1,500 *Titanic* deaths on Captain Stanley Lord of the *Californian*. Wrote the British Commission, "[The *Californian*] could have reached the *Titanic* if she had made the attempt when she saw the first rocket. She made no attempt."

Hearing actual testimony from the British Commission

The British Commission report is an enormous repository of *Titanic* information. It asks many relevant questions about the *Titanic*'s collision and foundering. It provides a concise snapshot of the events of April 14 and 15, 1912.

Following are key questions and answers from the report. Note that these questions and answers were written as summation to provide general information about the sinking. They were not credited to witnesses and are considered authored by unnamed members of the British Commission.

What was the number of boats of any kind on board the *Titanic?*

2 Emergency boats, 14 Lifeboats, 4 Englehardt boats.

What was the carrying capacity of the respective boats?

2 Emergency boats was for 80 persons. 14 Lifeboats was for 910 persons. 4 Englehardt boats was for 188 persons, or a total of 1,178 persons.

After leaving Queenstown [Ireland] on or about the 11th April last did information reach the *Titanic* by wireless messages . . . of the existence of ice in certain latitudes?

Yes.

Was her course altered in consequence of receiving such information, and, if so, in what way?

No.

Was a good and proper lookout for ice kept on board?

No. The men in the crow's nest were warned at 9:30 p.m. to keep a sharp lookout for ice; the officer of the watch was then aware that he had reached the reported ice region, and so also was the officer who relieved him at 10 p.m. Without implying that those actually on duty were not keeping a good lookout, in view of the night being moonless, there being no wind and perhaps very little swell, and especially in view of the high speed at which the vessel was running, it is not considered that the lookout was sufficient.

Were any, and, if so, what, directions given to vary the speed; if so, were they carried out?

No directions were given to reduce speed.

Were binoculars provided for and used by the lookout men?

No.

Is the use of them necessary or usual in such circumstances?

No.

Was ice seen and reported by anybody on board the *Titanic* before the casualty occurred?

Yes, immediately before the collision.

If so, what measures were taken by the officer on watch to avoid it?

The helm was put hard-a starboard and the engines were stopped and put full speed astern.

What was the speed of the *Titanic* shortly before and at the moment of the casualty?

About 22 knots.

Was such speed excessive under the circumstances?

Yes.

What was the nature of the casualty which happened to the *Titanic* at or about 11:45 p.m. on the 14th April last?

A collision with an iceberg which pierced the starboard side of the vessel in several places below the water line between the fore peak tank and No. 4 boiler room.

What steps were taken immediately on the happening of the casualty?

The 12 watertight doors in the engine and boiler rooms were closed from the bridge, some of the boiler fires were drawn, and the bilge pumps abaft No. 6 boiler room were started.

How long after the casualty was its seriousness realized by those in charge of the vessel?

About 15–20 minutes.

What steps were then taken?

The boats were ordered to be cleared away. The passengers were roused and orders were given to get them on deck, and lifebelts were served out. Some of the water-tight doors, other than those in the engine and boiler rooms, were closed. Marconigrams were sent out asking for help. Distress signals (rockets) were fired, and attempts were made to call up by Morse a ship whose lights were seen. Eighteen of the boats were swung out and lowered, and the remaining two floated off the ship and were subsequently utilized as rafts.

Did each boat carry its full load and, if not, why not?

At least 8 boats did not carry their full loads for the following reasons: 1. Many people did not realize the danger or care to leave the ship at first. 2. Some boats were ordered to be lowered with an idea of their coming round to the gangway doors to complete the loading. 3. The officers were not certain of the strength and capacity of the boats in all cases.

What vessels had the opportunity of rendering assistance to the *Titanic* and, if any, how was it that assistance did not reach the *Titanic* before the ss. *Carpathia* arrived?

The *Californian*. She could have reached the *Titanic* if she had made the attempt when she saw the first rocket. She made no attempt.

Watching for icebergs: The International Ice Patrol

In the preradar years of the early twentieth century (radar was patented in 1935), icebergs were a feared and dangerous threat to seagoing vessels. Iceberg alerts were sent from ship to ship, but only after crew members actually sighted ice and were able to send coordinates to warn other ships.

When the *Titanic* sank, mariners and governments around the world knew that something had to be done. About a year and a half after the disaster, the first International Conference on the Safety of Life at Sea convened in London. Delegates from the world's 13 maritime powers discussed how to monitor icebergs and alert ships to the presence of icebergs and ice fields

in the Arctic and North Atlantic oceans. The result of the conference was the founding of the International Ice Patrol (IIP). This organization patrols for icebergs in the shipping lanes between Europe, the United States, and Canada. It broadcasts information about the location of icebergs for the benefit of ships at sea.

Until World War II, U.S. Coast Guard cutters patrolled for icebergs, but now the job is done by aerial surveillance. Member nations reimburse the U.S. Coast Guard for its services.

Each year on April 15, to commemorate the sinking of the *Titanic,* the IIP drops wreaths in the North Atlantic where the *Titanic* sank.

Pulling No Punches and Laying Blame: Excerpts from a Joseph Conrad Essay

The legendary Polish-born British writer Joseph Conrad was uniquely qualified to comment on the *Titanic* tragedy. An orphan at age 11, at age 16 Conrad became a sailor with the French and then the English merchant marine. During his 20-year career, he sailed to many of the major ports of the world, as well as the Gulf of Siam, the Belgian Congo, the Malay Archipelago, and Australia.

After retiring from the sea, Conrad wrote such classics as *Heart of Darkness* (1899), *Lord Jim* (1900), *Nostromo* (1904), and *The Secret Agent* (1907). He was 55 in 1912 when the *Titanic* sank. By this time he was famous the world over for his gripping tales of dangerous adventures at sea and the deep psychological profiles of his characters.

Conrad must have felt obligated (or at least justified) to weigh in on the disaster that was making headlines around the world, and he did so with an essay called "Some Reflections, Seamanlike and Otherwise, on the Loss of the Titanic," excerpts of which are presented here. The essay was published originally in the May 1912 edition of *The English Review*. Subsequently, it appeared in an essay collection by Conrad called *Notes on Life & Letters*.

Conrad pulls no punches in his essay. He bluntly warns that his gloves are off by describing his "reflections" as "seamanlike and otherwise" in its title. Conrad tears into the *Titanic*'s owners and builders, the wealthy swells who lined up for tickets for her maiden voyage, the British Board of Trade, American railroads, and especially the senators who made up the U.S. Senate Subcommittee *Titanic* Hearing into the disaster.

In the opening paragraph of the essay, Conrad describes the scope of the tragedy:

> It is with a certain bitterness that one must admit to oneself that the late S.S. *Titanic* had a "good press." . . . And if ever a loss at sea fell under the definition, in the terms of a bill of lading, of Act of God, this one does, in its magnitude, suddenness and severity; and in the chastening influence it should have on the self-confidence of mankind.

When Conrad wrote his essay, the U.S. Senate was holding its subcommittee hearing into the *Titanic* tragedy. He took the Senate to task for grandstanding:

> One asks oneself what these men are after, with this very provincial display of authority. I beg my friends in the United States pardon for calling these zealous senators men. I don't wish to be disrespectful. They may be of the stature of demigods for all I know, but at that great distance from the shores of effete Europe and in the presence of so many guileless dead, their size seems diminished from this side. What are they after? What is there for them to find out? We know what had happened. The ship scraped her side against a piece of ice, and sank after floating for two hours and a half, taking a lot of people down with her.

Next Conrad asserts that the officers of the *Titanic,* as seamen, are answerable to only one authority:

> [W]hy an officer of the British merchant service should answer the questions of any king, emperor, autocrat, or senator of any foreign power (as to an event in which a British ship alone was concerned, and which did not even take place in the territorial waters of that power) passes my understanding. The only authority he is bound to answer is the Board of Trade.

And he takes the Board of Trade to task for not properly considering whether a ship the size of the *Titanic* had enough lifeboats or was fit to travel the oceans:

> But with what face the Board of Trade, which, having made the regulations for 10,000 ton ships, put its dear old bald head under its wing for ten years, took it out only to shelve an important report, and with a dreary murmur, "Unsinkable," put it back again, in the hope of not being disturbed for another ten years, with what face it will be putting questions to that man who has done his duty, as to the facts of this disaster and as to his professional conduct in it — well, I don't know! . . .

> Years ago I remember overhearing two genuine shellbacks of the old type commenting on a ship's officer, who, if not exactly incompetent, did not commend himself to their severe judgment of accomplished sailor-men. Said one, resuming and concluding the discussion in a funnily judicial tone:

"The Board of Trade must have been drunk when they gave him his certificate." . . .

The Board of Trade is composed of bloodless departments. It has no limbs and no physiognomy, or else at the forthcoming inquiry it might have paid to the victims of the *Titanic* disaster the small tribute of a blush. I ask myself whether the Marine Department of the Board of Trade did really believe . . . that a ship of 45,000 tons, that ANY ship, could be made practically indestructible by means of watertight bulkheads? It seems incredible to anybody who had ever reflected upon the properties of material, such as wood or steel. You can't, let builders say what they like, make a ship of such dimensions as strong proportionately as a much smaller one.

Later in the essay, Conrad ridicules the very idea of a luxury liner, which he compares to a floating hotel:

You build a 45,000 tons hotel of thin steel plates to secure the patronage of, say, a couple of thousand rich people (for if it had been for the emigrant trade alone, there would have been no such exaggeration of mere size), you decorate it in the style of the Pharaohs or in the Louis Quinze style — I don't know which — and to please the aforesaid fatuous handful of individuals, who have more money than they know what to do with, and to the applause of two continents, you launch that mass with two thousand people on board at twenty-one knots across the sea — a perfect exhibition of the modern blind trust in mere material and appliances. And then this happens. General uproar. The blind trust in material and appliances has received a terrible shock. I will say nothing of the credulity which accepts any statement which specialists, technicians and office-people are pleased to make, whether for purposes of gain or glory.

Conrad sarcastically suggests that the size of "unsinkable" ships like the *Titanic* requires a new kind of seamanship:

We shall have presently, in deference to commercial and industrial interests, a new kind of seamanship. A very new and "progressive" kind. If you see anything in the way, by no means try to avoid it; smash at it full tilt. And then — and then only you shall see the triumph of material, of clever contrivances, of the whole box of engineering tricks in fact, and cover with glory a commercial concern of the most unmitigated sort, a great Trust, and a great ship-building yard, justly famed for the super-excellence of its material and workmanship. Unsinkable! See? I told you she was unsinkable, if only handled in accordance with the new seamanship. . . .

You perceive suddenly right ahead, and close to, something that looks like a large ice-floe. What would you do?" "Put the helm amidships." "Very well. Why?" "In order to hit end on." "On what grounds should you endeavour to hit end on?" "Because we are taught by our builders and masters that the heavier the smash, the smaller the damage, and because the requirements of material should be attended to."

Conrad suggests that false belief that the *Titanic* was unsinkable contributed to the tragedy:

> All the people on board existed under a sense of false security. How false, it has been sufficiently demonstrated. And the fact which seems undoubted, that some of them actually were reluctant to enter the boats when told to do so, shows the strength of that falsehood. Incidentally, it shows also the sort of discipline on board these ships, the sort of hold kept on the passengers in the face of the unforgiving sea. These people seemed to imagine it an optional matter: whereas the order to leave the ship should be an order of the sternest character, to be obeyed unquestioningly and promptly by every one on board, with men to enforce it at once, and to carry it out methodically and swiftly.

Finally, Conrad comes to the defense of Captain Edward J. Smith:

> [T]he calumnious, baseless, gratuitous, circumstantial lie charging poor Captain Smith with desertion of his post by means of suicide is the vilest and most ugly thing of all in this outburst of journalistic enterprise, without feeling, without honour, without decency.

> But all this has its moral. . . . Yes, material may fail, and men, too, may fail sometimes; but more often men, when they are given the chance, will prove themselves truer than steel, that wonderful thin steel from which the sides and the bulkheads of our modern sea-leviathans are made.

Part III
Exploring Enduring Titanic Mysteries

The 5th Wave   By Rich Tennant

In this part . . .

Even after a century, some parts of the *Titanic* story remain a mystery. For *Titanic* buffs, this part looks into all the little details of why the *Titanic* sank and explores whether tragedy could have been averted. It attempts to unravel what really happened on the chaotic night of April 14–15, 1912. And it describes an eerie 1898 novella that seemed to foretell the sinking of the *Titanic*.

Chapter 11

Doomed from the Start? Studying What Went Wrong

Certain types of *Titanic* aficionados have a penchant for conspiracy theories. They relish reeling off instances when fate seemed to have played a hand in the great liner's demise. These types keep a list of suspicious events that defy explanation.

For example, they ask why the champagne bottle used to christen the *Titanic* didn't break at the christening ceremony (which is interesting because the White Star Line *never* christened its ships; when asked about the lack of tradition, one of the shipyard workers was quoted as saying, "We just builds 'em and shoves 'em in").

And why did a soot-covered face appear in the funnel of one of the smokestacks (this omen surely wasn't a good one)? And what about that cockerel that crowed as the *Titanic* set sail — that's a very bad sign to sailors, isn't it? Heck, some *Titanic* aficionados even believe that the name *Titanic* itself was a curse.

But could *Titanic*'s fate have been sealed by more mundane causes, such as human error, faulty materials, and bad decision-making? This chapter looks at some of the circumstances surrounding her sinking, with an eye on the more ordinary conditions and decisions that could have caused — or prevented — her demise.

Examining Whether the Watertight Doors Should Have Remained Open

In April 1998, WPIX-TV in New York broadcast a *Titanic* documentary called *Titanic: Secrets Revealed.* It was hosted by none other than Bernard Hill, a dignified British actor who played Captain Edward J. Smith in James Cameron's 1997 blockbuster film *Titanic.* The two-hour special presented interviews and computer simulations to explore some of the more tenacious "secrets" surrounding the sinking of the great liner.

At the time, the documentary wasn't of enormous interest to *Titanic* buffs who possessed even a perfunctory knowledge of the facts and rumors that had surfaced over the years. But *Titanic: Secrets Revealed* did provide new information in one critical area: the question of whether the *Titanic*'s watertight doors should have remained open.

The *Titanic* had 16 watertight compartments located in the hull of the ship, which were divided by 15 transverse watertight bulkheads (walls that were each one half inch thick). The doors and compartments were designed as a safety feature. In the event of a leak in the hull, the doors were to be closed automatically, which would prevent seawater from inundating the entire hull of the ship. Instead, water would be confined to the one or two compartments where the leak occurred.

Could Captain Smith have bought the *Titanic* time and kept her afloat long enough for everyone to be rescued if he had ordered the watertight compartment doors to be opened after they had been automatically closed? If the *Titanic* had been allowed to fill evenly with water, would she have remained on the surface long enough for the *Carpathia* and the *Californian* (see Chapter 7) to arrive on the scene and transfer each of the ship's passengers and crew to their decks?

The producers of *Titanic: Secrets Revealed* commissioned a scientific experiment to answer this important question. The following sections explain the experiment and the results.

Setting up and performing the experiment

The producers of *Titanic: Secrets Revealed,* with the assistance of naval architect Arthur Sanderford and technical consultant Bill Sauder, built a transparent Lucite model of the *Titanic* precisely to scale. The great liner's size, weight, and buoyancy — as well as all of her watertight compartments — were carefully duplicated in the model. The plan for testing the watertight doors was twofold:

✔ To sink the *Titanic* in a tank with her watertight-compartment doors shut, meticulously duplicating the conditions under which she foundered on the night of April 14–15, 1912.

✔ To sink the ship a second time with her watertight doors open to see whether keeping them open delayed the sinking of the ship.

First, the team allowed Boiler Rooms 5 and 6 to fill with water. The watertight-compartment doors were all quickly closed after the model ship struck the iceberg. Water filled the hull, and the model ship *Titanic* sank in just over two hours. This is precisely what happened in 1912.

The experiment then moved to its next phase. This time, the team started the clock on the experiment at 11:40 p.m., the same moment the *Titanic* struck the iceberg. The team began filling the *Titanic* model with water, only this time they left all of her watertight doors open. By 11:50 p.m., water was pouring into the six watertight compartments opened by the iceberg, only now the water was also flowing the entire length of the ship instead of pooling in just the six front compartments in the hull.

Seeing the results of the experiment

According to the experiment, here's how the *Titanic* would've sunk had its watertight doors been opened:

1. At 12:20 a.m., the first lifeboat is launched, and water continues to pour into the *Titanic* at the rate of 350 tons per minute. The ship is sinking more evenly as the water fills the hull along the entire length of the keel.

2. At 12:40 a.m., the *Carpathia* receives *Titanic*'s distress signal and begins steaming toward her. The *Carpathia* is 58 miles away. By now, more than 20,000 tons of water have flooded the *Titanic.* Remarkably, she is still level.

3. Around 12:50 a.m., the icy water of the Atlantic floods the *Titanic*'s last boiler and kills all power on the ship. The *Titanic* is now dark a full 90 minutes earlier than she was in 1912. Hundreds and hundreds of passengers and crew are now trapped below decks in the frigid cold, in pitch darkness.

4. By 1:30 a.m., 14 of *Titanic*'s lifeboats are away, and her bow remains above water, but the *Carpathia* is still 40 miles away.

5. At 1:40 a.m., the *Titanic,* now filled with close to 40,000 tons of water, begins to roll over. The remaining lifeboats can't be launched.

6. At 1:45 a.m., the ship is terribly unstable.

7. At 1:47 a.m., the *Titanic* rolls completely over on her side and capsizes, sinking a full 33 minutes earlier than she did in 1912. Her heavy list would have prevented the loading of the remaining lifeboats, and more people would have died. At this time, the *Carpathia* was still more than 30 miles away.

According to technical consultant Bill Sauder, "A heavy list makes it very difficult to launch lifeboats, so instead of the relatively calm sinking that we saw actually happen in 1912, we would have wound up with a ship in the dark for over an hour with a heavy list, panic; possibly stampedes on the lifeboats. It would have been a catastrophe." He concluded, "If Smith had left the watertight doors opened, contrary to his instructions, contrary to his training, the loss of life would have been catastrophic."

The experiment performed by the crew of *Titanic: Secrets Revealed* showed that nothing within the captain's power could have saved the ship.

Investigating Whether the Titanic's Rivets Were Fatally Flawed

Naval architect William H. Garzke, who went down to the wreck of the *Titanic* in 1996, said this about the *Titanic*'s sinking: "Everything that could go wrong, did."

For decades, experts believed that the 300,000-ton iceberg that the 46,000-ton *Titanic* collided with sliced a 300-foot gash in her hull. But a 1996 dive to the site of the wreck revealed that the damage to the *Titanic*'s side was much smaller than anyone could have imagined. The total area of damage was between 12 and 13 square feet — about the total size of a human body.

So if a giant gash in the hull wasn't the culprit in the *Titanic*'s sinking, what was? In this section, I walk you through a theory that focuses on some suspects considerably smaller than a 300,000-ton iceberg: the ship's rivets.

Considering whether rivets were to blame

The 3 million rivets that held the *Titanic* together are a source of fascination for *Titanic* fanatics who call themselves "Rivet Heads." The Rivet Heads often ask whether the rivets on the ship were metallurgically flawed. Were they so flawed, in fact, that their composition played a major role in the great liner's demise? Recent research on two retrieved rivets from the *Titanic*'s hull seems to confirm that the answer to that question is a qualified "yes."

Before I explain how scientists have arrived at that qualified "yes," allow me to explain how the spotlight was turned away from the iceberg itself and onto the rivets. When the French oceanographic group IFREMER (the French Research Institute for Exploration of the Sea) made a dive to the *Titanic* in August 1996, it brought along Paul Matthias, president of the Rhode Island–based company Polaris Imaging. Matthias used a device called a sub-bottom profiler to image the wreck of the *Titanic* with the goal of identifying the exact cause of her sinking. After establishing an analytic baseline with images of the port side, Matthias then examined the starboard side — the side that struck the iceberg.

"There's no gash," Matthias said in a postdive interview. "What we're seeing is a series of deformations in the starboard side that start and stop along the hull. They're about 10 feet above the bottom of the ship. They appear to follow the hull plate."

So instead of the *Titanic*'s hull plates being ripped open by the iceberg, as had been believed for decades, it now appeared that iron rivets holding the plates to the hull's crossbeams popped open, creating six splits the size of a hardcover book. These small slits, because they were about 20 feet below the waterline, would have allowed water to shoot into the watertight compartments under tremendous pressure, ultimately filling the *Titanic* with approximately 39,000 tons of water before she sank.

The *Titanic* had been designed to survive total flooding of three of her watertight compartments and, in some cases, four, depending on which four were opened to the sea. But the ship wasn't designed to withstand the flooding of six compartments, an eventuality that no one — not the owners, builders, crew, or passengers — even considered a remote possibility.

Right all along

In the British Commission of Inquiry hearings (see Chapter 10), a 32-foot-long section plan of the *Titanic* was hung on the wall. The White Star Line's naval architect, Edward Wilding, testified that — based on his calculations and the rate and nature of the ship's sinking — there was no long gash but only a series of a few small tears. He testified that the tears totaled about 12 square feet over a length of 200 feet.

On the plan, he marked in red where he calculated those slits to be. Those red marks are still visible on the plan today and are almost identical to the damage actually discovered on the *Titanic* wreckage in 1996. Wilding's theory was generally ignored for more than eight decades. It wasn't until Paul Matthias's 1996 discovery that Wilding's calculations proved to have been correct all along.

Understanding why the iron rivets popped

Two wrought-iron rivets retrieved from the wreck of the *Titanic* were examined and found to contain high concentrations of *slag,* which is the glass residue left over from the smelting of metallic ores. Manufacturers add slag in small quantities — usually, around 2 percent — to wrought iron to give it strength. "Otherwise it would be taffy," said Paul Foecke, the metallurgist who performed the microscopic examination of the *Titanic's* rivets.

Foecke discovered that the slag content of the two rivets retrieved from the *Titanic* was a dangerously high 9.3 percent, a concentration that would have made the rivets extremely brittle and substantially weaker than they would have been with an appropriate level of slag. He also found that the slag streaks, which are supposed to run lengthwise along the rivet, made a sharp 90-degree turn at the head end, thereby causing further weakness in the rivet. "To have the slag turned around this way," Foecke said, "this is a major area of weakness."

A conclusion from this new finding could be that the structurally weak rivets allowed the hull plates to pop. If the rivets weren't flawed, they might have held the plates together after striking the iceberg.

William H. Garzke, Jr., a naval architect who heads a team of marine forensic experts investigating the disaster, after learning of Foecke's findings, told the media, "We think they popped and allowed the plates to separate and let in the water." However, Garzke said these findings should be considered tentative because of the small sampling (only two rivets) used in testing.

Homing in on the slag content

A question that immediately arose after the slag results went public was one of standards: Based on the prevailing technologies, was a 9 percent slag content acceptable in 1912? In an attempt to answer this question, metallurgist Paul Foecke dug up a 1906 metallurgical reference book that defined "medium quality" wrought iron as containing 2 to 2.5 percent slag. So the 9.3 percent slag content of the *Titanic's* rivets appeared too high even for the time.

This information appears damning, yet Foecke wouldn't assign too much weight to the 1906 text. "As far as I can tell," he said in an interview, "there was no standard of the time." Foecke also noted that the *Titanic's* rivets conceivably could have been "state of the art back then."

It's quite possible that the high slag content of the two rivets tested could have been a fluke. After all, two out of 3 million rivets is a minuscule test sample. For results to be conclusive, many thousands of rivets would have to be tested with identical results for these findings to become *Titanic* gospel.

Defenders of Harland and Wolff and the quality of the iron point to the *Titanic*'s sister ship, the *Olympic,* for refutation of the flawed-rivets claim. "[The *Olympic*] sailed for 27 years," Foecke said in an interview. "It collided with two ships. It ran over and sank a submarine. It was hit by a dud torpedo. And it was called 'Old Reliable' and was scrapped in 1936. So it's not what it's made of, and what its design is. It's also circumstance."

Weighing What's Known about the Lack of Lifeboats

Titanic survivor Eva Hart once said, "The sound of people drowning is something I cannot describe to you. And neither can anyone else. It is the most dreadful sound. And there is a dreadful silence that follows it."

Far fewer people would have drowned if the *Titanic* had carried enough lifeboats. The *Titanic* had the capacity to carry 48 lifeboats, which would have provided enough lifeboat seats for all her passengers. However, to cut costs and to keep the decks from being too crowded, the White Star Line decided to carry only 20 lifeboats on board.

Carrying only 20 lifeboats, which provided enough seats for 52 percent of the *Titanic*'s passengers, didn't violate British Board of Trade laws regarding the number of lifeboats a ship must carry (see Chapter 10). Board laws stated that ships weighing more than 10,000 tons must carry at least 16 lifeboats with a capacity of 5,500 cubic feet. The *Titanic* exceeded this requirement (but, at 46,000 tons, actually needed many more lifeboats than the 16 required).

This section looks at what experts know and don't know about the woefully inadequate number of lifeboats aboard the *Titanic* and how they were subsequently used to save passengers.

Looking at conflicting reports

Reports about the *Titanic*'s lifeboats have revealed conflicting information and have raised many questions, including the following:

- ✔ When was each lifeboat launched?
- ✔ Who occupied each lifeboat?
- ✔ How many survivors were on each lifeboat?
- ✔ When was each lifeboat picked up?
- ✔ What happened to each lifeboat after the rescue?

The British Commission of Inquiry tried to answer some of these questions, as did the U.S. Senate Subcommittee *Titanic* Hearing (see Chapter 10). Colonel Archibald Gracie IV attempted the same in his book *The Truth about the Titanic* (first published in 1913 and now published by Adamant Media Corporation). But each reached different conclusions.

The total number of people put into the lifeboats according to the British Commission report was 854. However, according to the White Star Line, the total was 757. What's more, figures for the number of survivors also vary:

- The British Commission of Inquiry reported 711 survivors. (Initially, on April 25, 1912, the Board reported 703 survivors.)
- The U.S. Senate Subcommittee *Titanic* Hearing reported 706 survivors.
- *Carpathia* Captain Arthur Henry Rostron reported picking up 705 survivors from the lifeboats.

Further research suggests that the number of passengers put into lifeboats may actually have been 708.

The reality is that the complete truth cannot be known when it comes to the *Titanic*'s lifeboats. Why? Because the confusion, panic, and multiple observers that night contributed to an inevitable distortion of the actual events that took place between the time when the first boat was lowered (Lifeboat 7 at 12:45 a.m.) and when the last lifeboat was loaded aboard the *Carpathia* (Lifeboat 2 at 8:10 a.m.).

Reviewing the solid facts

Even though information on how the boats were used is sketchy, experts do know for sure that the *Titanic* carried a total of 20 lifeboats:

- **Two emergency cutters, numbered 1 and 2, with a capacity of 40 persons each:** These boats were designed to be lowered into the water quickly in emergencies, such as if a passenger were to fall overboard. The cutters were 25 feet long by 7 feet wide and 3 feet deep.

- **Fourteen standard wooden lifeboats, numbered 3 through 16, with a capacity of 65 persons each:** These lifeboats were 30 feet long by 9 feet wide by 4 feet deep. Lifeboats on the port (left) side were even-numbered; lifeboats on the starboard (right) side were odd-numbered.

- **Four Englehardt collapsible lifeboats with a capacity of 47 persons each:** These boats were 27 feet long by 8 feet wide by 3 feet deep. They had wooden bottoms and canvas sides. Because they could be laid flat, they took up little space on the top deck, where they were stored.

Experts also know that Fifth Officer Harold Lowe was in charge of Boat 14 and that he was the only one to go back to look for survivors floating in the cold, dark sea. And finally, they know that Marconi operator Harold Bride survived atop Englehardt Boat B after it floated off the ship as she foundered.

Table 11-1 shows the British Commission of Inquiry's final findings regarding the lifeboats. In the table, the "Number of Passengers" column includes a bracketed number if later research by the Board resulted in a different number.

Table 11-1		Lifeboat Findings by the British Board of Inquiry (with Revisions)			
Launch Order	Boat Number	Port or Starboard	Time	Capacity	Number of Passengers
1	7	Starboard	12:45 a.m.	65	27 [28]
2	5	Starboard	12:55 a.m.	65	41
3	6	Port	12:55 a.m.	65	28
4	3	Starboard	1:00 a.m.	65	50 [40]
5	1 (cutter)	Starboard	1:10 a.m.	40	12
6	8	Port	1:10 a.m.	65	39 [28, 35]
7	10	Port	1:20 a.m.	65	55
8	9	Starboard	1:20 a.m.	65	56
9	12	Port	1:25 a.m.	65	42 [43; 71 with transfers]
10	11	Starboard	1:25 a.m.	65	70
11	14	Port	1:30 a.m.	65	63 [60]
12	16	Port	1:35 a.m.	65	56
13	13	Starboard	1:35 a.m.	65	64
14	15	Starboard	1:35 a.m.	65	70
15	Englehardt C	Starboard	1:40 a.m.	47	71
16	2 (cutter)	Port	1:45 a.m.	40	26 [25]
17	4	Port	1:55 a.m.	65	40
18	Englehardt D	Port	2:05 a.m.	47	44
19	Englehardt B	Port (floated off)	2:15 a.m.	47	20–30?
20	Englehardt A	Starboard (floated off, passengers transferred from 14)	2:15 a.m.	47	12

Women and children first?

The "women and children first" rule of maritime survival isn't a hard-and-fast rule; it's open to interpretation. When it was a certainty that the *Titanic* would founder, Captain Edward J. Smith ordered the lifeboats uncovered and swung out and the passengers loaded, with women and children being taken aboard first. Yet there were lots of male survivors. How did this happen?

The spirit of the rule mandates that all women and children aboard a ship must be safely put onto lifeboats before any men can board. But on the *Titanic,* those given the responsibility of loading the lifeboats — including Officers William Murdoch, Harold Lowe, Charles Lightoller, Henry Wilde, and James Moody — in some cases winged it. If no more women or children were standing nearby when a lifeboat was being loaded, some loading officers allowed the remaining men to board.

Was this the right thing to do? In hindsight, it's clear that hundreds of women and children, many of them third-class passengers who were still below decks, should have been evacuated onto lifeboats before men were taken aboard. But if you imagine being a lifeboat loader, you can see why they made the decisions they did. If you're standing next to a lifeboat filled with 30 women and children, and no more women and children are on deck awaiting transfer, yet 30 or 40 men are waiting, it's easy to understand why the loaders would allow men to board. They were thinking about how to save more lives. Right or wrong, in the big picture, it's reasonable and fair to assume that the loaders' main concern was saving as many passengers as they could.

If you compare the last two columns of Table 11-1, you see the disparity between how the lifeboats should have been loaded and how they actually were loaded. Most of the lifeboats weren't filled to capacity, as they should have been.

The lifeboats' capacity was 1,178 people (including the collapsible boats). So depending on the number of survivors reported (which, as I explain in the previous section, isn't a hard-and-fast number), approximately 60 percent of the people who could have been saved actually survived. An additional 470 or so people died because the lifeboats weren't filled to capacity.

Speculating about a Head-On Collision with the Iceberg

What if First Officer William Murdoch hadn't given the orders he gave? Murdoch was the officer in charge on the bridge when the *Titanic* struck the iceberg. Upon learning of the presence of the iceberg, he ordered the rudder hard left and then he ordered the engines to full reverse. His goal was to "port around" the iceberg, a common tactic employed by ships at sea in ice fields.

But what if no one had seen the iceberg and the ship had continued on its straight-ahead course? Or what if Murdoch hadn't ordered a change in the ship's direction? Could the *Titanic* have survived a head-on collision with the iceberg?

The *Titanic* had four collision-watertight bulkheads at her bow (the front of the ship). These bulkheads were almost identical in principle to the "crumple zone" of a car. Hitting the iceberg would have collapsed the front immediately.

Regarding the question of whether the *Titanic* could withstand a head-on collision, Daniel Allen Butler, author of *"Unsinkable": The Full Story of RMS Titanic* (Stackpole Books), says this in his book:

> As for damage to the ship, the shock of the impact would have traveled the length of the hull, causing the entire ship's structure to flex, popping rivets and splitting seams just as occurred in the actual collision, but in this case along the entire length of the hull, opening up several more compartments to the sea. This is a scenario where the ship would have sunk in minutes, rather than hours.

It's a matter of physics: When a 46,000-ton ship traveling at 22 knots hits an iceberg weighing a minimum of 100,000 tons, the collision will create a powerful force that causes incredible destruction.

Some experts still believe the *Titanic* would have "ridden up" onto the iceberg, got stuck, and just sat there with little or no damage. This would have allowed plenty of time for rescue ships to arrive; the loss of life in that situation would have been minimal. But whether a great steamship like the *Titanic* can ride onto an iceberg is pure speculation. (The White Star Line's naval architect, Edward Wilding, strongly believed that the *Titanic* would not have sunk had it hit the iceberg head-on. He believed that the first two compartments would have "telescoped," but the ship still would have remained seaworthy.) Butler's scenario, that striking the iceberg head-on would have been devastating and would make the ship sink much faster than it did, makes much more sense.

Even though the ship sank, Murdoch and company did make the right decision to try to avoid the iceberg. Now, if the *Titanic* had only been going a little slower . . .

Questioning Whether Binoculars Could Have Helped

A few days before the *Titanic* sailed, *Olympic* Chief Officer Henry Wilde was assigned to the ship, resulting in Second Officer David Blair's being removed from the roster. In his haste to pack his belongings and deboard, Blair left the ship carrying the key to a locker in his room. In the locker was stored one pair of binoculars. The fact that these binoculars were locked away raised some serious questions. Why weren't they in the crow's nest with Frederick Fleet, the lookout? And if Fleet would have had the use of the binoculars, would he have spied the iceberg sooner and thereby prevented the *Titanic* from striking the iceberg?

Experts have mixed opinions, but the prevailing view is that using binoculars wouldn't have made a difference for a couple of compelling reasons:

- ✔ **Because it was a moonless night, the iceberg didn't reflect any ambient light.** Even when seen through binoculars, the iceberg would have looked like so much blackness.

- ✔ **Lookouts often identified icebergs by the waves breaking against them.** However, the sea was perfectly calm on the night the *Titanic* struck the iceberg. There were no waves for Fleet to have seen.

During the British inquiry into the sinking (refer to Chapter 10), Fleet was asked whether having the binoculars would have made a difference. Interestingly, he took the position that they *would* have made a difference. In so many words, he stated that he believed that the *Titanic* wouldn't have sunk if he would have had the use of binoculars. When asked what help they might have been, he responded that binoculars would have allowed them "to get out of the way" of the iceberg.

A century of review of the circumstances seems to refute Fleet's supposition. Many people believe Fleet was simply trying to steer blame for the disaster away from himself.

By the way, the infamous key that Blair took with him when he left the *Titanic* was passed on to his daughter, Nancy. It was put up for auction in September 2007. It fetched an astonishing £90,000 (almost $150,000).

Chapter 12

Lingering Questions about the Titanic's Final Hours

*W*hen it comes to reporting, recording, and remembering history, we now have the technology to chronicle every single moment of an event. During the *Titanic* era, there were cameras, of course, but no one filmed the sinking at the time it happened. We must rely on firsthand accounts. And as in a decades-long game of telephone, accounts of what happened get told and retold until they take on a life of their own. These differing accounts of events have in some cases become part of the historical record.

Firsthand accounts of what went on in the *Titanic*'s final hours paint a picture of a chaotic time. It was night, and what people thought they saw may or may not have happened. However, as with all oral histories, assumptions can be made based on the repeated appearance of a story or fact. If 8 out of 10 people saw something, and they describe it similarly, odds are what they describe did in fact happen.

This chapter looks at whether gunshots were fired on the *Titanic*, at First Officer William Murdoch's ultimate fate, at Captain Edward J. Smith's last stand, and at the final moments of the ship's existence above water.

Were Shots Fired on the Titanic?

Were shots fired on the *Titanic* as she sank? In a word, yes. There are simply too many credible accounts of shots being fired to dismiss the story as apocryphal.

The question of whether shots were fired is a relatively big deal because, except for military honors and burials at sea, guns are rarely fired aboard ship. Steamships always carried weapons, though, and certain crew members had access to guns. Some of the *Titanic*'s crew must have immediately armed themselves upon learning of the ship's fate. (Can you blame them?)

Fifth Officer Harold Lowe is the crew member most often named as the shooter, although survivor Jack Thayer also recalled seeing Chief Purser Herbert (or Hugh) McElroy fire his revolver to prevent people from rushing one of the lifeboats. Even though Lowe tried to prevent passengers from getting into an overcrowded lifeboat (thereby sealing their fate), he was also hailed after his rescue for being the only *Titanic* officer to go back to the site to pick up four men from the water.

Confirming three instances of shots fired

Based on testimony by passengers and crew members given at both the British and U.S. inquiries into the disaster (see Chapter 10), three instances of shots being fired can be considered accurate beyond a reasonable doubt:

- ✔ Lowe fired three warning shots along the side of the ship while loading Lifeboat 14. When asked during the British Commission of Inquiry hearings into the *Titanic* disaster why he fired his revolver, Lowe replied, "Because while I was at the boat deck two men jumped into my boat. I chased one out and to avoid another occurrence of that sort I fired my revolver as I was going past each deck. The boat had about 64 persons in it and would not stand a sudden jerk."

  When Frederick Clench, Able Seaman, was asked at the U.S. Senate Subcommittee *Titanic* Hearing if he heard any shooting from his lifeboat, he responded, "Yes, sir; Mr. Lowe was in No. 14 boat, and he sings out, 'Anybody attempting to get into these boats while we are lowering them, I will shoot them.' And he shot three shots." When asked if he saw Lowe actually shoot anyone, Clench replied, "He shot straight down in the water."

- ✔ Either First Officer William Murdoch or Purser McElroy fired two warning shots in the air while loading Collapsible C. This was reported by first-class passengers Hugh Woolner and Colonel Archibald Gracie.

- ✔ Second Officer Charles H. Lightoller fired two shots in the air while loading Collapsible D. This was also reported by Gracie.

Hearing from the survivors

The eyes and the ears lie. Emotions, stress, lack of light, noise, and other stimuli can affect the way we perceive what's going on. Detectives and police officers are continually confronted with two eyewitnesses seeing widely different events. This is clearly what happened in the final hours of the *Titanic,* as evidenced by the differing stories and versions of events.

One of the most frustrating realities for *Titanic* historians is that none of the accounts of what went on aboard the *Titanic* after it struck the iceberg can be incontrovertibly confirmed. No empirical evidence in the form of photographs or recordings can confirm what has been reported. However, as the old adage goes, if it walks, quacks, and swims like a duck, the odds are strongly in favor of its in fact being a duck. We can look to repeated, almost identical accounts from survivors to paint what must be considered a fairly accurate picture of events aboard the *Titanic* between 11:40 p.m. Sunday, April 14, 1912, and 2:20 a.m. Monday, April 15, 1912.

Several people who survived the *Titanic* were clear about their recollections of shots being fired onboard. Here are a few of their firsthand accounts:

- **Abraham Hyman, third-class passenger:** In the April 19, 1912, edition of *The New York Times,* Hyman said, "When [some of the steerage passengers] got on deck, they found a rope drawn closer to their quarters than usual, and this made some of them think there was danger. One or two of the women began to cry, and a panic began to spread. An officer came forward, stood close to the rope and waved the people back. . . . The officer who was standing at the rope had a pistol in his hand, and he ordered everybody to keep back. First, one woman screamed and then another, and then one man (I think he was an Italian) pushed toward the boat and the officer fired at him."

- **Jules Sap, Belgian, third-class passenger:** In the *Chicago Tribune* of Sunday, April 21, 1912, Sap reported being threatened with death twice by officers with revolvers: first on the Boat deck and then in the water when he tried to get into a lifeboat.

- **George Rheims, first-class passenger:** Rheims wrote a private letter dated April 19, 1912, to his wife, in which he stated that he personally saw an officer shoot a passenger who was trying to force his way into a lifeboat. His account read: "When the last boat was leaving, I saw an officer fire a shot and kill a man who was trying to climb into it. As there remained nothing more for him to do, the officer told us, 'Gentlemen, each man for himself, Good-bye.' He gave a military salute and then fired a bullet into his head. That's what I call a man!!"

- **Eugene Daly, third-class passenger:** Daly wrote a private letter to his sister in which he reported seeing an officer shoot two men who were trying to get into a lifeboat. After praying with two female passengers, Daly wrote, "We afterwards went to the second cabin deck, and the two girls and myself got into a boat. An officer called on me to go back, but I would not stir. They then got hold of me and pulled me out.

    "At the first cabin, when a boat was being lowered, an officer pointed a revolver and said if any man tried to get in he would shoot him on the spot. I saw the officer shoot two men dead because they tried to get into the boat. Afterwards there was another shot, and I saw the officer himself lying on the deck. They told me he shot himself, but I did not see him.

"I was up to my knees in water at the time. Everyone was rushing around and there were no more boats. I then dived overboard and got in a boat."

Did Murdoch Commit Suicide?

On December 12, 1997, one week before the movie *Titanic* opened in the United States, someone posted the following on an Internet *Titanic* news-group: "I will say this though. If the movie has Murdoch committing suicide I'll scream." Another poster immediately responded to this threat with just two words: "Start screaming." Thus the debate raged on.

The question of First Officer Murdoch's reported suicide has never been defini-tively answered, but so much has been written about the alleged incident that a review of the various accounts can help us draw our own conclusions.

Reconstructing Murdoch's final moments

So exactly what happened to Murdoch? How did he actually behave during the *Titanic*'s final moments? Several survivors reported seeing Murdoch (who is shown in Figure 12-1) assigning passengers to lifeboats and helping with their loading and launching. *Titanic* expert Walter Lord, in *The Night Lives On* (Avon), his sequel to *A Night to Remember,* noted that when last seen, just as Second Officer Lightoller jumped into the sea, Murdoch was still on deck trying to attach a collapsible lifeboat to the falls. If Murdoch had considered suicide, Lord wrote, it was understandable. He was, after all, the officer who had been in charge of the bridge at the time of the colli-sion with the iceberg and had been the one to give "the orders that failed to save the ship."

Yet surviving *Titanic* officers who knew Murdoch well all agreed that he would not be the type to kill himself. This is, of course, a subjective judg-ment by Murdoch's colleagues; no one can state with certainty what another person will or won't do under the right (or wrong) circumstances.

Some survivors also claimed to have seen Murdoch shoot two passengers and then kill himself. Thomas Whitely, one of the *Titanic*'s saloon stewards, said that he watched Murdoch "shoot one man . . . and then shoot himself." Whitely's testimony is unclear, however, because he also said, "I did not see this, but three others did," and it isn't clear whether Whitely is talking about Murdoch's shooting a man or shooting himself.

Figure 12-1:
First Officer
William
Murdoch.

On the Bridge at the Moment of Contact
Mr. Murdock was the officer in charge at the moment the
Titanic encountered the ice floe. He was not rescued,
and the manner of his death is at present uncertain

Mary Evans/© Illustrated London News Ltd/Everett Collection

Third-class passenger Carl Jensen said that he "glanced toward the bridge and saw the chief officer place a revolver in his mouth and shoot himself. His body toppled overboard."

The question of whether or not Murdoch killed himself arose almost immediately after the sinking. In a story that ran in the Friday, April 19, 1912, edition of Britain's *Daily Sketch* newspaper, the subject of Murdoch's ultimate outcome was already being discussed:

> [T]he . . . suggestion that it was the first officer, Mr. Murdoch, who shot himself on the bridge is disproved . . . by the quartermaster at the wheel, Robert Hitchens, who declares that Mr. Murdoch was in charge of the vessel at the time of the accident and that he acted in the coolest possible manner, closing the watertight doors and stopping the engines.

But in the *Daily Sketch*'s April 30, 1912, edition, survivor Charles Williams was quoted as saying, "[The Captain] did ask what had become of First Officer Murdoch. We told him Murdoch had blown his brains out with a revolver."

Living with the unknown

There is, in the end, no definitive answer to the question of whether Murdoch killed himself as the *Titanic* sank beneath the waves. What is clear, though, is that someone killed himself on the *Titanic*'s deck. Too many detailed accounts from credible witnesses exist to dismiss the story as fiction.

There are no final answers, and perhaps this unavoidable uncertainty is part of what has kept the *Titanic* legend alive for a century.

Murdoch's survivors get an apology

According to the depiction of Murdoch and his actions in James Cameron's film *Titanic* — the most recent rendering of his story — the first officer, in his final hours, accepted bribes for places on lifeboats, shot two panicked third-class passengers attempting to get into an already-overcrowded lifeboat, and ultimately committed suicide by shooting himself in the head.

This is not, however, the version of Murdoch's story that his family and townsfolk believe. In fact, the residents of Dalbeattie, Scotland, Murdoch's hometown, believe that Murdoch's actions during the *Titanic*'s final hours were heroic and selfless, and that he dutifully went down with the ship instead of killing himself.

At an April 15, 1998, ceremony in Dalbeattie commemorating the 86th anniversary of the sinking, Scottish-born Twentieth Century Fox executive Scott Neeson tried to paint a prettier picture than the one in the film. "[*Titanic*]," Neeson told the media, "never intended to portray him as a coward. I believe he was portrayed as a hero in the film. In the film and in real life, he is saving an enormous number of lives."

Neeson, in an attempt to mollify supporters of Murdoch's memory, gave Dalbeattie High School a check for $8,000 and an inscribed silver tray. He also officially apologized to Dalbeattie and Murdoch's family on behalf of Twentieth Century Fox for causing them all "so much distress."

Linda Kirkwood, head of Dalbeattie High School, praised the studio's donation to the school but said it did not make up for Murdoch's memory being "besmirched." She also said, "People in Dalbeattie and the rest of Britain know he was a hero, but filmgoers all over the world will see him portrayed as a coward."

Murdoch's nephew, Scott Murdoch, who was 80 at the time, was more magnanimous about the incident. Saying he was "very pleased" that the studio had issued an apology, he noted that "it was important to clear the name of my uncle. I don't think I can forget, but today certainly makes it easier to forgive."

Apology notwithstanding, Cameron's film will serve to carve in stone the version of the story that has Murdoch killing himself. But as with many elements of the *Titanic* tale, much of what we believe is what we personally want to believe. Murdoch's loved ones want to believe he died a hero. Cameron and other *Titanic* historians want to believe he killed himself.

The Riddle of Captain Smith's Death and Last Words

How did the *Titanic*'s Captain Smith die, and what were his final words? There are at least three notable accounts of his death: standing calmly in the wheelhouse, committing suicide, and swimming to a lifeboat holding a baby.

Piecing together details of Smith's death

We can only imagine Captain Smith's profound embarrassment and the over-whelming feeling that he had let down his passengers, his crew, and his ship as the *Titanic* foundered. Captain Smith, shown in Figure 12-2, was where the buck stopped. When the *Titanic* left Southampton, England, under Captain Smith's command, he was the one ultimately responsible for more than 2,200 lives and the $7.5 million vessel.

Figure 12-2:
Captain
Edward J.
Smith.

© Mary Evans Picture Library/Everett Collection

In the end, Smith lost his life, just as he lost the ship. However, the accounts of Smith's death vary widely. Some people said he went down with the ship. Others claim they saw him jump overboard. A few people believed that the captain committed suicide. Here's a sampling of their stories:

✔ **Robert W. Daniel of Philadelphia, survivor:** In the April 19, 1912, issue of the *New York Herald,* Daniel said that Captain Smith stood calmly on the bridge as it was submerged under the icy Atlantic waters: "I saw Captain Smith on the bridge. My eyes seemingly clung to him. The deck from which I had leapt was immersed. The water had risen slowly, and was now to the floor of the bridge. Then it was to Captain Smith's waist. I saw him no more. He died a hero." Daniel also said, "Captain Smith was the biggest hero I ever saw. He stood on the bridge, shouting through the megaphone, trying to make himself heard."

- ✔ **Dr. J. F. Kemp, a passenger on the *Carpathia*:** According to a *New York Times* article on April 19, 1912, Dr. Kemp said that Captain Smith committed suicide by shooting himself in the head. Kemp said he spoke with a young boy — a *Titanic* passenger — who claimed to have seen "Captain Smith put a pistol to his head and then fall down." Some other survivors confirmed also seeing this happen, but *Titanic* crew members passionately denied even the possibility of Smith's killing himself instead of going down with his ship.

- ✔ **Harold Bride, *Titanic* Marconi operator:** According to his U.S. Senate subcommittee testimony (see Chapter 10), Bride said he saw Captain Smith dive into the ocean just as Collapsible B was levered off the roof of the officers' quarters and fell onto the Boat deck: "The last I saw of the Captain, he went overboard from the bridge. He jumped overboard from the bridge when we were launching the collapsible lifeboat."

- ✔ **G. A. Brayton of Los Angeles, survivor:** An August 19, 1912, article in *The Star* quotes Brayton as saying, "I saw Captain Smith while I was in the water. He was standing on the deck all alone. Once he was swept down by a wave, but managed to get to his feet again. Then, as the boat sank, he was again knocked down by a wave, and then disappeared from sight."

- ✔ **Charles Williams, survivor:** Williams said he saw Captain Smith swimming around in the icy water with an infant in his arms and wearing a life belt. He reportedly handed the infant to someone in a lifeboat but refused to get in himself. Smith then asked what had become of Murdoch, and when told Murdoch had killed himself, pushed himself away from the boat, took off his life belt, and sank beneath the surface to his death. This version of the story was confirmed by a steward named John Maynard, who claimed to have personally taken the baby from Captain Smith, and by *Titanic* fireman Harry Senior, who reported having seen the captain rescue the child.

Why so many stories of his final actions and last words, though? Possibly because it was a fluid situation and Captain Smith was all over the place. Different passengers and crew members could easily have seen him and heard him say different things.

It is feasible that the majority of the accounts of the captain's final moments are true — except for the suicide story. There are not enough credible accounts of the captain shooting himself for it to be considered seriously, yet there are repeated accounts of both the "swimming with the baby" story and of seeing the captain on the bridge just before the ship went under.

Regardless of how Captain Smith died, I don't doubt that he did his duty as ship's captain and went down with his ship. Based on survivors' accounts and the belief that Captain Smith would probably have done everything in his power to save as many passengers as possible, one possible scenario could be that he did indeed swim to one of the lifeboats with a baby in his arms and then swam back to the ship, where he returned to the wheelhouse and awaited his and his ship's destiny.

Uttering six different "last words"?

Regarding Captain Smith's last words, history is also inconclusive yet consistent: Regardless of precisely what the doomed commander said, all post-rescue accounts of his last words emphasized Smith's heroism and self-sacrifice. He was reported to have said all, some, or none of the following:

✔ "Be British, boys! Be British!"

✔ "Every man for himself!"

✔ "Goodbye, boys! I'm going to follow the ship!"

✔ "I will follow the ship!"

✔ "Well, boys, do your best for the women and children, and look out for yourselves."

✔ "All right, boys. Good luck, and God bless you."

Debating the Band's Final Song

As you can read in Chapter 8, the *Titanic*'s junior Marconi operator, Harold Bride, in his *New York Times* article of April 28, 1912, said this of the ship's final moments: "The ship was gradually turning on her nose — just like a duck that goes down for a dive. I had only one thing on my mind — to get away from the suction. The band was still playing. I guess all of the band went down. They were playing 'Autumn' then."

Was "Autumn" the final song that the stalwart *Titanic* orchestra played before the band members put down their instruments and prepared themselves for their inevitable deaths? No one knows for sure, but there are three main contenders for the band's last song:

✔ "Autumn," a popular song of the time

✔ "Nearer, My God, To Thee,"a hymn

✔ "Songe d'Automne," a traditional waltz by Archibald Joyce

The band's playlist

It was quite a responsibility, being the sole source of musical entertainment on a gigantic liner like the *Titanic,* and the eight members of the *Titanic*'s main orchestra (shown in Figure 12-3) performed admirably. (The figure does not show Roger Bricoux, who was a guest cellist and who perished in the sinking.) Their official playlist included 120 songs — everything from operatic and classical pieces for accompanying dining to ragtime and waltzes for post-prandial dancing, including the "William Tell Overture," songs from *Rigoletto* and *Carmen,* and a variety of waltzes. The playlist included a wide assortment of national anthems, sacred hymns, and popular songs of the day.

Survivors have mentioned hearing songs that are not on the official playlist, and considering the vast range of musical expertise the members of the orchestra possessed, it is likely that this official repertoire was probably just a starting point for their performances. (For example, Edwina Troutt remembered hearing Edward Elgar's "Pomp and Circumstance" performed by the musicians, yet there is nothing specifically by Elgar on the playlist.)

"Autumn" or "Nearer, My God, To Thee"?

In the complete repertoire of the orchestra, "Nearer, My God, To Thee" and "Autumn" were not specifically listed, but "Songe d'Automne" was. However, the orchestra's list of music included the categories "Popular Songs" and "National Anthems, Hymns, etc. of all Nations," and these categories would almost certainly include "Nearer, My God, To Thee" and "Autumn."

Throughout the years, "Nearer, My God, To Thee" has become ensconced in the *Titanic* legend as the band's final song. Many survivors are on record as recalling hearing the song being played as the lifeboats were being loaded and the ship continued to sink. One 1912 newspaper account even stated that some of the lifeboat passengers actually hummed along with the band as it played the popular hymn.

Edward Wheelton, one of the *Titanic*'s saloon stewards, said this in his account of the *Titanic*'s final moments (from the Saturday, April 20, 1912, *Daily Sketch*): "As the boats were being lowered the orchestra was playing operatic selections and some of the latest popular melodies from Europe and America. It was only just before the liner made her final plunge that the character of the pro-gramme was changed, and then they struck up 'Nearer, My God, To Thee'."

Bride remembered hearing "Autumn," but he did not specify whether it was the Joyce waltz, which appears on the orchestra's playlist, or the popular song "Autumn," which does not appear (by name, that is). Considering that Bride is the only one on record who recalled hearing "Autumn," it seems more likely that "Nearer" was the band's final song.

THE ILLUSTRATED LONDON NEWS, APRIL 27, 1912.— 636

BRAVE AS THE "BIRKENHEAD" BAND: THE "TITANIC'S" MUSICIAN HEROES.

1. MR. F. CLARKE, OF LIVERPOOL. 2. MR. P. C. TAYLOR, OF CLAPHAM.
3. MR. G. KRINS, OF BRIXTON, SOMETIME OF THE RITZ HOTEL ORCHESTRA. 4. MR. W. HARTLEY (BANDMASTER), OF DEWSBURY. 5. MR. W. T. BRAILEY, OF NOTTING HILL.
6. MR. J. HUME, OF DUMFRIES. 7. MR. J. W. WOODWARD, OF HEADINGTON, OXON.

One of the most dramatic incidents of the great shipwreck was the heroic conduct of the band, which, led by Mr. W. Hartley, of Dewsbury, continued to play up to a few minutes of the end. On this subject, as on others connected with the disaster, there have been conflicting statements, but of the main fact there is no doubt. In its careful summary of the various reports, the "Times" said: "That the band played as bravely as that other band in the 'Birkenhead' during a great part of the time that the 'Titanic' was sinking seems indisputable . . . 'Nearer, my God, to Thee,' and other hymn tunes were, as reported, played for some time. Then the music changed to something lighter (which would explain Bride's statement about the rag-time he heard), and continued until about ten minutes before the end. As they played, the bandsmen are said to have tried to fix on life-belts. It may well be, indeed, that it was not until they were flooded out that they gave up their heroic and self-appointed task." In addition to those of whom we give photographs, there was Mr. R. Bricoux, of Lille.

Figure 12-3:
The members of the *Titanic's* main orchestra.

It's not surprising that the popular belief that "Nearer, My God, To Thee" was the band's final song still holds today. The lyrics of the second verse are

> Though like the wanderer, the sun gone down
>
> Darkness be over me, my rest a stone
>
> Yet in my dreams I'd be nearer, my God, to Thee . . .

It's easy to imagine someone going down with the *Titanic* thinking those thoughts, isn't it? Believing that their loved ones heard these words must have been a comfort to relatives of the ones who perished.

"Nearer, My God, To Thee" was immediately embraced as the band's final song. An April 22, 1912, article in the British paper *Daily Sketch* revealed that Wallace Hartley, the band's leader, had once told a fellow musician that if he were ever on board a sinking liner, he would get his men together and play music as the ship sank. When asked what he would play, Hartley replied, "Well, I don't think I could do better than play 'Oh God Our Help in Ages Past' or 'Nearer, My God, To Thee.' They are both favorite hymns of mine, and they would be very suitable to the occasion."

These words seem to confirm that what many survivors remembered hearing the band play was, indeed, what Hartley had his band perform.

Laying the bandmaster to rest

In early May 1912, the crew of the *Mackay-Bennett,* the ship sent to the site of the *Titanic's* sinking to search for bodies still afloat, found and identified bandmaster Wallace Hartley's body. Poignantly, Hartley's music case was still strapped to his body. (According to British news reports, Hartley's music case was returned to the White Star Line.) On Friday, May 17, 1912, his body was returned to Liverpool on the liner *Arabic* and claimed by his father. Hartley's coffin was driven by hearse to his hometown of Colne, where his funeral took place the following day.

The following account from the Monday, May 20, 1912, *Daily Sketch* details Hartley's funeral and again asserts the "Nearer, My God, To Thee" story:

> In keeping with the heroism of the man who led the *Titanic's* band as they stood on the deck of the doomed liner calmly playing "Nearer, My God To Thee," while the last of the lifeboats pulled away from the sinking ship were the striking scenes witnessed Saturday when the remains of Mr. Wallace Hartley were laid to rest in the cemetery of his native town of Colne, Lancashire. The Bethel Choir and the Colne Orchestral Society played "Nearer, My God, To Thee" as Hartley's remains were interred.

Chapter 13

Foreshadowing the Tragedy? The 1898 Novella *The Wreck of the Titan*

*T*his chapter examines what is a remarkable mystery, a remarkable coincidence, or a remarkable example of foresightedness. In 1898, Morgan Robertson, a popular adventure writer of the time, published a novella called *Futility*. The novella told the thrilling story of the largest passenger steamship ever built, how this steamship struck an iceberg in the North Atlantic and how it sank to the ocean floor, killing close to 3,000 of its passengers.

Does Robertson's novella sound familiar? It does, I wager. And if the similarities between Robertson's novella and the sinking of the *Titanic* aren't spooky enough, consider this fact: The ship in Robertson's novella was called (drum roll, please) the *Titan!*

Shortly after the *Titanic* was lost, Robertson's publishers re-released *Futility*, but this time it had a different title: *The Wreck of the Titan.*

Did Robertson predict the sinking of the *Titanic* 14 years before the great liner's maiden voyage? Keep reading, and see what you think.

Meeting Morgan Robertson

Morgan Robertson (1861–1915) was the son of a sea captain and grew up poor. He was a cabin boy on ships when he was young, thus making him familiar with ships at sea and helping him understand sailing, navigation, and other aspects of maritime life. When he started writing, it was not surprising that he would incorporate elements from his own life and experiences into his stories.

Robertson was a fascinating guy. In his 1905 novel *The Submarine Destroyer,* he claimed to have invented the periscope (he didn't). And in 1914, he wrote a short story called "Beyond the Spectrum," which was about a war between the United States and Japan precipitated by a sneak attack on the United States by Japan.

Robertson never made much money writing and died in a hotel in Atlantic City, New Jersey, in 1915 at the age of 53. His cause of death was an overdose of *protiodide,* an over-the counter mercury-based drug used to treat acne, kidney disease, syphillis, and other diseases.

How was Robertson able to somewhat accurately tell the story of the *Titanic* 14 years before she sailed? It was likely a combination of imagination, an ability to glimpse the future of shipbuilding, and fortuitous coincidence.

Did the Titanic's Builders Know about the Novella?

Very likely, the *Titanic*'s builders, Harland and Wolff, were unaware that a novella called *Futility* about a ship called the *Titan* had been published in 1898. While we can't know for certain that the *Titanic* builders hadn't read the novella, *Futility* had long been out of print when ideas for the building of the *Titanic* were taking shape.

Speculation that the *Titanic* builders could somehow have been influenced by the ideas in the novella seems far-fetched. J. Bruce Ismay, chairman and managing director of the White Star Line, and Harland and Wolff were highly regarded names in the shipbuilding field; it's difficult to imagine them taking direction from a novella when designing the greatest ship ever built. Had they taken any cues from *Futility* and the word got out, it would have been enormously embarrassing for them.

More likely, coincidence and an imaginative fiction writer with foresight were the real fountainheads for the story of the doomed ship *Titan.*

Foretelling Fact with Fiction

What did the *Titanic* have in common with the fictional *Titan?* The similarities included the ships' lengths, number of watertight compartments, gross tonnage, number of lifeboats, and speed. Also, the two ships had *identical* passenger capacity and the same number of propellers. Their fateful voyages began in the same month. Both struck an iceberg on their starboard (right) side. Both sank to the bottom of the North Atlantic.

Some of the passages in *The Wreck of the Titan* come remarkably close to journalistic accounts of the *Titanic*'s demise. Following are some examples.

The opening paragraph

The Wreck of the Titan begins this way:

> She was the largest craft afloat and the greatest of the works of man. In her construction and maintenance were involved every science, profession, and trade known to civilization. On her bridge were officers, who, besides being the pick of the Royal Navy, had passed rigid examinations in all studies that pertained to the winds, tides, currents, and geography of the sea; they were not only seamen, but scientists. The same professional standard applied to the personnel of the engine-room, and the stewards' department was equal to that of a first-class hotel.

The first sentence alone has two key points that pertain to the *Titanic:* She was the "largest craft afloat" at the time, and she was considered by her builders, her passengers, and much of the media at large to be the "greatest of the works of man."

The second sentence, which talks about every science, profession, and trade being involved in the building of the *Titan,* also applies to the *Titanic,* as does Robertson's description of the crew and his use of "first-class hotel" to describe the stewards' department. The entire opening paragraph could have been written verbatim about the RMS *Titanic.*

The "unsinkable" moniker

Later in Chapter 1 is this passage:

> From the bridge, engine-room, and a dozen places on her deck the ninety-two doors of nineteen watertight compartments could be closed in half a minute by turning a lever. These doors would also close automatically in the presence of water. With nine compartments flooded the ship would still float, and as no known accident of the sea could possibly fill this many, the steamship Titan was considered practically unsinkable.

This paragraph describes the ship's watertight compartments. The *Titan* had 19; the *Titanic* had 16. Before the *Titanic* launched, there was a great deal of talk about how many watertight compartments could flood before the ship would begin to sink.

Notice the use of the word *unsinkable* at the end of the paragraph. That word was routinely applied to the *Titanic* before its launch and used ironically after its sinking.

A major difference

Robertson wasn't entirely prescient. His crystal ball could sometimes get cloudy. A few paragraphs later in Chapter 1, he wrote:

> Built of steel throughout, and for passenger traffic only, she carried no combustible cargo to threaten her destruction by fire; and the immunity from the demand for cargo space had enabled her designers to discard the flat, kettle-bottom of cargo boats and give her the sharp dead-rise — or slant from the keel — of a steam yacht, and this improved her behavior in a seaway.

This description is totally at odds with the *Titanic* reality. The *Titanic* carried tons of cargo, including an automobile, books, clothing, furniture, grandfather clocks, orchids, and hundreds of cases of wine.

A sad, tragic similarity

This paragraph from Robertson's work parallels the *Titanic* reality in a remarkable way:

Unsinkable — indestructible, she carried as few boats as would satisfy the laws. These, twenty-four in number, were securely covered and lashed down to their chocks on the upper deck, and if launched would hold five hundred people. She carried no useless, cumbersome life-rafts; but — because the law required it — each of the three thousand berths in the passengers', officers', and crews' quarters contained a cork jacket, while about twenty circular life-buoys were strewn along the rails.

As I detail in Chapters 6 and 11, the *Titanic* carried just enough lifeboats to satisfy the (wholly inadequate) legal requirements. The *Titan* had 24 of them; the *Titanic* had 20.

The collision

Robertson's description of the *Titan* striking an iceberg isn't identical to what happened to the *Titanic,* but it's pretty darn close:

"Ice," yelled the lookout: "ice ahead. Iceberg. Right under the bows." The first officer ran amidships, and the captain, who had remained there, sprang to the engine-room telegraph, and this time the lever was turned. But in five seconds the bow of the Titan began to lift, and ahead, and on either hand, could be seen, through the fog, a field of ice, which arose in an incline to a hundred feet high in her track.

Frederick Fleet, who was lookout on the *Titanic* when she struck the iceberg, shouted, "Iceberg right ahead," which is very close to the *Titan* lookout's "Ice, ice ahead. Iceberg." Granted, most nautical lookouts would probably have shouted something very similar, but there's no denying Robertson got it right.

Comparing the Titan and Titanic Side by Side

How similar were the *Titanic* and the fictional *Titan?* Table 13-1 provides a side-by-side look at some of the most amazing parallels. Whatever you think of Robertson's precognitive abilities, there is no denying that *The Wreck of the Titan* is one of the stranger elements of the *Titanic* legend.

Table 13-1   **Similarities between the *Titan* and *Titanic***

	Titan	*Titanic*
Length	800 feet	882.5 feet
Number of propellers	3	3
Watertight compartments	19	16
Watertight doors	92	12
Passenger capacity	3,000	3,000
Passengers onboard	3,000	More than 2,200
Displacement (in tons)	45,000 (1898 edition) 70,000 (1912 edition)	52,310
Gross tonnage	45,000	46,328
Reputation	"Unsinkable" (Chapter 1)	"Unsinkable"
Horsepower	40,000 (1898 edition) 75,000 (1912 edition)	46,000
Lifeboats	24	20
Speed at time of collision	25 knots	22.5 knots
Month voyage began	April	April
Side of ship that struck iceberg	Starboard	Starboard
Time iceberg was struck	Near midnight	11:40 p.m.
Itinerary	New York to England	England to New York
Location of collision	North Atlantic, a few hundred miles off the U.S. coast	North Atlantic, a few hundred miles off the U.S. coast
First warning of danger	"Ice, ice ahead. Iceberg. Right under the bows."	"Iceberg right ahead."
Ship's owner/ headquarters	British company — Liverpool	British registry but owned by the U.S.- based International Mercantile Marine Company
Ship's owners' U.S. office location	New York	New York
Deaths	2,987	More than 1,500

Part IV
The Quest to Recover the Titanic

The 5th Wave   By Rich Tennant

1982 — BACK FROM ANOTHER UNSUCCESSFUL
SEARCH FOR THE TITANIC, SYLVIA AND
LEO DECKER REMAIN UNDAUNTED.

In this part . . .

The first proposal for raising the *Titanic* from the ocean floor was made only a few days after she sank. This part looks at plans and schemes — cockamamie and otherwise — to find, recover, and even raise the *Titanic*. It also describes the 1985 discovery of the wreck by Dr. Robert Ballard and IFREMER (the French Research Institute for Exploration of the Sea) and subsequent expeditions to the ocean floor to explore and salvage artifacts from the *Titanic*.

Chapter 14

Looking at Early Attempts to Raise the Titanic

*I*t's all about pressure — water pressure, that is. Two and a half miles below the surface of the North Atlantic, the water pressure on the *Titanic* is 6,500 pounds per square inch. Water pressure alone deterred and prevented recovery expeditions from reaching the *Titanic* until the technology could catch up with the brute force of nature. However, these technological limitations didn't stop folks from trying. And they tried everything — I mean everything.

In Clive Cussler's 1976 bestselling novel *Raise the Titanic!* (Berkley), the plan was to patch the holes in the hull, fill the ship with compressed air, raise the ship to the surface, and then sail it to New York. However, the whole premise of Cussler's novel was based on the false assumption that the ship sank intact and lay on the ocean floor in one piece. Dr. Robert Ballard and IFREMER (the French Research Institute for Exploration of the Sea), who found the *Titanic* wreck site in 1985, changed this assumption. They discovered that the *Titanic* had split in two when it sank.

As far-fetched as the Cussler idea sounds now, the attempts discussed in this chapter are much more outrageous. They involved balloons, magnets, and explosives, among other things. I start with the earliest attempts to raise the ship; then I move on to some more current claims of discovering and owning the *Titanic*. Finally, I round out the chapter with some of the most absurd ideas that salvagers have had throughout the years.

Considering the problems that are inherent in the physical realities of raising the *Titanic,* maybe we should just leave her alone.

Realizing the Challenges of Raising the Titanic

In 1998, George Tulloch and his team successfully raised (after two tries and two years) the Big Piece, a 20-ton piece of the *Titanic*'s hull. (See Chapter 16 for the full story of salvaging the Big Piece.) Tulloch's endeavor provides an idea of what it would be like to bring up much larger pieces of the ship. Raising the Big Piece was difficult enough. Anyone trying to raise even larger pieces of the ship would face the same problems that Tulloch and company faced, but the problems would be magnified by an unimaginable exponent.

The logistics of raising the whole *Titanic* are overwhelming. A salvage team would have to secure thousands of tons of steel 2.5 miles below the surface of the frigid North Atlantic. After successfully securing the ship, the team then would have to slowly pull her to the surface. Consider just a couple of things that can go wrong with a salvage of this magnitude:

- ✔ Cables can break at any point.
- ✔ Ocean currents can cause shifts in the ship's position, unleashing the ship from its cables and sending it plummeting back to the ocean floor.

Even if these key obstacles can be overcome, the question of what to do with a multiton piece of the *Titanic* after it reaches the surface may be unanswerable. Do you tow it over the water or winch it to a gigantic vessel? An aircraft supercarrier would probably be the only vessel able to take it.

And let's say that you successfully bring the *Titanic* to shore. Then what? It took almost two years of treatment to prepare the Big Piece for display. How long and how many resources would it take to treat the entire *Titanic* in a similar manner?

Bringing the *Titanic* up from the bottom of the ocean is almost certainly futile. The question must be asked: Why is it necessary to raise her anyway? According to most estimates, approximately 1 million shipwrecks sit in the waters of the planet. You could argue that these shipwrecks are gravesites. These ships, like many of their passengers and crew members, were in effect buried at sea and perhaps shouldn't be disturbed.

Surveying the First Efforts to Raise the Wreckage

Hardly had the *Titanic* sunk when people began thinking of ways to bring her back to the surface. For some of these people, it wasn't a matter of recovering the bodies or the ship; instead, they saw an opportunity to get rich.

The *Titanic*'s cargo manifest (its official list of passengers and cargo) was readily available. The manifest was rather mundane; it listed some valuable items, including an automobile, but it listed no diamonds or gold bullion. What excited people's imaginations was the generic "merchandise" listing. Everyone wanted to know what constituted "merchandise" for the wealthy first-class passengers aboard the *Titanic*. Jewelry? Furs? (See Chapter 19 for details about valuable artifacts believed to have sunk with the *Titanic*, including a gem-encrusted copy of the *Rubaiyat* known to be on the ship.)

People fantasized and bought into rumors and hearsay about the riches that went down with the *Titanic*. They dreamed of the treasures that awaited them if they were able to, if not raise the *Titanic*, at least get to and plunder her. After all, maritime law essentially boils down to "You find it, you own it."

The following sections provide a look at some of the most notable (and strange!) plots to raise the *Titanic* in the early years after her sinking.

The Astor plan of 1912: Blowing up the ship

Multimillionaire John Jacob Astor IV (see Figure 14-1) didn't survive the sinking. After seeing his young wife, Madeleine; her maid; and her nurse into a lifeboat, Astor retreated to the deck of the *Titanic*. (After her rescue, Madeleine Astor refused to talk about the sinking except to describe her last memory, which was seeing her husband's pet Airedale, Kitty, pacing the *Titanic*'s deck.)

Figure 14-1:
John Jacob
Astor IV.

© CSU Archives/Everett Collection

Astor's son Vincent was beside himself with grief when he learned of the sinking. On Tuesday, April 16, 1912, he visited the Marconi office in New York, desperate for news about his father. He also went to the Associated Press office and the White Star Line offices. A Wednesday, April 17, 1912, *New York Times* article notes, "The young man was grief-stricken for he was a chum as well as a son of John Jacob." The *Times* article continues

> He was told that his stepmother, who was Miss Madeleine Force, was known to be among them saved but that the worst was feared concerning the fate of his father, whose name was missing from the slender list that has been wirelessed from the *Carpathia* . . .

> He was almost hysterical from grief and one of the operators said he cried out that he would give all the money that could be asked for if the operator would only tell him that he had news of his father's safety.

After Vincent learned of the rescue of his stepmother, Madeleine, he realized that his father must have gone down with the ship. Almost immediately, he came up with a macabre idea for recovering his father's body: blow up the wreckage of the *Titanic* so that his father's body would float to the surface.

A Saturday, April 20, 1912, *New York Evening Journal* article discussed Vincent Astor's newly hatched plan to blow up the wreckage: "Young Astor, who is grief-stricken over his father's death, it was said, will to-day take up the matter with one of the large wrecking companies. He has been assured that it is feasible by his friends and is prepared to go to any expense, it was said, to recover his father's body."

The *New York Evening Journal* consulted Merritt Chapman Wrecking Company about Vincent's plan. Its owner, I. J. Merritt, said of the plan:

> It is certainly feasible. The most difficult problem would be to locate the wreck. I understand that the White Star Company has a fairly good idea as to where the *Titanic* sank, but it would take some time to find her by the use of soundings. Having found the boat, the rest would not be difficult, although we would be compelled to completely wreck the boat. A large quantity of gun cotton, between 300 and 400 pounds, heavily weighted, would be dropped into the wreckage. An electric wire, connected with a battery, would be "touched off." We could use other explosives, if necessary, and the force of the explosions would be sure to bring all of the bodies to the surface.

The gun cotton that I. J. Merritt recommended using to blow up the *Titanic* wreckage is nitrocellulose, a combustible material suitable for blasting. It's made by steeping cotton in nitric and sulphuric acids.

Whatever arrangements Vincent made to blow up the *Titanic* and recover his father's body were made irrelevant on Monday, April 22, when John Jacob Astor's body was recovered at sea by the *Mackay-Bennett*. The White Star Line chartered this cable steamer out of Halifax, Nova Scotia, to go to the wreckage site and recover bodies floating in the ocean. John Jacob Astor's was body #124. He was found fully dressed, complete with almost four grand in cash, a blue handkerchief, and a monogrammed shirt. His body was transported to Halifax, where it was immediately claimed and then embalmed. The moment Vincent Astor heard of the recovery of his father's body, he abandoned the plan to drop explosives on the *Titanic*.

Even though I. J. Merritt was confident in Astor's plan, it wouldn't have worked for several reasons, not the least of which was that no one really knew where the *Titanic* lay. Randomly dropping explosives where they thought she landed on the ocean floor would have been futile. And considering the 46,000-ton weight of the *Titanic,* would "between 300 and 400 pounds" of gun cotton have done the job?

The 1913 magnet plan: Using "monster leeches"

Some people get so involved with their ideas that they come up with ludicrous plans without thinking things through. And even if they do think things through, they make unproven assumptions and accept them as not only possible, but also executable.

One such person was Charles A. Smith, a Denver engineer. Smith was fascinated by the *Titanic*. Immediately after the sinking, he came up with a plan to not only find her, but also to raise and tow her to Nova Scotia, where she would rest in no more than 100 feet of water. This way, he figured, divers could easily get to her and then inside her.

Smith's plans involved what were known as electromagnetic lifting magnets. The April 24, 1914, *Oelwein Daily Register* ran an article titled "Hopes To Raise the *Titanic*" that described Charles Smith's imaginative yet far-fetched plan to raise the great liner in detail. Here's the newspaper's synopsis of his plan (kudos to the long-gone author of this article for coming up with the evocative image of the magnets as "monster leeches"):

> Briefly, it is his purpose to make use of a great many powerful electric lifting magnets, which when energized will cling to the steel body of the *Titanic* like so many monster leeches.

> When these magnets are firmly attached to the skin of the ship lines leading surfaceward will be secured to buoyant caissons, or camels, of steel built especially for the purpose, and then the inventor counts upon the cumulative lifting force of all these cylindrical tanks to raise the *Titanic* clear of the bottom so that the wreck and the floating camels can be towed into shallower water.

> Each time the *Titanic* is halted by the rising sea bed the connecting lines will be shortened, the vessel raised a few feet, and with this clearance she will be towed nearer land. Thus step by step the foundered ship is

to be raised and moved shoreward until the next to the last stage of the operation finds her in water of such moderate depth that the ordinary diver can be employed. This would involve bringing the *Titanic* from her present supposed resting place, two miles down below the surface of the sea, and transporting her to some point near the Nova Scotian coast, where a temporary resting place could be found at a depth of not more than 100 feet.

This plan, of course, made a bunch of assumptions that couldn't adequately be proved, including the following:

✔ The *Titanic* was still in one piece and could be found quickly.

✔ A submersible could be built and survive at the depths where the *Titanic* rested.

✔ The electromagnetic magnets could handle the 46,000-ton load.

✔ The towing would go smoothly.

✔ Buoyant caissons equivalent to the amassed buoyancy of 215 *Titanic* ships could easily be constructed and shipped to the site.

✔ The money for such an endeavor would be easy to raise.

Smith's plan never got off the ground . . . er, out of the water.

Laying Claim to the Titanic

Folks came out of the woodwork after the *Titanic* sank. Everyone wanted a piece of history, but the two men in the following sections wanted history all to themselves. Jack Grimm believes he holds the historic record of being the first to find the *Titanic* wreckage. And Douglas John Faulkner-Woolley says he was awarded ownership of the great ocean liner by the British court. I provide their stories so you can come to your own conclusions.

Scouring the ocean floor with Jack Grimm

Jack Grimm was an Oklahoma-born Texas oilman who was fascinated with the search for lost legends. Grimm, who died in 1998, searched at various times during his life in the Pacific Northwest for Sasquatch, in Scotland for the Loch Ness Monster, in Turkey for Noah's Ark, and in Nepal for the Abominable Snowman. (In the 1970s, Grimm claimed to have found Noah's Ark. He said he kept a piece of the Ark with him in his briefcase at all times.) In 1980, 1981, and 1983 expeditions, Grimm explored the bottom of the North Atlantic for the *Titanic*. He put together his first team of scientists to accompany him on an expedition to find the wreckage of the *Titanic* in 1980. One of his team members was geophysicist Dr. William B. F. Ryan of Columbia University. Grimm raised money from Texas oilmen he knew, and he developed equipment for undersea exploration that Columbia University, by prior agreement, got to keep when the expedition was over.

In the August 4, 1980, issue of *People* magazine, Ryan said, "My team is as excited about this as anything we've done. It has given us a chance to buy or build some equipment we couldn't have afforded, and it allows us to do some tests from our wish list."

Grimm's team set out after mapping a 15-by-15-mile search area they had determined was the actual position of the *Titanic* (as reported by her crew before she sank). They towed an underwater sled with sonar equipment for mapping the ocean floor on a 4-mile-long cable. The plan was to send down cameras if the *Titanic* was found.

Grimm's claim to have found the wreckage of the *Titanic* was based on a photo of what he believed was the *Titanic*'s propeller. This artifact was later determined *not* to be a part of the *Titanic* (it was a rock). After the confirmed discovery of the *Titanic* wreckage in 1985 by Dr. Ballard and IFREMER, Grimm's claims to the initial discovery were dismissed by a court of law. (You can read about the 1985 discovery in Chapter 15.)

In spite of their three tries, Grimm and company never found the *Titanic*. However, Grimm always claimed they did. He even wrote a book called *Beyond Reach: The Search for the Titanic* (Beaufort Books). He never backed off his belief that he had been the first to find the great ship. He died in 1998 still believing that he'd beaten Dr. Ballard to the finish line.

Grimm seemed to be less interested in the actual history of the *Titanic* and more intrigued by the fame and spectacle that would accompany his discovery of the wreckage. His three missions were all failures, but many historians believe that Grimm did at one point sail right over the location of the ship.

Douglas John Faulkner-Woolley: Is he the real owner of the Titanic?

Douglas John Faulkner-Woolley says he owns the *Titanic,* and he's not kidding.

Born in Liverpool in 1936, Faulkner-Woolley got hooked on the history of the *Titanic* and the idea of raising her when he learned that two of his great-aunts, Sally and Ellen, had booked passage on the *Titanic* but canceled because of a dark premonition. Their cancelations came too late for them to retrieve their luggage, however, and their luggage ended up going down with the ship.

His claim to the wreckage and its contents is based on a late-1960s ruling by a British court and the British Board of Trade. The court that awarded him ownership of the *Titanic* apparently did so with one condition: Faulkner-Woolley owned the *Titanic* only if he could locate and raise her.

Regardless of the discovery of the *Titanic* by Dr. Ballard and IFREMER in 1985 and the subsequent explorations of the wreckage, Faulkner-Woolley still considers the letter to be valid legal confirmation of his ownership. He's currently trying to collect enough money to raise her. To him, just because he hasn't raised her yet doesn't mean he forfeits his claimed owner's right to do so.

Faulkner-Woolley also is on record as challenging Dr. Ballard's claim to be the first to locate the *Titanic,* as well as challenging RMS Titanic, Inc.'s court-sanctioned claim to be salvor-in-possession of the *Titanic* and everything found in her debris field. He claims that the *Hecate,* a British Royal Navy ship, was the first to find the *Titanic* in the 1970s, but the discovery was kept secret.

I was in contact with Faulkner-Woolley in 2011, and he sent me a copy of his book (written with Clive Amphlett), *Titanic: One Man's Dream: Douglas John Faulkner-Woolley: His Claims on Britain's Two Most Famous Liners* (Seawise Publication). In this book, Faulkner-Woolley defends his claims by providing extracts from British maritime laws that he claims support his legal ownership. Faulkner-Woolley's own words are in parentheses:

- "Finding an object does not make it the property of the finder . . ."

- "The rights to items of the wreck lie firstly with the owner." (These rights have been handed to D. J. Woolley.)

- "Salvors should not assume a wreck has no owner."

- "Not every finder (Grimm, Ballard and later finders) necessarily has salvage rights. Nor does the raising of the items confer any rights to a site." (D. J. W. made his claims on the *Titanic* . . . in accordance to the law. The U.S. courts have no bearing in these matters and the claims of the Americans are not valid.)

- "Anyone who interferes with a designated site without a license is guilty of an offense."

No one can say with certainty whether Faulkner-Woolley's claims will bear fruit. He continues to recruit investors for his company and collect money to raise the *Titanic.* RMS Titanic, Inc., meanwhile, continues to retrieve artifacts and display them in *Titanic: The Artifact Exhibition.* One thing is certain: If Faulkner-Woolley's plans come to fruition, and the *Titanic* ends up in a tourist museum in England, the legal battles among Faulkner-Woolley, his company, his successors, and RMS Titanic, Inc., will rage on for ages.

Miscellaneous and Cockamamie Schemes for Raising the Titanic

Since the *Titanic* sank in April 1912, people have schemed and planned not only to find the great liner, but also to bring her to the surface. Before 1985, when Dr. Ballard and IFREMER confirmed that the ship was in two pieces on the ocean floor, ideas for raising the *Titanic* were based on the assumption that the ship was in one piece and, perhaps, still capable of sailing.

Today, people still talk about raising one or both halves of the ship even though the science is extremely tricky and the ship is in no condition to be moved. Douglas John Faulkner-Woolley, for example, plans to raise both halves, put them back together, and then spray the ship with some kind of silicon treatment that will hold the ship together so it can sail again. The majority of scientists don't believe this plan to be feasible in the least. But people can dream, right?

This section describes some cockamamie schemes to raise the *Titanic* and sail her to port. In Clive Cussler's bestselling novel *Raise the Titanic!,* the ship sails into New York amid great cheers and celebration. Maybe the dreamers who scheme to raise the *Titanic* have similar visions of themselves sailing the ship into New York Harbor to the cheers and adulation of many.

Scooping her up

Because the *Titanic* is crumbling, any attempt to lift her would probably result in the ship's coming apart and collapsing. A video shows an exploratory submarine accidentally bumping into a part of the *Titanic*'s deck and the deck disintegrating from the impact.

Because the *Titanic* is so fragile, some proponents of the "bring her up" school of thought have concluded that the best way to pick her up without her own weight collapsing her is to construct a giant scoop or shovel and slide it under her hull.

The idea makes sense, but frankly, it's a tad ridiculous. Each half of the *Titanic* measures around 400 feet; where do you find a scoop that big? The biggest payloader in the world is the Le Tourneau L-2350. Its bucket is less than 23 feet wide (and I'm not sure payloaders can swim).

The numbers alone render the "scoop her up" idea impossible. And even if a bucket loader were built that could get beneath each 400-foot half of the wreck, no submarine could summon enough power to lift the scoop (and wreckage) 2.5 miles to the surface. A 12,000-foot arm attached to the boat, you say? Once again, the numbers render that idea impossible.

Filling her hull with ping-pong balls

The idea of filling the *Titanic*'s hull with ping-pong balls sounds simple enough: Because ping-pong balls are filled with air, the balls can float the *Titanic* to the surface.

Is this idea anywhere close to plausible? According to Donald Duck, it is. In a 1949 Walt Disney cartoon, Donald Duck and his nephews, Huey, Louie, and Dewey, were faced with the problem of raising their Uncle Scrooge's sunken yacht. They filled the yacht with ping-pong balls to bring it to the surface.

But that's a cartoon, and as anyone who has seen a Road Runner cartoon knows, the laws of physics, physical vulnerability, and mortality don't apply in the universe inhabited by Bugs Bunny and Wile E. Coyote.

A real-world application of the ping-pong-ball plan, and the specifics and logistics of its execution, provides a clue as to whether the plan would work for the *Titanic*. In 1964, the freighter *Al-Kuwait* sank in the Persian Gulf. About 1 million ships have sunk in the waters of the world, so you may expect the prevailing attitude to be "What's one more?" However, the *Al-Kuwait* carried 6,000 head of sheep when it went down. If left to nature, their rotting carcasses would do serious damage to Kuwait's primary source of drinking water. Some of the world's largest desalination facilities were located near the shipwreck.

What to do? The answer came from a Dutch manufacturer by the name of Karl Kroyer. He remembered seeing the 1949 Donald Duck cartoon and decided to duplicate Huey, Louie, and Dewey's plan to raise their uncle's yacht. Rather than transport ping-pong balls to the site, Kroyer actually had them manufactured at the location of the sinking. He pumped the ping-pong balls into the freighter *Al-Kuwait,* and his plan worked.

In theory, the ping-pong-ball scheme could work with the *Titanic* as well (*MythBusters* proved it on a 2004 TV show), but the logistics of the salvager's supplying or manufacturing more than 600 million ping-pong balls for the *Titanic* make the plan completely implausible. Furthermore, the *Titanic* is no longer intact. Pumping ping-pong balls into each half of the ship would probably succeed only in littering the ocean surface with little plastic balls; the balls would likely float out of the wrecked hull to the surface.

Another factor to consider in the ping-pong-ball scheme is the depth of the ocean where the *Titanic* rests. The depth of the Persian Gulf is rarely more than 200 feet. The *Titanic,* on the other hand, is 2.5 miles down. At that depth, the water pressure is 6,500 pounds per square inch. Under that much pressure, the ping-pong balls would likely be crushed instantly.

Packing her hull full of molten wax

Wax freezes at around 45 degrees Fahrenheit and, when frozen, floats in water. So one idea for raising the *Titanic* was to pump the ship full of molten wax, wait for the wax to harden or possibly freeze, and then float the *Titanic* to the surface. (I can find no record of who came up with the molten-wax idea, by the way.) A similar idea was floated (pardon the pun) to use petroleum jelly to raise the *Titanic*. After the petroleum jelly froze and hardened, you could use it to float the ship from the depths of the ocean.

What's amazing about these fanciful ideas is that they always begin with the premise that pumping hundreds of thousands of tons of a thick substance 2.5 miles below the surface of the North Atlantic is easy. Actually getting substances to the wreck is always taken for granted.

Whether the salvager used molten wax or petroleum jelly, he would need approximately 180,000 tons of the stuff to fill the body of the *Titanic* wreckage. But keep in mind that the ship isn't in one piece, so again, the substance would likely just float out into the ocean.

Turning the Titanic into an iceberg

In the early 1980s, British salvager John Pearce proposed an idea to raise the *Titanic* by using liquid nitrogen. His plan was to first wrap the entire ship in a strong metal wire mesh, creating a gigantic basket of sorts to hold her. (Remember that before the 1985 discovery of the *Titanic*, everyone thought the ship was still in one piece.) Liquid nitrogen would then be pumped throughout the entire ship, which would presumably cause her to freeze solid. The *Titanic* would then become a kind of seafaring 46,000-ton iceberg that, Pearce assumed, would float to the surface and could then be towed to port.

Pearce's idea is a quixotic one that science can quickly rule out as not only unfeasible, but also scientifically impossible. The temperature of the water at the *Titanic* site is believed to be approximately 28 degrees Fahrenheit, a few degrees below freezing. (The water doesn't freeze, of course, because of its salt content.) Liquid nitrogen freezes at –346 degrees Fahrenheit. The idea that the nitrogen could freeze the *Titanic* is scientifically untenable because the water in which the ship sits isn't cold enough to freeze liquid nitrogen. What would likely happen is that the liquid nitrogen would remain liquid and simply dissolve into the surrounding water as it was pumped into the wreck.

Filling her with foam

Another plan (apparently first suggested in Clive Cussler's novel *Raise the Titanic!*) was to fill the ship with foam. What kind of foam did this plan call for? Not shaving cream — the wreckage would be pumped full of plastic foam, which is a form of polypropylene used for a variety of molded plastic parts. After the floatable foam was pumped inside the wreck, balloons would be attached to the hull, allowing the ship to rise to the surface.

As with the other far-fetched ideas in this chapter, the key problem here is that getting enough foam in a usable form to fill a hull 2.5 miles below the surface of the ocean is near impossible. And even if it were possible, you face the problem of lifting the wreckage by using balloons; the balloons would require the buoyancy of 215 ships the size of the *Titanic*.

Chapter 15

The Quest of the Century: The 1985 Discovery of the Wreck

*F*or a time in the twentieth century, the *Titanic* was essentially forgotten. The world had other things to think about. There were two world wars and a global depression. Massive technological change in the form of home appliances and the assembly line, not to mention the personal computer and the Internet, resulted in societal and cultural upheaval. The lost ship of dreams was not a high priority for most people.

A ship sank. There were an uproar and enormous public and media attention. Memoirs were published. Memorials were erected and unveiled. People were blamed. People were exonerated. Books were written. And then it all just faded away — but only temporarily. A few decades of indifference came to an end with the 1955 publication of Walter Lord's seminal account of the tragedy, *A Night to Remember.* And then, in 1985, Dr. Robert Ballard, on a joint mission with IFREMER (the French Research Institute for Exploration of the Sea), discovered the wreck of the *Titanic,* and interest in the great ship exploded.

This chapter looks at the 1985 discovery of the wreck, which launched renewed interest in the *Titanic* — an interest that has yet to wane. It explains how Ballard and IFREMER discovered the *Titanic,* how their work and that of explorers who came after them solved *Titanic* mysteries, and what high technology is helping researchers discover in the *Titanic* wreck.

Looking Back on the Titanic Century

As I write these words, there have been four defining years for global *Titanic* interest:

- ✔ **1912:** The unsinkable *Titanic* strikes an iceberg and sinks on its maiden voyage; more than 1,500 people perish for lack of enough lifeboats.

- ✔ **1955:** Walter Lord's account of the disaster, *A Night to Remember,* is published and becomes a bestseller.

- ✔ **1985:** Dr. Robert Ballard, IFREMER, and the *Argo* camera sled definitively locate the wreck of the *Titanic.*

- ✔ **1997:** James Cameron's epic film *Titanic* becomes the highest-grossing movie in cinematic history (until his *Avatar* breaks that record); untold millions see it and become fascinated with the *Titanic* story.

Shortly after I write these words, 2012 will prove to be another seminal year as the world marks the 100th anniversary of the ship's sinking. Worldwide commemorations will fuel the ongoing passionate interest in the complete *Titanic* story.

The 1985 discovery of the wreck was a monumentally important historical event. One of the first things Dr. Ballard said after the discovery was this:

> It was one thing to have won — to have found the ship. It was another thing to be there. That was the spooky part. I could see the *Titanic* as she slipped nose first into the glassy water. Around me were the ghostly shapes of the lifeboats and the piercing shouts and screams of people freezing to death in the water. Our little memorial service lasted five, maybe ten minutes. Then I just said, "Thank you all. Now let's get back to work."

The 1985 discovery brought the *Titanic* back to the public eye. Once again, the ship of dreams became an object of fascination. The "piercing shouts and screams" of the victims could be heard once more.

Following Ballard from First Hopes to First Sighting

In his 1987 book *The Discovery of the Titanic* (Grand Central Publishing), Dr. Ballard (shown in Figure 15-1) writes

> The first time I remember seriously thinking about going after the *Titanic* was in 1973. By then I had left the Navy and, as a junior scientist at Woods Hole, I was a brash 31-year-old member of the Alvin Group . . . a

small three-man submarine named after one of its early advocates — Al Vine — and the Alvin Group was then moving into the forefront of underwater research technology.

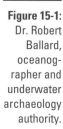

Figure 15-1:
Dr. Robert Ballard, oceanographer and underwater archaeology authority.

© Frank Capri/Getty Images

(See the sidebar "The Woods Hole Oceanographic Institution" for info about where Ballard was working.)

It would take nine years for Ballard's initial dream to be fulfilled. In 1982, Ballard asked the U.S. Navy if it would fund an expedition to find the *Titanic* using his new submersible, the *Argo*. Towed beneath a mothership, the *Argo* was an unmanned video-camera sled that could descend to and operate at depths of 20,000 feet (7,500 feet deeper than the *Titanic* wreckage).

The Woods Hole Oceanographic Institution

The Woods Hole Oceanographic Institution (WHOI) is, according to its website, "the world's largest private, nonprofit ocean research, engineering and education organization." Its mission statement says it is "dedicated to research and education to advance understanding of the ocean and its interaction with the Earth system, and to communicating this understanding for the benefit of society." WHOI is comprised of research departments, ocean institutes, labs, and subject-specific centers and programs. More than a thousand people are on staff, including scientists, technical and scientific support staff, a marine crew, and graduate students. Robert Ballard is a scientist emeritus in the Applied Ocean Physics & Engineering department.

The Navy said "no, thanks" to funding a mission to find the *Titanic,* but it did come up with a compromise plan that Ballard accepted.

This section looks at Ballard's initial discoveries with the help of the U.S. Navy, how he and IFREMER discovered the wreck site, the media frenzy that ensued, and plundering expeditions by various groups. It also takes you behind the scenes with Ballard to see some of the details of the expedition.

Starting from the Thresher and Scorpion

In the 1960s, the U.S. Navy lost two nuclear-powered submarines, the USS *Thresher* and the USS *Scorpion.* The *Thresher* went down in 1963 during deep-sea diving tests, killing all 129 aboard, including some civilians. It is believed that the sub imploded. The *Scorpion* went down in 1968, killing all 99 crew members. Why the *Scorpion* sank has never been determined, although sabotage and a collision with another vessel were never ruled out as possible causes.

The deal that the Navy offered Ballard was this: Use the French ship the *Knorr* and his camera sled the *Argo* to locate the *Thresher* and the *Scorpion,* and assess their nuclear reactors to determine whether radioactivity from these reactors was leaking into the ocean. The Navy also wanted to find out whether the rumor that the Soviet Union had shot the *Scorpion* and sunk it was true. After Ballard completed his assessment of the *Thresher* and the *Scorpion,* the Navy said, he could search for the *Titanic.*

Ballard originally pitched the additional "locate the *Titanic*" element of the mission to Deputy Chief of Naval Operations for Submarine Warfare Ronald Thunman, now retired. Thunman wasn't crazy about the idea of searching for the *Titanic* while on duty on a Navy mission. "I was a little short with him," Thunman told *National Geographic* in 2008. Ultimately, though, the Navy agreed to the mission.

Ballard accepted the Navy's offer to use the French ship the *Knorr.* In the summer of 1985, he and a French team from IFREMER used the *Knorr* and the *Argo,* Ballard's submersible, to successfully carry out the two classified missions. They discovered that the nuclear reactors on the *Thresher* and *Scorpion* were safe. They also found evidence that proved that the *Scorpion* had not been sunk by the Soviet Union. For these missions, Ballard was placed on temporary active duty with the Navy. He carried out both missions under the auspices of the U.S. Navy (this would become important later, when the question of who owned the rights to photos and video of the *Titanic* wreck was raised).

During the mission, Ballard learned a great deal about how very heavy objects sink in ocean currents. They sink fast, he discovered. This new information enabled him to project where the *Titanic*'s debris field was located. But with only 12 days left in the mission, he and the rest of the crew on the *Knorr* had to work fast to find the *Titanic.*

Homing in on the Titanic

After finding the two nuclear submarines, the *Knorr* headed for the site where, Ballard believed, the *Titanic* went down. This was why Ballard was at sea; this was why he accepted the Navy deal: He wanted to find the wreck of the *Titanic*. His new research findings suggested that the *Titanic* had broken in two and left a large debris field, and that notion proved to be correct. "That's what saved our butts," Ballard told *National Geographic* in 2008, explaining how findings from the new technology developed for the Navy allowed him to extrapolate that the *Titanic* likely left a large debris field. The knowledge that the debris field was a large one enabled Ballard and his team to conduct a broader search.

For 26,802 days, the great liner RMS *Titanic* rested peacefully on the ocean floor, her magnificent body broken in two, her bow buried 65 feet in the Earth 2.5 miles below the surface of the North Atlantic. On Sunday, September 1, 1985, *Titanic*'s sleep was interrupted.

Shortly after midnight on that day, crew member Bill Lange switched the *Argo*'s camera from forward-looking to down-looking. Watching the video monitor, he said one word: "Wreckage." Thus began the *Titanic*'s new era.

As the crew reconnoitered the site, time passed until Ballard realized it was close to 2 a.m., minutes away from the time that the *Titanic* sank. He made an announcement that he was going to the fantail of the ship in about 20 minutes and everyone was welcome to join him. He then raised the house flag of *Titanic*'s builders Harland and Wolff — a red, white, blue, and yellow flag with the company's logo on it — and at 2:20 a.m., Ballard and the crew paused for a few moments of silence.

Fighting over Titanic video and pictures

Dr. Ballard admits in his book *The Discovery of the Titanic* that he, Woods Hole, IFREMER, and the U.S. Navy never considered, if the *Titanic* were found, who would own valuable video footage and photographs of the sunken ship. Who owned the photos and video of the wreck? Who would profit from the sale of those materials? Who would profit from salvaged artifacts?

Ultimately, these questions were resolved in the courts. The Navy asserted no claim to anything pertaining to the *Titanic*. In 1987, IFREMER and the company that would become RMS Titanic, Inc., entered into an agreement to salvage artifacts from the wreck. They made 32 dives and recovered some 1,800 artifacts. In 1993, they recovered another 800 artifacts.

The following year, the court named RMS Titanic, Inc., salvor-in-possession of the *Titanic* and sole owner of all artifacts recovered from the site on the condition that the company remain "in possession," meaning that the company must travel to the *Titanic* on a fairly regular basis. RMS Titanic, Inc., has been traveling on a regular basis to the site since the court ruling and remains the salvor-in-possession.

The first real piece of the *Titanic* that the explorers saw was one of the ship's main boilers. Over the next few days, Ballard and his team used the *Argo* to determine several key facts about the lost liner, one of the most important being that the *Titanic* was upright. Also, they learned that the first funnel was gone and that a great deal of the ship seemed to be still intact. This finding confirmed what many survivors had reported: that the forward funnel had fallen into the water just before the ship went under, nearly hitting Collapsible B, one of the lifeboats that floated off the *Titanic* as she sank and to which Colonel Archibald Gracie IV, Harold Bride, Second Officer Charles Lightoller, and between 35 and 40 others clung desperately in the icy waters.

Dealing with the instant media frenzy

Finding the *Titanic* was big news, and the world had the right to know of the discovery. Woods Hole asked Dr. Ballard to speak to as many reporters as possible about the discovery. He conducted a live interview from the *Knorr* with Tom Brokaw of NBC News. Then came the media frenzy. Helicopters buzzed the *Knorr;* planes flew over, attempting to obtain the exact coordinates of the *Titanic* site.

Ballard and his team made what in hindsight was a pretty big mistake: They provided — to Canadian television — images of the *Titanic*'s boiler and of the jubilant reaction aboard the *Knorr* to its discovery. These images hit the airwaves almost immediately, which ruffled the feathers of American television networks. Ballard gave Canadian television an exclusive! Does that violate some law? Some American networks threatened to sue Woods Hole.

Ballard and his team tried to repair the damage by providing multiple copies of all the footage and photos to all the networks and to French TV. But French TV beat them to the punch by picking up the footage from satellites, infuriating IFREMER, which believed that it should have been the one to release the photos and video footage. IFREMER wanted to sell these valuable images, and here was an American giving them away!

All this hoopla served to damage the feelings of shared success and camaraderie that the team had enjoyed during their weeks at sea on the *Knorr.* Ballard describes taking a group picture on the fantail of the *Knorr* and having to beg his team members to smile for the photo.

Today, Dr. Ballard continues to explore the world's oceans, looking for lost ships. In the fall of 1997, he coauthored a book called *Lost Liners* (Hyperion Books), and in April 1998, he announced that he would lead an expedition to find and explore the USS *Yorktown,* the aircraft carrier that was sunk by Japanese torpedoes on June 7, 1942, during the Battle of Midway.

Plundering artifacts from the debris field

Since the memorable discovery of the ship of dreams in 1985, *Titanic* has been revisited many, many times. Dr. Ballard himself returned to the *Titanic* several times. A Russian film crew shooting an IMAX film went down in 1991. The late George Tulloch (see Chapter 16) and RMS Titanic, Inc., visited the *Titanic* many times. James Cameron went down at least a dozen times to research his 1997 film *Titanic*.

In the first decade of this century, visitors to the wreck have recovered more than 6,000 artifacts from the 3-by-5-mile debris field. So far, these visitors to the *Titanic* have drawn the line at plundering the interior of the wreck itself. Still, legal proscriptions notwithstanding, now that the debris field is essentially picked clean and interest in the *Titanic* continues to grow by leaps and bounds, how long visitors will keep their hands off the interior of the ship is an open question.

They did WHAT on Titanic?

In July 2001, David Leibowitz and Kimberley Miller outraged some *Titanic* buffs and survivors' family members, and likely brought a tear to the eyes of others not so deeply invested in viewing the *Titanic* as a gravesite. What did these two young people do to upset so many people? They got married on the bow of the *Titanic* — the *real Titanic,* two-and-a-half miles below the surface of the North Atlantic.

It all started when Leibowitz won a competition to dive to the site. The competition was sponsored by a British company called SubSea Explorer. Leibowitz, who was engaged to Miller, inquired whether he could bring his fiancée along for the ride. He was told that it was possible but that it would cost him $4,500 . . . unless they were willing to get married during the trip. If the couple got married, the company would foot the bill for Kimberley as well as fund their honeymoon.

The plan was for the sub to set down on the *Titanic*'s bow, a site deliberately chosen because the bow was where Jack and Rose met in James Cameron's 1997 move *Titanic.* Then Captain Ron Warwick, captain of the cruise ship the *Queen Elizabeth II* and along for the trip, would perform the marriage ceremony. (Princess Elettra Marconi, Guglielmo Marconi's daughter, was also aboard for the trip.) The plan went off without a hitch.

Titanic champions were outraged. Brian Ticehurst of the British Titanic Society told BBC News that the wedding idea was "utterly sick" and that it was "an insult to each one of those people that this couple should spoil the site by getting married." Leibowitz's response? "We don't really view this as a gravesite," said the groom. "[I]f you were to be married at a church, you'd have to treat that with reverence because you'd be near a graveyard, too."

On a Christmas Eve 1997 *Larry King Live* broadcast, Dr. Ballard proclaimed with certainty that if someone were to go deep enough into the *Titanic* (say, into the boiler rooms or third-class cabins), he or she would no doubt find human skeletons. (This assertion has since been widely refuted and disputed. Scientists now believe that all human remains were completely gone by the early 1940s at the latest. See "Not finding bodies" later in this chapter for more information.)

Titanic artifacts are irresistible to many. Somewhere in the front cargo hold of the *Titanic* is a brand-new Renault automobile. It may be only a matter of time before the wreck is plundered the way Egyptian tombs were plundered in the previous centuries.

Maybe plundering the ship for all its artifacts isn't a bad idea. The *Titanic* is decaying. Many experts believe that between iron-eating bacteria and the ongoing decomposition that seawater causes to other materials (to leather and wood, for example), the great steamer may be nothing more than a stain on the ocean floor in a hundred years. By some estimates, the *Titanic*'s total disintegration is only 20 years away.

Digging up details about the discovery

We all know the ending: Ballard and IFREMER found the *Titanic*. But that's not the whole story. This section looks at some interesting details about the 1985 discovery of the wreckage.

Being rejected by Disney

Ballard approached Roy Disney about funding an expedition to search for the *Titanic* in 1978. Disney turned him down, telling him, "Because of the enormous capital investment which you require immediately, it is simply not feasible for us to become involved." Ballard had asked Disney for the now-paltry sum of $1.5 million.

Listening to Vivaldi

On the way down to the *Titanic* (a trip that takes about two-and-a-half hours), Ballard and his dive mates usually listened to Vivaldi's *The Four Seasons* on cassette. They would turn the tape off when they got to the wreck so they could record their comments without a soundtrack.

Going HERE

Because there was no toilet on the *Alvin,* the submersible that was used to explore the *Titanic* wreck, Ballard and his diving companions had to urinate in a plastic bottle that they nicknamed HERE, an acronym for "Human Endurance Range Extender." In 2002, Bruce Strickrott, one of the *Alvin* pilots, answered questions from schoolchildren about deep-sea exploration during an online chat sponsored by the University of Delaware. One of the kids noted that there were no bathrooms on the *Alvin* and asked what the crew did when nature called. Strickrott replied, "It is possible to go to the bathroom in the sub using what is called a 'human range extender,' which basically is a bottle for urine. Most people are careful not to drink a lot of fluids before getting in the sub for an eight-hour dive."

Coining a word

During one of his tours of the *Titanic* wreck, Dr. Ballard noticed reddish-brown stalactites of rust hanging several feet from the *Titanic*'s railings. These formations were the result of iron-eating bacteria and had never been seen on what Ballard called "such a massive scale."

Ballard coined the term *rusticles* — a blend of the words *rust* and *icicles* — to describe these rust stalactites. This word is universally used today when referring to rust formations of this type on any shipwrecks. (See "Finding What the Wreck Actually Revealed," later in this chapter, for more on rusticles and the role they play in the disappearance of the *Titanic*.)

Not finding bodies

Perhaps the most common question asked of Dr. Ballard after he discovered the wreck was "Did you see any bodies?" During a 1986 dive, Ballard was horrified to see what he described as "a small, white smiling face" lying on the ocean floor. "For a split second I thought a corpse had actually materialized — and it scared the hell out of me," he wrote in his 1987 book *The Discovery of the Titanic*.

Other Ballard discoveries

In addition to finding the *Titanic*, Ballard discovered other ships on the ocean floor. In June 1989, Ballard found the *Bismarck*, the German battleship sunk in World War II off the northwest coast of France.

In 1998, he successfully located and photographed the USS *Yorktown*, the U.S. aircraft carrier sunk in the Battle of Midway in June 1942. The *Yorktown* is 3 miles below the surface (a half mile deeper than the *Titanic*), yet it is upright and in surprisingly good condition.

In 2002 near the Solomon Islands, he located the *PT-109*, the torpedo boat commanded in World War II by future American President John F. Kennedy.

The head turned out to be the ceramic head of a doll of French or German origin. (See Chapter 18 for more on the doll's head.) The doll's hair and clothes were long gone. After his initial reaction of fear, Ballard felt an overwhelming sense of sadness as he wondered who had owned the toy and whether the little girl had been one of the survivors. James Cameron used an image of a doll's head lying on the ocean floor in the opening sequence of his 1997 film.

Scientists now agree that there are no surviving human remains at the site of the *Titanic,* either inside the ship or in the surrounding debris fields. In fact, scientists believe that all human remains were completely gone by the 1940s at the latest. The human body is organic. It is subject to assault by all things natural. Decomposition is slow, but after many years at the bottom of the ocean in frigid water and with enormous pressure, mortal remains could not last.

Bemoaning "a freak show at the county fair"

In 2004, 19 years after the discovery of the wreck, Ballard wrote the following for *National Geographic* magazine:

> It had been 19 years since I'd discovered *Titanic* as part of a French-American team. I'd come back to see how she'd changed. I knew that a private salvage company, RMS Titanic, Inc., had dived on her many times, legally removing thousands of objects from what I consider a sacred grave. Russian submarines had taken Hollywood filmmaker James Cameron and others to the wreck, also breaking no laws but reportedly colliding with the hull. Cruise ships had circled the site while RMS Titanic, Inc. tried to raise a 20-ton piece of the ship. A beer company had sponsored sweepstakes to watch the salvagers recover bottles of ale. And a New York couple had even plunked down on *Titanic*'s bow in a submersible to be married. It was all such a comedy — exactly what I had hoped would not happen. I'd urged others to treat *Titanic*'s remains with dignity, like that shown the battleship *Arizona* in Pearl Harbor. Instead they'd turned her into a freak show at the county fair.

Ballard also described the retrieval of artifacts as "pulling the jewelry off the old lady in her grave." He is on record with *National Geographic* as comparing visiting the *Titanic* wreck site to "visiting a battle site or the World Trade Center."

Finding What the Wreck Actually Revealed

Before Ballard and IFREMER found her, the world knew far less about the *Titanic* and her sinking than it does now. Volumes of information were available about the building and outfitting of the ship. Passenger and cargo lists were in the public record. The Marconigram real-time record of her collision with the iceberg and her wait for the rescue that was not to come were available for all to see. The minute-by-minute actions of many crew members, and what passengers said and how they acted, were also well known. Survivors provided vivid descriptions of the sights and sounds of the fateful night when the *Titanic* sank.

But the sinking itself was always something of a mystery because survivors' stories varied and eyewitness accounts can be notoriously unreliable.

This section looks at the mysteries that the 1985 discovery of the *Titanic* and later dives to the ship solved.

It did break in two

For years, historians and even survivors believed that the *Titanic* went down intact. Yet there were eyewitness reports as early as a month after the sinking that the ship broke in two in its final death throes.

An article in the May 4, 1912, *Witney Gazette,* a newspaper published in Plymouth, England, reported on the basis of interviews with survivors that "The *Titanic* broke in two between the funnels. There were explosions. The men believe that the machinery fell out of the hull when she split and the bow went down. The stern rose straight up in the air before the final plunge."

Seaman Edward John Buley said at the U.S. Senate Subcommittee *Titanic* Hearing, "She went down as far as the after funnel, and then there was a little roar, as though the engines had rushed forward, and *she snapped in two* [emphasis added], and the bow part went down and the afterpart came up and stayed up five minutes before it went down . . . It was horizontal at first, and then went down."

Seaman Buley's account is absolutely accurate, yet eyewitness accounts, many of which were recounted in Walter Lord's book *A Night to Remember,* describe the entire ship standing perpendicular to the water and then sinking intact. Lord wrote

> The *Titanic* was now absolutely perpendicular. From the third funnel aft, she stuck straight up in the air, her three dripping propellers glistening even in the darkness. . . . Then slowly she began sliding under, moving at a steep slant. As she glided down, she seemed to pick up speed. When the sea closed over the flagstaff on her stern, she was moving fast enough to cause a slight gulp. 'She's gone; that's the last of her,' someone sighed to Lookout Lee in Boat 13.

The question must be asked: How could the people in the boats have missed the horrific sight of the *Titanic* breaking in half?

At any rate, the 1985 discovery of the *Titanic* wreck proved definitively that the ship did break in two. And Ballard and his crew had the photographs and video to prove it.

A tear, a puncture, or a dent?

Did the iceberg tear a 300-foot-long gash in the side of the *Titanic?* Or did it simply poke holes in the hull? Or did it cause a massive "dent" that popped the hull plates and caused the flooding?

The damage that was done to the ship by the iceberg was long a matter of contention among everyone from survivors and historians to ship designers and the ship's crew members. But no one knew with certainty just how the hull had been damaged. Even the ship's chief designer, Thomas Andrews, and Captain Edward J. Smith didn't know. By the time they went to look, the damage was underwater, and they couldn't inspect it.

As I note in Chapter 11, Harland and Wolff's Edward Wilding, who was an assistant to Thomas Andrews, testified that the total damage couldn't have been more than 12 square feet. His opinion was dismissed. For decades people thought that the iceberg had, as J. Kent Layton (author of the 2007 book, *Lusitania: An Illustrated Biography of the Ship of Splendor* [Lulu.com]), described, "disemboweled" the ship.

In a 1996 expedition to the wreck by RMS Titanic, Inc., however, the world got the answers it had been waiting for. In an excellent, comprehensive article titled "Mysteries: The Iceberg Damage," J. Kent Layton wrote:

> When the bow smashed into the berg . . . the impact caused a rupture [#1] described as a "trace" in length, which penetrated the Forepeak . . . .two quick blows [#2 and #3] in rapid succession . . . five feet and four feet long . . . [then] penetrated Cargo Hold No. 1. . . . The fourth rupture, at fifteen feet long, damaged Cargo Hold No. 2. . . . Next, the berg created a 32-foot long rupture [#5] — more than twice the length of the previous one — that started in Cargo Hold No. 2 and continued past the transverse bulkhead into Cargo Hold No. 3. . . . [The] sixth rupture was the coup de gras [sic] which sealed the *Titanic*'s fate and the fates of 1,500 people aboard her. This fatal blow tore open the forward coal bunker of Boiler Room No. 6, past the retaining wall and into the Boiler Room itself, all across the entire length of the compartment, through No. 6's aft coal bunker, past the watertight bulkhead, and ended between 2 and 5 feet inside Boiler Room No. 5's forward coal bunker. This wound was by far the longest of all six, being some 45 feet in length.

After analyzing the exact nature of the damage and calculating the results, it turns out that the total damage to the *Titanic*'s hull from the collision with the iceberg was approximately 12 square feet. Edward Wilding had been right all along.

The Titanic is disappearing: Rusticles (maybe) have sealed its fate

In 50 years or so, the *Titanic* may be nothing but a stain on the ocean floor. Some estimates have the wreck completely disintegrating in as short a period as 20 years. Henrietta Mann of Dalhousie University in Halifax, Nova Scotia, told *The Christian Science Monitor* in December 2010, "In 1995, I was predicting that *Titanic* had another 30 years. But I think it's deteriorating much faster than that now. Perhaps if we get another 15 to 20 years out of it, we're doing good . . . eventually there will be nothing left but a rust stain."

As I note earlier in the chapter, Ballard coined the word *rusticles* — a combination of the words *rust* and *icicles* — after his discovery of the *Titanic* wreck. Rusticles are rust formations. They are about a third iron oxide (iron from the *Titanic* itself) and two thirds bacteria and fungi that are eating the rust, thus causing serious, ongoing corrosion.

The bacteria consuming the *Titanic*'s 46,000 or so tons of iron have been at work since the moment the ship hit the ocean floor. The combination of 27 bacteria — including the newly discovered *Halomonas titanicae* — quite simply *love* iron. They can't get enough of it. And apparently, they work together to eat as much as they can. From an April 2011 article on the Daily Galaxy website:

> Scientists believe that this strange super-organism is using a common microbial language that could be either chemical or electrical — a phenomenon called "quorum sensing" by which whole communities "sense" each other's presence and activities aiding and abetting the organization, cooperation, and growth.

How much of the iron comprising the *Titanic* has been consumed by the bacteria since 1912 is not known. Most scientists are content to describe the wreck as "rapidly deteriorating." What is known is that the stern is being consumed at a rate approximately 40 years ahead of the bow. So the rear half of the *Titanic* wreck will disappear well before the bow at this rate.

Halomonas titanicae, a member of the salt-loving *Halomonas* genus, was a never-before-seen bacterium discovered within the rusticles hanging off the *Titanic* wreck. The *International Journal of Systematic and Evolutionary Microbiology* describes this bacterium as "a gram-negative, heterotrophic, aerobic, non-endospore-forming, peritrichously flagellated and motile bacterial strain." Whatever that means, it doesn't sound good.

Recently, Dr. Lori Johnston, a microbial ecologist, told UK TV that she estimates that 667 pounds of the *Titanic* iron are being eaten every day by the bacteria. Doing the math, this means that in a hundred years, just over 12,000 tons of the *Titanic* would have been consumed, which is a small percentage of the total wreck. However, scientists also know that the deterioration increases over time; the rate of consumption isn't steady. Future generations of historians and researchers will be the ones who learn how quickly the great ship disappears.

Taking a 3D, High-Def Visit to the Titanic

In the summer of 2010, salvor RMS Titanic, Inc., in collaboration with the Woods Hole Oceanographic Institution, carried out an unprecedented photographic mission to the *Titanic,* using autonomous underwater vehicles (AUVs) and remote-operated vehicles (ROVs). These devices can be controlled remotely from ships on the ocean surface. The RMS Titanic, Inc., team took high-definition photos and 3D photos of the *Titanic.* The images they came back with are the clearest and most vivid seen of the wreck to date.

The two AUVs were named *Ginger* and *MaryAnn* after the heroines of the *Gilligan's Island* TV show. The mission was helmed by expedition leader David Gallo, Woods Hole's director of special projects.

Ginger and *MaryAnn* "mowed the yard with sound," as Gallo put it. The two AUVs, which were completely wireless, slowly traveled back and forth across the wreck site, "mowing" row after row of the ocean floor with sonar (sound waves), which, when translated into imagery, provided more detail than anyone had ever seen before. The AUVs provided a staggering amount of new information, including the fact that the debris field was 3 miles by 5 miles.

In fall 2010, Michael Dessner of the Waitt Institute, a nonprofit scientific research organization, visited the imaging lab where the new 3D footage of the *Titanic* was being put together by a team of scientists, engineers, and technicians. He described the lab in the Waitt Institute's "Expedition Blog" as the "most amazing sprawl of technology." It had two 47-inch HD monitors and five other monitors of various sizes. Dessner described the other "tech" in the room: "Five monster Mac tower computers, seven large computer screens, six smaller monitors, four huge armored computer cases and a couple other stacks of arcane technology that I can only guess at."

The images taken are spectacular and show the *Titanic* in amazing detail. The lighting alone is impressive, considering that the wreck sits in absolute pitch darkness, with no ambient light or light from the surface managing to make its way down the two-and-a-half miles to the wreck. *The Wall Street Journal*'s website — www.wsj.com — offers video of the new HD footage.

Part V
The Titanic in Popular Culture

In this part . . .

After the *Titanic* sank, the ship became a part of history and popular culture. This part explores whether salvaging artifacts from the *Titanic* serves history or is essentially grave robbing. It explains where you can see *Titanic* salvaged artifacts on display and how to join historical societies and visit commemoration sites in person and online. It also goes behind the scenes of movies made about the tragedy, including James Cameron's 1997 masterpiece.

Chapter 16

Salvaging the Titanic and Its Artifacts

*W*hen the *Titanic* foundered and ended up on the bottom of the ocean, it became a part of history. Objects on the ship became much more than what they were before. A mundane teacup, for example, instantly became a collectible item and a valuable artifact.

This chapter looks at *Titanic* artifacts and the efforts to salvage those artifacts from the ocean floor. It examines the ethics of salvaging and explains how George Tulloch and RMS Titanic, Inc. (a salvage company focused on the artifacts of the *Titanic*), salvaged a part of the ship — a piece so big, in fact, that it's now called the Big Piece.

You also find information about where to see *Titanic* artifacts, museums, and memorials. As this chapter explains, you can even pay a visit to the *Titanic* herself on the floor of the North Atlantic! (As of 2007, experts calculated that there had been more than 75 visits to the wreck. The total now could easily be double that number.)

If you're curious to see examples of the types of artifacts that have been salvaged to date, be sure to turn to this book's color photo section.

Mementos from the Sea: Seeing Which Artifacts Have Been Salvaged

Titanic artifacts are very popular. Tens of thousands of people have visited the traveling *Titanic: The Artifact Exhibition* (which you can read about later in this chapter), and many of these folks come away awed and subdued after seeing the items. A man's suit. A woman's perfume bottle. A pair of gloves. A doll. These are personal things. They belonged to real people who lost their lives in the 28-degree water of the North Atlantic when the *Titanic* went down. People are certainly animated and engaged when walking through *Titanic: The Artifact Exhibition,* but you don't get a sense of celebration or "fun," so to speak. The overall tone is one of quiet respect.

Why is value placed on mementos of misery? For those people who feel compassion and empathy, the mementos provide a human connection to the passengers who suffered.

Here's a partial list of artifacts that have been recovered from the *Titanic* debris field (nothing has been taken from inside the ship itself):

> alligator purse, bank receipts, bars of soap, brushes, calling cards, cane from a damaged seat, chandeliers, children's shoes, clothing of all types, coal, coins, collection of sample perfumes, cooking and dining room items, currency, cutlery, damask drawstring bag, deck chair, dolls, equipment from the ship, flags from the lifeboats, furniture, gloves, handkerchiefs, jewelry, kitchen pots and pans, letters from passengers, life jackets, liquor bottle, luggage, menus, name boards from the lifeboats, ornate combs, passenger lists, perfumes, plaque signs from the ship, pocket watches, reading glasses, safes, seat supports, shoes, smoking tins, stairwells, stemware, suitcases, suspenders, syringe and glass vial, ticket stubs, vases, wallets, and wine bottles.

As you can see, in addition to equipment from the ship, the artifacts represent a veritable treasure trove of personal effects from the passengers and crew. The artifacts personalize the tragedy more than any documentary or book could.

Hearing What the Courts Said about the Artifacts

As I explain in Chapter 15, the initial discoverers of the *Titanic,* Dr. Robert Ballard (of the Woods Hole Oceanographic Institution) and Jean-Louis Michel (of IFREMER, the French Research Institute for Exploration of the Sea), video-taped the wreck but didn't collect any artifacts during their 1985 expedition. What's more, in 1986, Ballard placed a plaque at the site urging that the site never be disturbed. Ballard wanted the site to be a permanent memorial to the people who perished with the *Titanic*.

In 1987, however, a U.S.-based company called Titanic Ventures contracted with IFREMER to salvage artifacts from the *Titanic* wreckage. Titanic Ventures recovered some 1,800 artifacts, drawing protests from some *Titanic* survivors and praise from others. For example, survivor Eva Hart called the salvagers "fortune hunters, vultures, pirates," while survivor Louise Kink Pope said, "I feel that if research and salvage will benefit all people, then such activities should be encouraged."

Titanic Ventures sold its interest in salvaging the *Titanic* to a company called RMS Titanic, Inc., and in 1994, nine years after the *Titanic* was discovered, a U.S. District Court awarded salvor-in-possession rights to the wreck to RMS Titanic, Inc. (Check out the sidebar "What does salvor-in-possession mean?" for more information.)

RMS Titanic, Inc., had begun making expeditions to the site two years after the ship's discovery. In 1993, a French administrator awarded recovered relics to RMS Titanic's predecessor (Titanic Ventures), but this ruling was overturned, and full ownership and salvor-in-possession rights were awarded back to RMS Titanic, Inc.

The case was then remanded to a U.S. District Court. It ruled on August 15, 2011, that RMS Titanic, Inc., owned everything "post-1987" from the *Titanic*. This ruling means that RMS Titanic, Inc., owns the almost 6,000 *Titanic* arti-facts. The ruling included these conditions:

What does salvor-in-possession mean?

Under *admiralty* (maritime) law, the person or company that owns the right to salvage a shipwreck is called the *salvor-in-possession*. Initially, the salvor-in-possession is the owner of the ship. The owner has the right to all objects recovered from the wreck.

Seems simple enough, right? But what if the ship's owner makes no salvage efforts? Or what if a long period of time elapses after the ship sank before anyone wants to salvage? In these cases, a third party can become the salvor-in-possession by recovering objects from the site of the wrecked ship.

✔ The artifacts must, however necessary, be preserved forever.

✔ If the artifacts are ever sold, they must be sold as a collection.

✔ If the artifacts are sold, the purchaser (and any subsequent purchasers) must be approved by the court and by NOAA (the National Oceanic and Atmospheric Administration); must agree to maintain the artifacts to museum standards; must agree to keep the artifacts on public display; and must agree to all other covenants set forth by the court. (RMS Titanic has made it a priority to preserve for posterity even the tiniest of artifacts recovered from the *Titanic*.)

The court estimated the value of the artifacts to be in the $110 million range.

Salvaging the Titanic: Serving History or Robbing a Grave?

Here's the perfect college essay question: Write a 300-word essay comparing and contrasting the views regarding salvaging artifacts from the *Titanic* and putting them on display.

People who are *against* salvaging believe that the ship is a gravesite and, for that reason, should be left undisturbed. People who are *for* salvaging believe that recovering and displaying *Titanic* artifacts serves history and scholarship (perhaps now even more so because the last survivor has passed on). This latter camp says artifacts from King Tut's tomb serve as an example of how artifacts can be presented and preserved respectfully for scholars and the general public.

Is salvaging items from the *Titanic*'s debris field akin to grave robbing? Or is salvaging important for educational and historical purposes? This section provides survivor and commentator perspectives, and explains the differing opinions of Dr. Robert Ballard and George Tulloch.

Listening to Titanic survivors and commentators

Everyone has an opinion on whether salvaging at the site of the wrecked *Titanic* is ethically permissible. Here's a look at some of the dialogue that has taken place about the ultimate fate and treatment of the *Titanic* wreck and everything on and around her:

Dr. Robert Ballard, co-discoverer of the *Titanic* wreckage: "When I sailed away from the *Titanic* wreck site in 1986, I did so with the reasonable hope that the ship's last resting place would be left undisturbed." (from the epilogue to the 1995 edition of his book *The Discovery of the Titanic,* published by Warner Books)

George Tulloch, founder of RMS Titanic, Inc.: "Our philosophy at RMS Titanic echoes the thoughts of the *Titanic*'s designer and builder, Thomas Andrews, as he expressed them in his 1910 Christmas card: 'It is not what you say, it is not what you think, it is not what you feel. It is what you do.' RMS Titanic is dedicated to preserving and protecting the memory of the *Titanic* with dignity and respect." (from the epilogue to the RMS Titanic–sponsored book *Titanic: Legacy of the World's Greatest Ocean Liner,* published by Time-Life Books)

"There's hardly a day goes by that I don't say to myself, life would be so much easier if we could sell [the *Titanic* artifacts]. But there's a real problem with selling them. And the real problem is, it's wrong." (*Civilization,* December 1997/January 1998)

Millvina Dean, *Titanic* survivor: "If they want to make money, I don't honestly mind." (from *People,* May 19, 1997)

Eva Hart, *Titanic* survivor: "[*Titanic* salvagers are] fortune hunters, vultures, pirates." (*Civilization,* December 1997/January 1998)

Edward Kamuda, president of the Titanic Historical Society: "The wreck is a grave site. There's nothing that can be learned there that's worth disturbing the site. There's no reason to do this except for greed." (*Civilization,* December 1997/January 1998)

Charles A. Haas, president of the Titanic International Society: "Children of the future will never have the experiences our generation has had in meeting and learning first-hand from *Titanic*'s survivors. Books crumble into dust. Photographs fade into blurs. Videotapes have estimated lives of seven years. Memories fade. Recovered artifacts won't." (*Voyage* 18, Autumn 1994)

Walter Lord, author of *A Night to Remember:* "To me, the mystique of the *Titanic* was one of the wonderful things about it — the mystique of not knowing what happened once it slipped beneath the waves. And they've certainly ended that. Pulling these things up out of the water, you take away the mystery." (*Civilization,* December 1997/January 1998)

John Whitehead, Media Service, The U. S. Commemorative Fine Art Gallery: "Official and authentic *Titanic* historical items are finally being made available to the public for a very limited period of time and while certain supplies last. These historic items are being made available by the U. S. Commemorative Fine Art Gallery, a division of SCI. SCI, along with RMS Titanic, Inc., financed and carried out the now famous Titanic Expedition and Cruise, as seen on The Discovery Channel and a *National Geographic* television special." (from a full-page ad in the January 5, 1998, issue of *USA Today*)

Robert Ballard versus George Tulloch: A difference of opinion

At a 1998 lecture and book signing, Ballard spoke out against RMS Titanic, Inc., President George Tulloch for his company's salvage efforts. Ballard said that he didn't think the responsibility for the great liner — and ownership of all the artifacts recovered from her — should be in the hands of a car dealer from Connecticut.

The crowd's reaction to the criticism was mixed, but it seemed that a majority of attendees sympathized with Ballard and felt that the *Titanic* should be left alone. However, audience members chose to be there, meaning that they wanted to see, hear, and meet Ballard. In other words, they were predisposed to agree with him.

Legal decisions aside, to salvage or not to salvage is a difficult question. Science has always endeavored to chronicle history. Recovering, restoring, and displaying *Titanic* artifacts would seem to serve that purpose. The antisalvagers, though, believe that the *Titanic* site is essentially a cemetery and that its hallowed ground shouldn't be disturbed.

Tulloch, who died in 2004, believed that salvaging artifacts from the wreck is educational, furthers historical knowledge, and makes great contributions toward the preservation of the memory of the lost liner and its passengers. He vowed never to sell artifacts that his company recovered from the site. However, RMS Titanic, Inc., did sell pieces of *Titanic* coal to raise money for future expeditions. (The *Titanic*'s coal was never considered an artifact, per se, by the courts because it is a natural substance — not manmade — and was intended to be consumed on the voyage.)

The Big Piece: Salvaging a Part of the Titanic

Until 1998, all the world knew of the *Titanic* wreck were its artifacts, the coal from its debris field on the ocean floor, and video footage of the wreckage. But in 1998, people throughout the world saw for the first time an actual piece of the *Titanic* being dragged out of the water under the bright light of the sun.

That year, salvagers recovered what came to be known as the Big Piece. This vestige of the great ship weighs 20 tons and measures 15 feet by 25 feet. It has four portholes, three of which still have glass in them.

The Big Piece has been identified as having been part of the outer wall of two C-deck first-class berths (berths C79 and C81). These two berths were next door to the cabin occupied by the British journalist William Thomas Stead, editor of *The Review of Reviews*.

The Big Piece was salvaged in two dramatic operations. The first operation, in 1996, failed to bring the piece to the surface, but it managed to port it from the wreck site 10 miles to the Grand Banks off the coast of Newfoundland. From there, the second operation, in 1998, brought the Big Piece to shore. In the following sections, I explain the process of raising the Big Piece.

Raising the necessary capital

The raising of the Big Piece came with a price tag of around $17 million. The ever-enterprising George Tulloch, owner of RMS Titanic, Inc., had to scramble to find investors to raise the necessary capital. One of the ways he and his company did so was to sell 2,000 tickets to the event at $5,000 apiece. The plan was for two luxury cruise ships, the MV *Royal Majesty* and the SS *IslandBreeze*, to accompany Tulloch's salvage vessel to the site where the 20-ton Big Piece was located, approximately 70 feet east of the *Titanic*'s stern wreckage.

Tulloch's cruise ships were equipped with closed-circuit TVs in each cabin so guests could monitor the progress of the expedition in relative comfort. If they got bored, they could always turn their attention to the Las Vegas–style floor shows and casino gambling on the ships. The presence of these amusements may have contributed to some of the backlash against Tulloch's plans.

"You can't bring this thing up with no one looking," Tulloch told the media before the expedition. "This is theater."

Following Tulloch's best-laid plan

The specifics of trying to raise a piece of the *Titanic* from the ocean floor — the nuts-and-bolts details — are fascinating. Reading the daily dispatches from Tulloch's initial expedition of August 1996, you can't help but be impressed with the thought and planning that went into raising a 20-ton piece of steel from 2.5 miles below the ocean's surface.

The salvage vessel *Nadir* and the submersible *Nautile* were the main actors in the ambitious attempt to bring the piece of the *Titanic* to the surface after being hidden for 84 years in unimaginable darkness on the ocean floor.

Eight flotation bags filled with a total of 20,000 gallons of diesel fuel borrowed from the *Nadir* would do the lifting. They would be tethered to the Big Piece with 25 tons of steel chain. Each bag would have a lift capability of 3.5 tons. The following sections show you the process Tulloch's team went through in order to raise the Big Piece from the sea.

Facing potential problems

Raising the Big Piece of the *Titanic* was quite a gamble on Tulloch's part. Many factors had to go precisely as planned in order to achieve a smooth lift. Consider the following:

- ✔ **The team faced the potential problem of underestimating the weight of the Big Piece.** The Big Piece was thought to weigh between 15 and 18 tons. If it actually weighed more, the eight flotation bags could have trouble lifting it.

- ✔ **The team had to carefully estimate the mud-slurp factor.** If the Big Piece was buried too deep in the ocean floor (a real possibility), the suction created by the mud could increase the lift requirement substantially — enough, in fact, that the chains would quickly snap and the Big Piece would settle back into the mud on the ocean floor.

- ✔ **The team had to consider the possibility of a warm-water thermocline.** A *warm-water thermocline* is a water layer separating the colder, heavier deep water from the warmer, lighter water closer to the surface. If the bags hit one of these layers, their lifting power would be neutralized, causing the Big Piece to rise most of the way to the surface and then just stop. The bags and the Big Piece would then simply float around the Atlantic, "holding hostage hundreds of thousands of dollars of equipment, and a good bit of the *Nadir*'s fuel" (in the words of expedition crew member Steve Allison).

Towing the Big Piece

On Thursday, August 29, 1996, Tulloch and his team members succeeded in the first part of their plan. They attached the green and red flotation bags to the Big Piece. Eventually, the bags broke the surface of the Atlantic. Beneath these bags, the Big Piece dangled some 200 feet below.

Because of worsening weather conditions, the team decided to tow the Big Piece to the Grand Banks off the coast of Newfoundland, where the water depth was only 250 to 300 feet. There, divers could more safely repair the rigging and ultimately raise the Big Piece again.

Moving slowly at 2 knots, the *Nadir* began its trek to shallower waters. The weather got worse, and the waves became rougher. Finally, the chains holding the Big Piece could take no more stress. They broke at 3 a.m. on Friday, August 30, 1996. The Big Piece planed slowly down to the ocean floor. It landed upright 10 miles from the site of the *Titanic* wreck.

Passengers on the first Big Piece mission talk about their experience

Ernest Eldridge, the mayor of Windham, Connecticut, and his wife, Anita, were passengers on George Tulloch's first expedition in 1998 to raise the Big Piece. In a 2011 interview, Ernest told me about his experience on the mission, and he also offered his thoughts on the pro-salvaging versus anti-salvaging debate:

> My wife Anita and I have been *Titanic* collectors for a long time and we also put on *Titanic* presentations for schools and groups. A few months after we bought a piece of *Titanic* coal that had been advertised in the local paper, George Tulloch called us and asked if we would be interested in an "Expedition to *Titanic*." We agreed immediately.
>
> When we arrived at the dock for boarding there was a handful of protesters, along with TV stations. The protesters called it the Ghoul Cruise and accused Tulloch of disrupting the gravesite.
>
> We arrived on site after the *Nadir* and looked at the workboat and the nylon ropes. Frankly, the ropes immediately looked inadequate to us. We were aware of the size and weight of the Big Piece and the ropes did not look like they'd be capable of holding it. Interestingly, before we were even out of Boston Harbor we received lifeboat instructions and a lifeboat drill.
>
> There were several fascinating "offerings" on the cruise, not the least of which was *Titanic* survivor Eleanor Shuman, who we were honored to meet. The cruise also boasted artifacts on display which had been brought up on prior dives, book authors on board who lectured about *Titanic,* and reenactments of the shooting of emergency rockets, rockets which had been made to 1912 specifications. The *Nadir* and our ship separated the exact distance between *Titanic* and the *Californian* the night of the sinking so we could see what the *Californian* saw. The rockets were very easy to see and the firing of them gave us the chills. There were also special commemorative services at the *Titanic* site and the names of all who perished were read, a ritual that seemed unending.
>
> The ropes began to smoke and burn as the Piece rose higher and higher. We saw parts of the Piece via underwater cameras, but the diesel-filled flotation bags covered most of it. Certainly contributing to the stress on the ropes was the fact that the water, which had been smooth and calm, became quite choppy and rough as the Piece got closer to the surface.
>
> Some of our shipmates came onboard with trunks and Victorian clothes and made it a true *Titanic* first-class experience.
>
> Astronaut Buzz Aldrin, the second man to walk on the moon and one of the few who have traveled down to see the *Titanic* wreck, was also onboard and we had a chance to speak with him.
>
> As for salvaging *Titanic* artifacts and displaying them, Anita and I subscribe to the education and historical importance view regarding the retrieval of artifacts. Within our lifetimes the wreck will be close to disintegration. However, we also believe that great care should be taken when exploring and salvaging so as not to disturb or damage the site unnecessarily.

Preparing the Big Piece for display

After the Big Piece was raised, Conservation Solutions of Santa Fe, New Mexico — the company tasked with restoring the Big Piece for display — placed the piece in a pool filled with a water–and–sodium carbonate solution. The team then attached aluminum/magnesium anode blocks to the hull, which the salt in the metal attacked. The Big Piece was soaked in two phases: once for 18 months and then a second time for 3 months. After that, it was suspended in air and hosed down to remove loose pieces and any remaining rusticles. The Big Piece was then coated with tannic acid and treated with a microcrystalline wax to prevent further corrosion.

The crew of the *Nautile* eventually cut loose the flotation bags that were still attached to the Big Piece, recovering the fuel from them for the *Nadir*. Before leaving the site, the team dropped a plaque onto the Big Piece that read, "I will come back. George Tulloch."

Tulloch later told the media, "The ocean gives no quarter. We failed on this attempt because we neglected to carefully coordinate the 21st century technology of deep ocean recovery with the 19th century technology of winching and rigging. We won't make that mistake again."

Making the final leg of the journey

After a two-year delay, the Big Piece of the *Titanic* was successfully brought to the surface on Monday, August 10, 1998, by Tulloch and his team. This time, the team spent a month at sea. Besides raising the Big Piece, they retrieved artifacts and photographed the wreck.

When Tulloch and company returned to the Grand Banks off the coast of Newfoundland, they found the Big Piece still standing upright on the ocean floor. Using GPS devices, the team found it quickly.

They raised the Big Piece using techniques similar to those they used the first time around. After attaching six diesel-filled flotation bags to the Big Piece with 5-inch nylon ropes, they brought it to the surface. Then they hauled it onto the deck of their research vessel, the *Abeille Supporter;* winched it to an A-frame section of the ship; and sailed it to Boston Harbor.

The Big Piece is now on display in Las Vegas in *Titanic: The Artifact Exhibition* at the Luxor Hotel, where it will remain until 2018. Rumors have suggested that it may return to Belfast, but RMS Titanic, Inc., is in charge of deciding what to do with it.

Glimpsing Artifacts from the Ship

Artifacts from the *Titanic* are fascinating relics not only of a lost ship, but also of the Gilded Age, a time when men carried calling cards, women never appeared in public without being dressed to the nines, and travel —for the well-to-do — was leisurely and luxurious. The artifacts tell stories of what it was like to live in that age, when England and the United States had their own subtle, yet very real, caste system.

If you want to see artifacts from the *Titanic* in person or get involved with the history of the great ocean liner, you have many options. You can visit exhibitions, museums, and memorials, and you can participate in a variety of *Titanic* societies. I explain each of these options in the following sections.

Seeking out Titanic exhibitions

If you want to see some great artifacts that have been collected from the *Titanic*, you can visit one of the traveling exhibitions, or you can head to the permanent exhibition in Nevada. Here's the lowdown on each of these exhibits:

- **Traveling exhibitions:** The traveling exhibitions, called *Titanic: The Artifact Exhibition,* are owned and operated by Premier Exhibitions, of which RMS Titanic, Inc., is a division. More than 20 million people worldwide have viewed these exhibitions. Go to `www.rmstitanic.net/exhibitions.html` for details on current touring Titanic artifact exhibitions. Each exhibition is different, but each includes dozens of artifacts of note — and always an iceberg that visitors are encouraged to touch.

- **The permanent exhibition:** The largest and most important artifact exhibition is stationed permanently at the Luxor Hotel and Casino in Las Vegas, Nevada. From the Luxor's website, here is a description of *Titanic: The Artifact Exhibition* in Las Vegas:

  The 25,000-square-foot exhibit features numerous items from the *Titanic,* including luggage, the ship's whistles, floor tiles from the first-class smoking room, a window frame from the Verandah Café and an unopened bottle of champagne with a 1900 vintage. In addition, the exhibit features a piece of *Titanic*'s hull, a full-scale re-creation of the Grand Staircase as well as a newly expanded outer Promenade Deck, complete with the frigid temperatures felt on that fateful April night.

Seeing the *Titanic* for yourself

Many people have seen photos and video of the *Titanic* wreckage, but few people have seen the ship herself in three dimensions. However, the wreck is accessible, and yes, those who can afford to can visit the *Titanic* in person.

Deep Ocean Expeditions (www.deepocean expeditions.com) is the only company granted permission to take visitors to the wreckage of the *Titanic*. The company scheduled two expeditions comprised of 25 divers each for 2012. The cost of a submersible ride to the *Titanic* for the 2012 expeditions is approximately $60,000 per person.

The trip down in the submersible takes two and a half hours. The submersible spends three to four hours at the wreck site. The tour concentrates on the bow area, the main deck, and the promenade areas; you see where the Grand Staircase was, a boiler, and one propeller. Passengers are given time to photograph and observe the sites.

Is it dangerous for ordinary, untrained civilians to travel almost 13,000 feet below the surface of the Atlantic? With supervision and instruction, the trips are safe for most people.

The Luxor exhibition is enormous and is the only artifact exhibition to include a full-scale re-creation of the Grand Staircase from the *Titanic*. The Luxor exhibition is also the home of the Big Piece. It took days to move the Big Piece into the display area, and it's not going anywhere — at least until 2018, when the current agreement with Premier Exhibitions expires.

For complete details on visiting the Luxor exhibition, including admission fees, visit the Luxor's *Titanic* site at www.luxor.com/entertainment/titanic.aspx.

Taking a stroll through Titanic museums

A select few museums offer *Titanic* artifacts. Here are a few notable ones:

- ✔ **Ulster Folk & Transport Museum (Belfast, Northern Ireland):** This museum has an exhibition called *Titanica,* which provides a great deal of information about the *Titanic*'s construction. You can get more information at www.nmni.com/uftm.

- ✔ ***Titanic* Museum (Branson, Missouri):** This museum is a half-size replica of the ship (only two steam funnels); a giant iceberg stands next to the front door. To get in, the museum says, visitors have to successfully navigate the iceberg. Visitors can stroll through replicas of the lobby, cabins, and Marconi wireless room (where they also can send an SOS message). The museum features an 18-foot, one-of-a-kind *Titanic* model. Visit www.titanicbranson.com to discover more.

✔ **Maritime Museum of the Atlantic (Halifax, Nova Scotia, Canada):** This museum has an enormous collection of wooden *Titanic* artifacts. It also houses what has come to be called the "Shoes of the Titanic Unknown Child." This pair of leather shoes was discovered on "Body No. 4," a 2-year-old unknown male child found in the waters of the sinking site. The museum also has other artifacts in its permanent *Titanic* exhibition, including railroad tycoon Charles Hays's gloves. Head to `http://museum.gov.ns.ca/mmanew/en/home/default.aspx` for more information.

✔ **The Titanic Museum (Indian Orchard, Massachusetts):** This museum belongs to the Titanic Historical Society. Although it's small, the museum boasts some memorable *Titanic* artifacts, including original *Titanic* blueprints (donated by the builders of the ship), John Jacob Astor's life jacket, and the original *Titanic* wireless that received the warning transmission saying where the fatal iceberg was located. You can read more about this museum at `www.titanichistoricalsociety.org`.

✔ **Merseyside Maritime Museum (Liverpool, England):** This museum presents the original 20-foot-long builder's model of the *Titanic,* a survivor's life jacket, a bank note, a ventilation grille, tie pins, a watch, spectacles, and a lifeboat nameplate. Visit `www.liverpoolmuseums.org.uk/maritime` for details.

✔ **East Hants Historical Society (Maitland, Nova Scotia, Canada):** This rather eclectic museum displays one item of interest to Titaniacs: the embalming table used to preserve John Jacob Astor's body! Check out `http://ehhs.weebly.com` for more.

✔ **Titanic — The Experience (Orlando, Florida):** This large museum offers "guided tours led by trained actors in period dress portraying actual *Titanic* notables." It also offers full-scale re-creations of the Grand Staircase, the Verandah Café, a first-class parlor suite, and the Promenade deck. More than 200 *Titanic* artifacts are on display. You can read more at `http://titanictheexperience.com`.

✔ **Titanic Museum (Pigeon Forge, Tennessee):** This museum is owned and operated by the Branson Titanic Museum Company. Visit the website at `www.titanicpigeonforge.com`. This exhibition has more than 400 artifacts on display, as well as re-creations of the Grand Staircase and hallways, cabins, and parlors. Visitors can also put their hands into 28-degree water and simulate shoveling coal into a burning furnace.

Visiting Titanic memorials

Memorials in honor of the *Titanic* and its crew, victims, and survivors can be found in Europe, Canada, the United States, Australia, Ireland, and elsewhere. Here's a look at some notable cenotaphs and other monuments:

- **Titanic Memorial Bandstand (Ballarat, Victoria, Australia):** This bandstand is a memorial to the *Titanic* musicians. It has an interesting Edwardian design with multiple oriental-design roofs. It's located in front of the Mechanics Institute on Sturt Street.

- **Titanic Memorial (Belfast, Northern Ireland):** This memorial, opening in April 2012, features a marble figure of the goddess Thane designed by Sir Thomas Brock. You can read more at www.titanicbelfast.com.

- **Cobh Titanic Memorial (Cobh, Ireland):** This memorial in Cobh, formerly known as Queenstown, is a large marble sculpture with two plaques on it, one of which reads in part, "Commemorating RMS *Titanic* and her last port of call on her maiden and final voyage, April 12, 1912." Queenstown was the last place the *Titanic* docked before steaming to her destiny in the North Atlantic.

- **Titanic gravesites (Halifax, Nova Scotia, Canada):** One hundred fifty *Titanic* victims are buried in Halifax, Nova Scotia, of whom 121 are buried in Fairview Lawn Cemetery. A large sign simply reads "Titanic." The graves are arranged in a manner that seems to suggest the shape of the *Titanic*'s bow. Read more about the gravesites and those buried there at http://titanic.gov.ns.ca/graves.html.

- **Memorial to the Engine Room Heroes of the Titanic (Liverpool, England):** This granite monument, which is a stunning 48 feet tall, is located in St. Nicholas Place. It's dedicated to the 244 engineers who died when the *Titanic* sank. The monument was damaged by shrapnel from bombs dropped on England during World War II. The damage hasn't been repaired.

- **Titanic Memorial Lighthouse (New York, New York):** This lighthouse has stood since April 13, 1913, a year after the sinking of the *Titanic*. Before it was moved to its present location at the corner of Pearl and Fulton streets in Lower Manhattan (in front of the South Street Seaport Museum), it was located atop the Seamen's Church Institute on Water Street. The wooded area in front of the museum is known as Titanic Memorial Park.

- **The Isidor and Ida Straus Memorial (New York, New York):** The memorial is a fountain sculpture located in Straus Park at Broadway and West 106th Street. The memorial was erected in 1915 to commemorate the couple who founded the Macy's department store and who later died together on the *Titanic*. The inscription reads, "Erected by voluntary contributions from many fellow citizens and accepted for the City of New York by Mayor John Purroy Mitchel and Cabot Ward, Commissioner of Parks, AD MCMXV."

- **Memorial to Titanic's Engineers (Southampton, England):** This magnificent, enormous granite sculpture shows a giant winged angel watching over the *Titanic*'s engineers as they continue to do their jobs while the ship sinks. Its inscription reads, "To the memory of the Engineer Officers of the R.M.S. *Titanic* who showed their high conception of duty and their heroism by remaining at their posts. 15th April 1912." The memorial was unveiled on April 22, 1914. A reported 100,000 people attended the ceremony.

✔ **Titanic Musicians Monument (Southampton, England):** This monument is a duplicate of the original Titanic Musicians Monument that was destroyed when the building where it stood was demolished to make room for new construction. It's a granite-inscribed block affixed to a building at the intersection of Cumberland Road and London Road. It pays tribute to Wallace Hartley and the *Titanic* musicians for remaining at their posts and playing as the ship sank.

✔ **Titanic Stewards' Memorial (Southampton, England):** This marble, towerlike memorial was unveiled on July 27, 1915. It was originally located in public in Southampton. Over the years, the memorial was, sadly, vandalized, and in 1972 it was moved into a locked alcove in Holyrood Church. Its inscription reads, "This memorial was erected in memory of the crew, stewards, sailors and firemen, who lost their lives in the SS *Titanic* disaster on April 15, 1912. It was subscribed for by the widows, mothers, and friends of the crew. Alderman Henry Bowyer, Mayor, 1912–1913."

✔ **Women's Titanic Memorial (Washington, D.C.):** This memorial sits on the shore of the Washington Channel. It's a granite statue of a 13-foot-tall male with his arms outstretched as though he were flying. It was erected by the Women's Titanic Memorial Association. The inscription on the front reads, "To the Brave Men Who Perished in the Wreck of the Titanic April 15 1912. They Gave Their Lives That Women and Children Might Be Saved. Erected by the Women of America." The back reads, "To the Young and the Old the Rich and the Poor the Ignorant and the Learned All Who Gave Their Lives Nobly to Save Women and Children." The memorial was unveiled in 1931 by First Lady Helen Taft.

Joining Titanic societies

If you're a history buff and love to read about all things *Titanic,* you'll be glad to know that *Titanic* societies offer all kinds of information about the ship. In addition to those I describe here, others can be found through an online search. Some of these societies present conventions, some publish newsletters and journals, and others provide websites chock full of information. Here are five societies you may want to check out:

✔ **British Titanic Society:** Formed in 1987, this organization hosts a convention, publishes a newsletter, and offers educational material about the *Titanic* and the White Star Line. Its website at `www.titanic-titanic.com` is excellent.

✔ **Canadian Titanic Society:** Founded in 1998, this organization publishes a journal called *The Wireless: The Voice of the Canadian Titanic Society.* The society states that it won't ever dictate to members any position on salvaging *Titanic* artifacts, and it says that it won't take an editorial position that assigns blame for what happened in 1912. You can read more at `www.canadian-titanic-society.com`.

✔ **Titanic Historical Society:** Established in 1963, this is the oldest and largest *Titanic* society in the world. It maintains a museum, publishes a glossy quarterly magazine called *The Titanic Commutator,* and hosts conventions and events with notable guest lecturers and *Titanic* experts. *Titanic* survivors were frequent guests at Titanic Historical Society conventions. Visit www.titanic1.org for more details.

✔ **Titanic International Society:** This society was founded in 1989. It publishes a quarterly journal, *Voyage,* hosts annual conventions, and provides research and information about historical ocean liners. You can view its website at http://titanicinternationalsociety.org.

✔ **Titanic & Nautical Resource Center:** I highly recommend this group, which hosts a superb website and publishes a quarterly journal. Check out the website at www.titanic-nautical.com.

Chapter 17

Presenting the Titanic Story on Screen and on Stage

In This Chapter

▶ Surveying *Titanic* movies

▶ Checking out the award-winning *Titanic* musical

A Hollywood cliché says that some real-life stories are so implausible, no one would pay to see them on the silver screen. The *Titanic* story is one of those "too unbelievable to believe" stories. Imagine someone trying to pitch this to a movie producer: "I've got a disaster movie for you. The biggest ship ever built hits an iceberg and sinks on its very first voyage." Odds are that the producer would reject that idea outright for being too far-fetched.

Yet the *Titanic* did sink on its maiden voyage, and of course, movies were made about it. This chapter looks at the *Titanic* legend as it has been told in movies and on stage.

If your taste in film favors the nonfictional over the fictional, Chapter 20 describes ten terrific *Titanic* documentaries.

Sailing on the Titanic to Hollywood

Many movies have been made about the *Titanic* disaster. The first, a 10-minute short, debuted in 1912, only two months after the *Titanic* sank. The gold standard of *Titanic* movies — James Cameron's epic *Titanic* — was made in 1997.

Here's a thumbnail list of notable *Titanic* films, starting with the earliest:

▸ **Saved from the Titanic (1912):** A 10-minute short (also known as *I Survived the Titanic*) that starred Dorothy Gibson, a true *Titanic* survivor (see Chapter 3). In the next section of this chapter, I provide details about this movie.

- ✔ *Titanic* **(1943):** A Nazi propaganda film designed to make the greedy British owners of the White Star Line (and, by implication, all British business-people) look bad. Although the hero, fictional German First Officer Herr Petersen, begs the other crew members to slow down the ship, his warnings are ignored. "The deaths of 1,500 people remains unatoned, forever a testament of Britain's endless quest for profit," says the movie's epilogue.

- ✔ *Titanic* **(1953):** The story of a down-home girl from Mackinac, Michigan, fed up with European high society, who decides to bring her 17- and 10-year-old children back to her hometown on the *Titanic.* Her estranged husband, however, buys a ticket in steerage with an eye to thwarting her plan. This movie stars Clifton Webb, Barbara Stanwyck, and a 23-year-old Robert Wagner.

- ✔ *A Night to Remember* **(1958):** The most memorable and accurate rendering of the *Titanic* story — until 1997, when James Cameron's epic came out. See "A Night to Remember (1958)" later in this chapter for information on this movie.

- ✔ *The Unsinkable Molly Brown* **(1964):** Strictly speaking, this musical isn't about the *Titanic* tragedy — it's about the life and times of Margaret Tobin Brown, a *Titanic* survivor. You can read about this movie, which stars Debbie Reynolds, in the later section "The Unsinkable Molly Brown (1964)."

- ✔ *S.O.S. Titanic* **(1979):** A made-for-TV movie with David Janssen and Cloris Leachman. This narrative version of the story highlighted previously little-known passengers and crew. Some people allege that the movie used colorized versions of some scenes from *A Night to Remember.*

- ✔ *Raise The Titanic* **(1980):** The film version of Clive Cussler's bestselling novel of the same name. After the U.S. military determines that the *Titanic* carried a shipment of a rare mineral, byzanium, capable of powering a sound beam the military has developed to shoot down enemy missiles, the military hires renowned adventurer Dirk Pitt to assemble a team and raise the *Titanic* from the ocean floor.

- ✔ *Titanic* **(1996):** A TV miniseries starring Catherine Zeta-Jones and George C. Scott. This was the first *Titanic* movie made after the 1985 discovery of the *Titanic* shipwreck. In the miniseries, the *Titanic* breaks in two, a historical accuracy that previous movies were incapable of depicting because they were made before that fact was known.

- ✔ *Titanic* **(1997):** The James Cameron epic, winner of the Academy Award for Best Picture, starring Leonardo DiCaprio and Kate Winslet. See "Cameron's epic: Titanic (1997)" later in this chapter to read more about this film.

While I'd love to describe each of these movies in detail, I just don't have the space! So in the following sections, I provide a rundown of my favorites. You'll notice that I pay particular attention to Cameron's blockbuster because I feel that it's in a category of its own.

Saved from the Titanic (1912)

Saved from the Titanic has the distinction of being the first *Titanic* movie, and it's also the only one starring a survivor of the catastrophe. The movie starred Dorothy Gibson, a singer, model, and silent-screen star. Gibson escaped the sinking of the *Titanic* aboard Lifeboat 7, the first lifeboat launched.

Gibson made this 10-minute silent film almost immediately after her rescue. It debuted on May 14, 1912, only 29 days after the *Titanic* sank. In the movie, Gibson wore the same dress that she wore on the *Titanic*. Her character is a heroine who helps passengers board lifeboats. (In real life, Dorothy Gibson wasn't as heroic, however. Some reports have Gibson being one of the first passengers to board a lifeboat, which wouldn't have given her much time to help others.)

Unless a print of *Saved from the Titanic* is tucked away in someone's attic, the movie no longer exists. All known prints were destroyed when Éclair Studio, the maker of the movie, burned down in 1914.

A Night to Remember (1958)

The 1958 movie *A Night to Remember* (see Figure 17-1) was based in large part on the Walter Lord book of the same name. The movie portrays the night of April 14–15, 1912, when the *Titanic* sank. The movie starts with an error; it shows the *Titanic* being christened with a bottle of champagne, when in reality, the White Star Line never christened its ships. (I debunk this myth in Chapter 19.) After that error, however, the movie hits all the well-known beats:

- ✔ The luxuriousness and one-of-a-kind reputation of the ship
- ✔ The disparities among the three classes of passengers
- ✔ The shrugged-off ice warnings
- ✔ The chairman and managing director of the White Star Line, J. Bruce Ismay, pushing for speed (and later jumping into a lifeboat when women and children were still aboard)
- ✔ The collision with the iceberg
- ✔ The alleged dereliction of the *Californian*'s Captain Stanley Lord in not investigating the steamer he could see from his boat (see Chapter 7)
- ✔ Captain Edward J. Smith's announcement that "*Titanic* will founder" (although what Captain Smith says in the movie is "*Titanic* will sink")
- ✔ The mad scramble to load lifeboats
- ✔ The lights going out

Figure 17-1:
A scene from *A Night to Remember.*

- ✔ The band playing until the bitter end (see Chapter 12)

- ✔ The sinking (but the ship goes down in one piece)

- ✔ Margaret Tobin (Molly) Brown demanding that Lifeboat 6 turn back for survivors (see Chapter 3)

- ✔ The arrival of the *Carpathia* to rescue people from lifeboats (see Chapters 6 and 7) and the religious service for survivors

The movie's special effects are decent for the time, and the portrayal of the ship is mostly convincing. To build the sets, the filmmakers used actual *Titanic* blueprints. And the actors chosen resembled the people they were portraying.

The movie still holds up today and is reportedly the reason James Cameron decided to tackle the *Titanic* story. According to comments he made in the authorized companion book to his 1997 movie, he was watching *A Night to Remember* when the thought occurred to him that with modern special-effects technology, a *Titanic* movie could be made that showed exactly what happened, as realistically as possible.

The Unsinkable Molly Brown (1964)

The Unsinkable Molly Brown, based on the 1960 Broadway musical of the same name, starred Debbie Reynolds and tells the colorful story of Margaret Tobin Brown. The daughter of Irish immigrants, she married mining magnate James Joseph Brown in Leadville, Colorado, became a figure in high society in spite of her humble origins, and survived the sinking of the *Titanic*.

Kristen Iversen, author of a comprehensive 1998 biography of Molly Brown called *Molly Brown: Unraveling the Myth* (Johnson Books), told me, "Margaret Tobin Brown was never known as Molly; that was an invention of Hollywood. In fact, most of what people know of her life is from the Debbie Reynolds movie, which was 99 percent pure invention." When Brown set sail on the *Titanic,* her nickname was Maggie. Yet after her bravery on the *Titanic,* she became known as "Molly," and later, she became unsinkable, too.

If I had to pick one word to describe this 1964 movie, it would be *boisterous*. Star Debbie Reynolds dances, leaps, and gets flung around to the accompaniment of a raucous musical score while people in elaborate and gaudy costumes frolic in front of garish movie sets. The movie is dated and can come across (especially to the sensibilities of younger generations) as corny. Yet the movie has a certain appeal to other generations.

As for the scenes on the *Titanic* and its lifeboats, Reynolds's Molly is a "never-say-die" cheerleader who manifests an attitude and gumption more appropriate for a home game than a lifeboat filled with people watching the ship carrying their loved ones sink to the bottom of the ocean. When a woman starts screaming, "We're going to die!", Molly screeches, "No, we ain't! I ain't ready to die! Hell, I'm just learnin' how to live!" Then she slaps a woman who's crying and tells the other lifeboat passengers that she's going to teach them a song. She says, "That ship may be down, but not me, because I'm unsinkable! . . . So let's sing!"

Cameron's epic: Titanic (1997)

After its release on December 19, 1997, James Cameron's *Titanic* achieved a success unheard of in cinema history. The movie garnered 14 Academy Award nominations and 11 Oscars, tying *Ben-Hur* for the most Oscars won by a single motion picture. As of this writing, *Titanic* is still the second-highest-grossing film of all time (it took Cameron's own *Avatar* in 2009 to knock *Titanic* off its perch). The movie's soundtrack also became the biggest-selling movie soundtrack of all time.

Costars Leonardo DiCaprio (who plays the fictional Jack) and Kate Winslet (who stars as fictional Rose) became overnight sensations. Certain images from the film featuring DiCaprio and Winslet, such as the one shown in Figure 17-2, gained worldwide renown.

Behind the success of the movie was Cameron himself. He served as *Titanic*'s director, screen writer, co-producer, and co-editor.

This section looks behind the scenes at how Cameron struggled to make *Titanic,* and you can read more about the movie and its lasting impact in Chapter 1 as well.

Pitching the movie

In the January 1988 issue of *The Titanic Commutator,* the official journal of the Titanic Historical Society, Cameron explained why he wanted to make *Titanic:*

> I got infused with the emotionalism of the tragedy. It really just struck me as this magnificent, incredibly sad, very emotional occurrence which was real and which was well understood and which, in a way, couldn't have been better. It was as if history wrote a great novel for us, and it was all right there.

Figure 17-2:
Jack and Rose flying high in Cameron's film.

The real Jack?

Was there a real Jack Dawson on the *Titanic,* and was he James Cameron's inspiration for the character of the same name in his epic film? In a word, no. But there was a "J. Dawson" aboard the *Titanic* — later discovered to have the first name Joseph. Cameron has said repeatedly that he had no idea there was a "J. Dawson" on the ship's crew when he wrote his script.

Joseph Dawson worked the mammoth mounds of coal in the *Titanic*'s belly as a trimmer. He had to make sure that the coal mountains were always even so as not to weigh overly heavily on either side of the ship. His body was recovered by the *Mackay-Bennett* and buried in Halifax, Nova Scotia, on May 8, 1912. He was from Dublin, Ireland, and listed his residence as Briton Street in Southampton, England.

After the movie became a global phenomenon in 1997, interest in all things *Titanic* led fans to J. Dawson's grave. And because the story was just too romantic, and too dramatic, and too *perfect* to dismiss, "Jack & Rose" devotees embraced Joseph as their Jack and began leaving photos, ticket stubs, and all other manner of memorabilia at his grave in honor of the young man who saved Rose's life.

Alas, Joseph Dawson is not the fictitious "Jack Dawson." But wouldn't it have been amazing if he was?

When pitching *Titanic* to movie executives, Cameron provided the following list. Every item on the list describes a film not worth making, yet the film was made.

- The movie would cost "north of" $100 million.

- The movie would run more than three hours (which meant that theaters could show it only a limited number of times each day).

- The movie would be an elaborate historical period piece (meaning scads of costly costumes).

- The movie wouldn't be able to use big-name stars because of the youth of the characters.

- The movie had absolutely no possibility for a sequel or merchandise tie-in products.

Oh, and one more thing: Everyone already knows the end of the story.

This pitch contained a lot not to like, and Cameron knew it. Yet studio executives who heard Cameron pitch the movie expressed enough interest in the idea that Cameron decided to write a *film treatment* (a more detailed description of the storyline).

In a 1998 interview with Charlie Rose, Cameron said that the studio executives who read his *Titanic* treatment told him that they hated that they liked it so much, because they knew they would have to go ahead and make the movie despite their misgivings.

Making Titanic: An expensive three-year odyssey

It took three years to make *Titanic*. Cameron made a dozen trips to the bottom of the North Atlantic to film the actual ship. A replica of the great liner — at an amazing 92 percent scale — was built in Baja, Mexico. Shooting the film required an arduous seven months. *Titanic* was originally scheduled for a summer 1997 release, but Cameron decided (with not a little bit of grumbling from the studio) to push the release to December.

Just for fun: Titanic blunders and inaccuracies

Even a $200 million movie isn't historically perfect, as the following list of *Titanic* inaccuracies illustrates:

✔ The cabins Rose and her husband, Cal, stayed in — B52-54-56 — were occupied by White Star Line Chairman and Managing Director J. Bruce Ismay during the actual voyage.

✔ At the first-class dinner party, Rose mentions to Ismay the work being done by Sigmund Freud regarding "the male preoccupation with size." Freud didn't publish that work until 1920, eight years after the *Titanic* sailed.

✔ Rose, Ruth, Cal, Molly, and many other first-class passengers attend a worship service and sing the hymn "Eternal Father, Strong to Save" (also known as "The Navy Hymn"). The two verses that the group sings in the movie, however, weren't written until 1937.

✔ Jack is prevented from entering the worship service because he held a third-class ticket and his presence there wasn't "appropriate." Actually, the worship services held on the *Titanic* at 10:30 a.m. on Sunday, April 14, 1912, were open to all the passengers on the ship.

✔ Captain Smith can be seen wearing soft contact lenses, a convenience that wouldn't be available for another 59 years.

✔ When the *Titanic* is seconds away from striking the iceberg, First Officer William Murdoch runs onto the bridge and bumps into Second Officer Charles H. Lightoller, making him spill his tea. In reality, Lightoller was asleep in his bunk when the *Titanic* collided with the iceberg.

✔ Jack is handcuffed to a pipe in the Master-at-Arms' office, which is shown as having a porthole. On the *Titanic*, however, the Master-at-Arms' office was actually an interior room on E deck.

✔ When Captain Smith enters the wheelhouse to await his death, the ship's telegraph is set to "Full Reverse" instead of "All Stop" (the handle straight up in the air), which was the order Smith had actually given at around 1:40 a.m.

✔ Cal escapes the sinking ship in a solid-bottom lifeboat that floats off as the *Titanic* goes down. In reality, none of the *Titanic*'s 16 wood-bottom lifeboats floated off the ship. Two of the collapsible lifeboats floated off; the others were all lowered by ropes.

✔ A close-up of the Statue of Liberty's torch shows the restored, post-1986 version, not the original amber stained-glass torch.

✔ On the real *Titanic*, floor-to-ceiling Bostwick gates were installed *only* in areas separating passengers from crew. The gates that separated the different classes of passengers were only waist-high and were guarded by stewards.

The budget overruns on the film resulted in Twentieth Century Fox's bringing in Paramount Pictures as a partner to help defray some of the astronomical costs of production. After the film's budget broke the $100 million mark, Paramount signed on for $65 million — capped — in a deal that probably ended up being one of the most lucrative investments the studio ever made.

As production continued, however, even $165 million wasn't enough to finish the film, and for a time, talk surfaced of pulling the plug on the epic — something Cameron absolutely refused to consider. As a result, Cameron offered personally to give up a total of approximately $30–35 million — his $10 million director's fee and the $25 or so million he could conceivably earn in profit participation on the film — in order to complete the movie the way he wanted to. Twentieth Century Fox agreed; Cameron signed over his cut of *Titanic;* and the film was finally released on December 19, 1997.

As of 2011, *Titanic* had grossed more than $1.8 billion worldwide, and its projected total gross (including video release and cable and network airings) would probably be close to $2 billion.

Watching Titanic in 3D

On April 6, 2012, *Titanic* is being released to theaters in 3D. The date was chosen because it falls near the 100th anniversary of the sailing of the *Titanic* on April 10, 1912, and the 100th anniversary of its foundering on April 15, 2012.

As of this writing, the conversion to 3D is being overseen by Cameron and by Jon Landau of Lightstorm. Cameron told *The Hollywood Reporter,* "There's a whole generation that's never seen *Titanic* as it was meant to be seen, on the big screen. And this will be *Titanic* as you've never seen it before . . . . With the emotional power intact and the images more powerful than ever, this will be an epic experience for fans and newcomers alike."

Bringing the Greatest Ocean Liner to Broadway with Titanic: A New Musical

Titanic: A New Musical opened on Broadway in April 1997, and it gave its final performance in March 1999. (Several foreign productions have been done in Germany, Japan, Canada, and Australia since then.) The musical won five Tony Awards in 1997. The September 8, 1997, issue of *People* magazine gave the original cast CD a rave review: "It takes guts to write a musical about the century's most infamous disaster, yet Broadway's *Titanic* unflinchingly sails forth with its cargo of epic themes aboard what was the earth's largest man-made moving object, until it suddenly stopped moving on April 15, 1912."

Titanic: A New Musical succeeds in the extremely difficult task of synthesizing countless elements of an undeniably grand epic into a musical experience that tells the story but doesn't diminish its gravity because of its musical format.

One of the musical's most heart-wrenching moments is a scene when the third-class passengers, who had previously sung "I Must Get on That Ship" in anticipation of boarding the *Titanic* for their long-awaited journey to America (where "the streets are paved with gold"), reprise the song in Act II — only this time, they sing about getting on a lifeboat.

Interestingly, especially for a musical, *Titanic: A New Musical* takes on the subject of who was to blame for the disaster. In "The Blame," which is sung in Act II after the collision with the iceberg, writer Peter Stone and lyricist Maury Yeston have the characters of J. Bruce Ismay (the chairman and managing director of the White Star Line), Thomas Andrews (the *Titanic*'s chief designer), and Captain Edward J. Smith furiously hurling accusations at one another in an attempt to exonerate their own actions and absolve themselves of blame for the imminent sinking. At the conclusion of this powerful number, after all the desperate charges are hurled back and forth, Captain Smith steps forward and accepts full responsibility: "There's only one captain," he sings, "and I was in charge . . . this is my ship, no one else's . . . ."

Part VI
The Part of Tens

The 5th Wave   By Rich Tennant

Titanic Exhibit →

Old corroded relics from the past

"Walter, will you please step away from that sign?"

In this part . . .

Each chapter in this part offers ten tidbits of good, solid information about the *Titanic*. Turn here to read about the ten most interesting *Titanic* artifacts, ten *Titanic* myths (which I debunk), and ten worthwhile *Titanic* documentaries.

Chapter 18

Ten Fascinating Titanic Artifacts

In This Chapter

▶ Traveling to Vegas to see the Big Piece

▶ Eyeing the Grand Staircase and a deck chair

▶ Finding a watch frozen in time

▶ Examining menus, perfumes, and handwritten sheet music

*N*o human remains were found during any of the expeditions to retrieve artifacts from the *Titanic* debris field (see Chapter 15). It is believed that all human bodies were completely decomposed, disintegrated, and consumed by the 1940s. Based on photos of pairs of shoes lying on the ocean floor, we know precisely where bodies landed after the ship sank. The feet and the rest of the bodies are long gone; only the shoes survive.

To feed more than 2,000 people three times a day for several days at sea, the *Titanic* carried massive stores of foodstuffs (as I detail in Chapter 4). But food, like human flesh, is organic and was consumed by sea creatures and organisms at the bottom of the North Atlantic.

Most of the *Titanic*'s wood is gone as well, having served as food for, most likely, deep-sea worms.

So what did survive? Items made of leather, glass, metal, and ceramic. Gems, soap, and other nonorganic, nondigestible materials also survived. This chapter looks at ten of the most fascinating artifacts that survived the *Titanic*'s demise. To get a sense of what some of these items look like, be sure to check out this book's color section.

The Big Piece

The Big Piece is the name given to part of the *Titanic*'s hull — the outer wall of two C-deck first-class cabins (numbers C79 and C81, which were unoccupied during the voyage) and extending down into D deck. The Big Piece is probably the most fascinating of all the *Titanic* artifacts that have seen the light of day. It is a huge piece of the actual ship that broke off upon impact, probably with the ocean floor, and was brought to the surface, preserved, and put on display. People who were born decades after the *Titanic* launched can now see, close up, a piece of the ship's hull precisely as it looked to those onboard and to those on the dock seeing her off on her maiden voyage.

Raising the Big Piece was not an easy task; in fact, it took two tries. (See Chapter 16 for details about how the Big Piece was salvaged.) And it took two years of cleaning, restoration, and preservation before the Big Piece could be moved to its home, the Luxor Hotel in Las Vegas. The Big Piece is now part of *Titanic: The Artifact Exhibition* at the Luxor. It will remain there until at least 2018. After that, the owners of the Big Piece (RMS Titanic, Inc.) will decide where it goes. (Considering the success of the Luxor's exhibition, there's a good chance that the contract will be renewed and the Big Piece will remain there until 2028. But that's purely speculation.)

In May 2011, Heritage Auctions announced that it was auctioning a much smaller, 4-inch by 7-inch piece of the *Titanic*'s hull. This piece, which was found apart from the Big Piece on the ocean floor, ended up in the possession of writer and *Titanic* historian Charles Pellegrino. The question immediately arose as to who actually owned this particular piece of the hull. Soon after its initial announcement, Heritage announced that Pellegrino was pulling three other pieces from the auction, described as "rusticles," which he gave to RMS Titanic, Inc. The 2011 auction ultimately did include the offer of the signed Pellegrino hull piece; the donation of the rusticles seemed to have cleared the way for Pellegrino to retain ownership of the small piece and auction it off.

In other "hull" news, in 2007, Geneva-based watchmaker Romain Jerome announced that it was manufacturing 2,012 limited-edition timepieces made from metal from small hull pieces of the *Titanic*. The hull metal was mixed with other metals to make the watches' cases, and hull metal and coal from the *Titanic* were mixed to manufacture the watches' dials. The watches were expected to sell for around $125,000 each. In 2011, the price for the watches was approaching $150,000.

What are the chances of other hull pieces being raised from the ocean floor? It's still possible, considering that other scattered hull pieces rest in the debris field. But the cost and time it took to raise the Big Piece make it seem unlikely that another salvage expedition so large will be mounted in the near future. Quite possibly, the Big Piece may be a one-of-a-kind relic of the great ship (and a great excuse to schedule a trip to Las Vegas).

Coal

Why is the *Titanic*'s coal fascinating? Because the tons of coal that were spilled into the debris field when the *Titanic* crashed onto the ocean floor were meant to feed the ship's mighty boilers. If the ship had survived, this coal would have been the ship's source of power. The coal's retrieval allows

Titanic buffs to literally own a piece of history. And the coal is relatively inexpensive compared with other artifacts.

Coal from the *Titanic*'s bins is available in a variety of sizes and configurations. A common, reasonably priced collectible is a 5×7-inch photograph of the *Titanic* with a piece of authentic *Titanic* coal affixed to the photo in a plastic bag. Most pieces come with a certificate of authenticity. Much of the coal on the market is from the 1994 salvage expedition (see Chapter 16).

Titanic coal sculptures also exist. These sculptures are not made from *Titanic* coal; instead, they are pieces of coal sculpted into replicas of the ship. Pieces like this don't have great value to most collectors, but they may appeal to the completist: a *Titanic* collector who must have absolutely everything *Titanic*-related.

A Piece of the Grand Staircase

Part of the railing of the Grand Staircase in the ship's first-class section was recovered by the cable ship *Minia* in 1912. The *Minia* was the second ship chartered by the White Star Line to speed to the site of the *Titanic*'s sinking and retrieve bodies.

The *Minia* left Halifax, Nova Scotia, on Monday, April 22, 1912, one week after the *Titanic* sank. She met bad weather and was able to retrieve only 17 bodies, two of which were buried at sea. She did, however, recover a variety of floating wood and other remnants of the ship. The piece of the Grand Staircase was part of the haul.

Whoever initially took possession of the piece fashioned it into a picture frame. (More than one account has William Parker, the ship's carpenter on the *Minia*, doing the refashioning.) The frame changed hands, and its new owner cut the frame up into four pieces, each of which could be sold or given away.

One of the Grand Staircase pieces sold at auction for $23,000 in 2004. The others are in the hands of private collectors and have not become available for purchase.

The Deck Chair That Stayed Home

Thomas Barker was a newspaper photographer who boarded the *Titanic* in Queenstown, Ireland (now Cobh), on April 11, 1912, to take photos of the ship for his newspaper. As he was leaving, he noticed the dozens of beechwood deck chairs and asked a crew member if he could have one as a souvenir. The crew member, surprisingly, said yes, and Barker duly carted off a chair from the first-class promenade. (Did crew members have the authority to give away accoutrements of the ship? Did the crew member ask someone higher up if he could give away a chair?)

Barker said he wanted the chair for his garden, and that's where it stood until the *Titanic* went down. Then Barker apparently got spooked. According to www.luxist.com, Barker ultimately "wanted nothing to do with the chair." He gave it to his housekeeper, who took it with her to England. It then changed hands several times over the years until finally it was put up for auction by Bonhams & Butterfields in 2006.

Interestingly, the deck chair failed to sell in a May 2008 auction. The highest bid was lower than the price the anonymous owner had set for the chair. There are only six *Titanic* deck chairs in the world; you can see a photo of one in this book's color insert. A beechwood chair that is believed to have been thrown off the ship for passengers and crew in the water to use as a flotation device sold at auction in 2001 for close to $69,000.

For a period, the J. Peterman Company offered a miniature *Titanic* deck-chair replica. It was 8.5 inches by 5.5 inches and made of wood and cast polyurethane. The miniature deck chairs reportedly sold for around $100 or so each; these days, they're available only at collectibles auctions.

Carl Asplund's "2:19 A.M." Pocket Watch

Englishman Carl Asplund, his wife, and their five children boarded the *Titanic* at Southampton, England, bound for what they thought would be a new life in California. Asplund and three of his sons died in the disaster. (His wife and two youngest children, 5-year-old Lillian and 3-year-old Felix, survived.)

Twelve days later, Asplund's body was recovered at sea. A watch and *Titanic* ticket were found in his vest pocket. The watch, an American Waltham, was frozen at 2:19 a.m. It is believed to have stopped the moment Asplund hit the frigid water. (You can see a photo of a different pocket watch retrieved from the *Titanic* in this book's color section.)

The watch was purchased by a Swedish collector at auction in 2008 for $61,786. Also sold at the same auction was daughter Lillian Asplund's *Titanic* ticket, which went for $65,772.

The Doll's Head

In a June 6, 2004, article in *The New York Times,* writer James Barron asked an interesting question: "Will the day come when items from September 11 —

survivors' possessions or keepsakes from victims' relatives — are auctioned?" He asked the question as part of his coverage of an auction of personal items belonging to *Titanic* victims. Barron called the personal items a "gruesome-sounding trove of *Titanic* artifacts." His question speaks to the personal nature of many artifacts.

Probably no *Titanic* artifact is as personal as the doll's head that Robert Ballard discovered during one of his salvage expeditions (see Chapter 15).

For a moment, Ballard and crew thought they had found human remains, but they quickly remembered that no human remains can survive on the ocean floor. What they saw was the head of a child's doll.

Ballard did not recover the doll's head, nor did he record its location. But the video footage he took has appeared in *Titanic* documentaries, and James Cameron in his 1997 film *Titanic* (see Chapter 17) had the doll's head appear as well.

The doll's head is believed to have belonged to first-class passenger Loraine Allison, although it could have belonged to Marjorie Collyer, Eva Hart, or Elin Braf. There is no way of knowing with certainty to whom it belonged.

Leather Objects

Objects made of leather (such as a wallet shown on the last page of this book's color section) did not deteriorate over the past 100 years on the ocean floor. Leather objects survived because microorganisms cannot digest the tannic acid used during the manufacturing process to preserve leather. If microorganisms can't eat it, they leave it alone.

Leather objects retrieved include bags, shoes, belts, wallets, and handbags. Interestingly, leather's lack of appeal to the creatures foraging for food has also protected items stored in anything made of leather. In one leather travel bag, for example, salvagers found money, jewelry, and possibly items from one of the *Titanic*'s safes. What was this bag's story? Did it belong to a traveling salesman headed to New York to sweet-talk a client? Or was it stolen from a first-class cabin as the ship sank? Maybe a thief filled it with items he grabbed from abandoned cabins in an optimistic looting spree he thought would set him up after he was rescued? We'll never know.

Menus

Obviously, paper disintegrates rapidly under the pressure and temperature conditions 2.5 miles beneath the ocean. However, some *Titanic* menus were found on the recovered bodies of the victims. (Passengers were known to carry menus around in their pockets to peruse the offerings before dinner.) These recovered menus provide a vivid picture of what the great ship's passengers ate.

From all accounts, the food served on *Titanic* was magnificent. More than one account declares that the food served to second-class passengers was equal to or better than the first-class offerings on other ships.

First-class passengers could indulge in an astonishing ten-course meal, beginning with oysters and consommé; continuing with filet mignon, roast duckling, lamb, and roast squab; and concluding with pâté de fois gras and Waldorf pudding, complete with an array of wonderfully prepared vegetables, salads, and side dishes.

Second-class passengers were similarly well treated. They chose among baked haddock, curried chicken, spring lamb, and roast turkey accompanied by peas, turnips, rice, and potatoes, with ice cream, plum pudding, fresh fruit, and cheese biscuits for dessert.

Even third-class passengers, who had to bring their own food on other ocean liners, were in for a treat on the *Titanic.* They ate their big meal in the middle of the day, and their fare included roast beef with sweet corn, potatoes, and plum pudding, along with plenty of fresh bread and fruit.

The breakfast, lunch, and tea menus on the *Titanic* were equally rich with gustatory delights. See Chapter 4 for all the details about the food served onboard.

Perfume That Still Has a Scent

Glass vials of perfume were recovered from the ocean floor and are now on display in RMS Titanic, Inc.'s traveling *Titanic: The Artifact Exhibition.* What makes this artifact notable is that the scents of the perfume are still strong and vibrant.

Titanic: The Artifact Exhibition displays them in a sealed glass showcase that has a series of holes in its side. Visitors are invited to put their noses to the holes (which I did when I visited the exhibition) and smell 100-year-old perfume. Apparently, due to the chemical components of the liquid, very little scent deterioration has occurred over the decades. I was able to smell what the *Titanic* passengers smelled on the voyage.

In addition to perfume belonging to female passengers, *Titanic: The Artifact Exhibition* includes a leather satchel discovered in the *Titanic* debris field that originally held 65 vials of perfume samples. The recovered satchel held 62 vials; the missing three have not been found.

Replicating the Titanic's perfumes

In 2001, the perfumes and oils recovered from the *Titanic* were sent to a company in England that specializes in developing perfume and cosmetics. The company analyzed the liquids, identified their components, and mapped their DNA for easy duplication. Whether actual perfumes will be manufactured using the DNA maps is up to RMS Titanic, Inc.

In 2009, the Scents of Time company announced that it had successfully "cloned" a perfume based on Adolphe Saafeld's oils. The perfume was to be called RosaMaris — the Rose of the Sea. However, the company did not market the perfume, believing that Saafeld (as well as Eliza Gladys Millvina Dean, the last survivor to die) would not have approved. RMS Titanic, Inc., and Scents of Time instead produced a new perfume called Night Star, dedicated to Millvina Dean, which they market as a "Fragrance of the Future."

The perfume vials belonged to Adolphe Saafeld, a perfume maker from Manchester, England. Saafeld brought samples of his perfume and scented oils to New York with the hope of obtaining orders from department stores, boutiques, and other perfume retailers. Saafeld survived the sinking and was taken aboard the *Carpathia* from Lifeboat 3 without his perfume satchel. He continued in the perfume business until his death in 1926.

Handwritten Sheet Music

Handwritten sheet music was discovered in a leather satchel recovered from the *Titanic*. What makes this artifact fascinating is that the music may never have been performed. We don't know whether the music on the sheet was a new composition written by a passenger or orchestra member or whether it reflects a band member's attempt to write notes to a popular song of the day.

The romantic at heart may speculate that the handwritten sheet music was a song composed in someone's honor or dedicated to someone, and that the passenger who wrote it used the time on the *Titanic* to write the piece for someone waiting in New York. We'll simply never know.

Chapter 19

Ten Titanic Myths Debunked

*N*o sooner had the *Titanic* sunk than myths began to spring up around her, regarding why she sank or regarding some of her more peculiar passengers and cargo. This chapter explores and debunks some of these myths.

Read on to find out about the mummy in the *Titanic*'s cargo hold, the riches that sank along with her, and her champagne curse. This chapter also looks into the cryptic anti-Catholic message that supposedly was emblazoned on the *Titanic;* the dead worker riveted inside her hull; and the story of Frank Tower, purportedly the *Titanic*'s luckiest passenger.

The Titanic Carried a Cryptic, Anti-Catholic Message

Through the years, a pervasive myth concerning the *Titanic* said that its hull number, 390904, when looked at in a mirror (while squinting, I presume), spelled out the words *No Pope.*

In an experiment I conducted, the mirror image of number 390904 does indeed resemble the words *No Pope.* In a mirror, the numbers 9093 definitely look like the word *pope,* but the alleged word *No* looks like exactly what it is: a backward 4 and a zero.

With this myth, we see shades of the Beatles album *Sgt. Pepper's Lonely Hearts Club Band.* Rumors circa 1967 said that if you held up a mirror in the middle of the words "Lonely Hearts" on the cover of the album, you could read *I ONE IX HE <> DIE,* which meant, of course, that Paul McCartney was dead.

Was a hidden message deliberately created and emblazoned on the *Titanic*'s hull in order to make a 46,000-ton steamship a slur against Catholicism? In a word, no. How can you be sure? How about starting off with this piece of empirical evidence (y'know, a *fact*)?: The *Titanic* was constructed in Harland and Wolff Yard No. 401. That number was engraved into her propeller and is clearly visible on the wreck. The number 390904 doesn't appear *anywhere* in the Harland and Wolff records for the *Titanic*. The only six-digit number that Harland and Wolff records associated with the *Titanic* is her Board of Trade number: 131428. Case closed.

Is That You, Mummy?

Another *Titanic* myth said that a mummy was stowed on the *Titanic* and that's why the ship sank. According to the myth, the mummy was named Amen-Ra, and she hurled curses around like a lawn sprinkler throws water.

A very elaborate backstory as to who the mummy was, who owned her carcass, the death and destruction she wielded, and how she ended up on the *Titanic* goes something like this: The Princess of Amen-Ra, who lived about 1500 B.C.E., was buried on the shores of the Nile and dug up many centuries years later by archeologists. Her mummy ended up in a museum in London. Anyone who took possession of the princess died, including a child whose museum worker father disrespectfully struck the coffin with a dust rag. The museum put the Amen-Ra mummy in the basement. It was then removed, haunted a house, and was purchased by an American archaeologist who decided to take it to New York on the *Titanic*.

As is often the case, the truth is much less dramatic. There was no mummy on the *Titanic,* and her sinking had everything to do with an iceberg and nothing to do with a curse. Moreover, the genuine "mummy of Amen-Ra" was not really a mummy, but a sarcophagus cover that now resides in Room 62 of the British Museum.

Unlike most myths, the source of the mummy myth is well known. It originated with writer, journalist, editor, and spiritualist William Thomas Stead. Although he isn't well remembered today, Stead, an Englishman, was once called the most famous person to die on the *Titanic*. In 1912, he was known the world over for his humanitarian efforts and writings. When the *Titanic* sank, Stead was on his way to New York to speak at a peace conference at the request of President William Howard Taft.

On Friday evening, April 12, two nights before the *Titanic* sank, Stead regaled his dinner companions with ghost stories and tall tales. One tale recounted the legend of Amen-Ra, the mummy allegedly stowed in the cargo hold. Stead deliberately embellished his tale so that its conclusion occurred after midnight. The story spread, and the legend of the *Titanic*'s mummy was born. No one knows the particulars of Stead's story, but it almost certainly included details about the mummy's destructive past and her fateful encounters with others throughout her history. The only survivor of the group who actually heard Stead's story, Fred Seward, vowed never to retell the story for fear that the curse was real and it would doom anyone who heard it — just as it seemed to doom seven of the eight passengers who heard Stead tell the story aboard the *Titanic*.

In some reports, Stead was seen helping women and children into the lifeboats and was last seen in the water. Walter Lord, in his novel *A Night to Remember,* wrote that Stead was last seen sitting in a parlor reading a book. In the April 20, 1912, edition of the *Worcester* (Massachusetts) *Telegram & Gazette,* however, Philip Brock, a survivor, said, "Many men were hanging on to rafts in the sea. William T. Stead, the author, and Col. John Jacob Astor clung to a raft. Their feet became frozen and they were compelled to release their hold. Both were drowned."

After his death, two short stories that Stead wrote decades prior received renewed attention:

- ✔ "How the Mail Steamer Went Down in Mid-Atlantic, by a Survivor" (published in the March 22, 1886, *The Pall Mall Gazette*) tells of a steamer that collides with another ship with great loss of life because the steamer doesn't carry enough lifeboats for its passengers and crew.
- ✔ "From the Old World to the New" (published in the December 1892 *The Review of Reviews*) tells how the brave captain of the *Majestic* goes to the rescue of passengers and crew stranded on the iceberg that previously sank their ship.

This Stead was a spooky guy!

A Worker Was Trapped in the Titanic's Hull

One of the ghastliest myths about the *Titanic* purports that a worker was trapped inside the ship's hull during construction, and with nowhere to escape, he died, his body sealed in the hull of the ship. (This rumor has a long shelf life. The same was said about the Hoover Dam — that a worker was trapped inside the dam and left to die.)

Only two construction-related deaths occurred during the building of the *Titanic,* a remarkable safety record. The two deaths were recorded, and all workers were accounted for when the ship set sail. No workers were trapped inside the *Titanic*'s hull.

How did this myth start? One explanation says that older workers started it to put a scare into younger workers. At the end of the workday, riveters had to walk around the hull and tap the newly installed rivets to make sure they were installed correctly. Old-timers would tell stories of hearing the tapping of trapped workers inside the hull and leaving them to die. Must have been a real laughfest at the *Titanic* work site, eh?

Frank Tower Was the Luckiest Man on Earth

Frank "Lucky" Tower would be considered one of the luckiest men to ever walk the face of the earth if the stories about him were true. Or if he actually existed.

A *Titanic* myth tells us that Frank Tower was a stoker on the *Titanic* who survived the sinking in 1912. Two years later, he survived the sinking of the *Empress of Ireland*. A year later, in 1915, he survived the torpedoing and sinking of the *Lusitania*.

There is no Frank Tower on the crew rosters of the *Titanic,* the *Empress of Ireland,* or the *Lusitania*. However, a Frank *Toner* survived the sinking of the *Lusitania,* and a William Clark survived the sinking of both the *Titanic* and the *Empress of Ireland*. One theory holds that the stories of Toner and Clark somehow got conflated, and they became the mythical Frank "Lucky" Tower.

The Hope Diamond Went Down with the Titanic

The Hope Diamond is a 45.52-carat blue diamond. The story goes that a large stone weighing about 115 carats was discovered in India and was cut into the Hope Diamond. Over the years, it traded hands more than 20 times.

A myth says that the Hope Diamond was lost forever when the *Titanic* sank. This myth has persisted over the years, yet there isn't a whit of truth to it.

Adding to the confusion was the creation of a fictional giant blue diamond, Heart of the Ocean, for James Cameron's 1997 movie *Titanic*. The fictional Heart of the Ocean diamond was not meant to represent the Hope Diamond, but truth be told, the myth obviously influenced the movie's similar "lost diamond" storyline.

When the *Titanic* sailed in 1912, the Hope Diamond was owned by a wealthy American socialite named Evalyn Walsh McLean. She had it in her possession the entire time the ship was on the water, so it's impossible for the diamond to have been on the *Titanic*. From McLean, it went to jeweler Harry Winston, who in 1958 donated it to the Smithsonian Institution, where it now resides.

The "Priceless" Rubaiyat Was Lost

Priceless means "worth more than can be calculated in money." And *priceless* is the term Walter Lord used in his book *A Night to Remember* to describe a gem-encrusted, leather-bound copy of Omar Khayyam's *The Rubaiyat* that sailed on the *Titanic* and was lost when the ship went down.

But either words have meaning or they don't, and the myth of a "priceless" volume in the hold of the *Titanic* is just that: a myth. That the book sank with the *Titanic* has been confirmed by 1912 newspaper accounts and elsewhere, but its value hardly comes close to the epic numbers you imagine when you hear the word *priceless*.

According to some of the myths, the book, if recovered, would now be worth hundreds of thousands, if not millions, of dollars. It was supposedly bejeweled with 1,000 emeralds and rubies set in gold, and specially handcrafted to create a one-of-a-kind volume.

The truth is a bit more pedestrian. A few weeks before the *Titanic* sailed, the book was purchased at auction for around £405. Today, the identical book would fetch around $40,000, although that amount would climb significantly due to the book's association with the *Titanic*. But its value in no way would reach the astronomical heights the myth would have us believe.

The Purser's Safe Was Loaded with Valuables

The *Titanic* purser's safe is where the wealthy first-class women onboard stored their valuables during the voyage. A common belief had it that the safe was still aboard the *Titanic* and that it contained a treasure trove of diamonds, jewelry, gold, bank notes, and other valuables.

In truth, the purser's safe was retrieved from the *Titanic* and opened for a 1987 television special called *Return to the Titanic*. Inside the safe was what a representative from Van Cleef & Arpels said was a diamond bracelet. That's it: a diamond bracelet — not a jewelry-store cache of diamond bracelets or any other jewelry, for that matter.

The Titanic Sank Because of the Champagne Curse

The myth of the *Titanic* champagne curse tells us that the reason the *Titanic* sank was because the bottle of champagne used to christen her did not break. An ancient rule of the sea (probably found in some book called *Ancient Rules of the Sea*) says that if a ship's christening bottle remains intact, bad luck will befall the vessel.

In fact, one of the complaints about the movie version of *A Night to Remember* (Walter Lord's book about the *Titanic*) was that the opening scene was inaccurate. It shows a woman in a huge hat and fur stole christening the *Titanic*. She proclaims, "I name this ship *Titanic*," takes a mighty swing at the ship with a champagne bottle, and breaks the bottle cleanly. "That isn't true!" the myth's proponents declare about the movie. "In real life, the bottle didn't break, and that's why the *Titanic* sank!"

But there was no champagne bottle. The White Star Line most assuredly did not christen its ships with bottles of champagne or any other beverage. *A priori,* the *Titanic* did not sink due to a champagne curse, even if you believe in champagne curses.

The Titanic Vied for the Blue Riband

The Blue Riband was an unofficial title of achievement awarded to the fastest passenger ship making transatlantic crossings. No formal award was given for speed at crossing the Atlantic until 1935, when the Hales Trophy was awarded.

Twenty-five ships won the Blue Riband and, later, the Hales Trophy. The *Titanic* was not one of them, but a myth persists that the *Titanic* was vying for the Blue Riband on her maiden voyage. Because her captain and owners wanted her to win the award, the myth says, the *Titanic* didn't slow down in the ice fields, struck an iceberg, and sank.

But the *Titanic* was not vying for the Blue Riband, mainly because achieving the speeds necessary to win it was unlikely with her reciprocating-engines design. She was not built to be a fast ship, but a luxurious one.

This myth does correlate nicely, though, with the rumor that J. Bruce Ismay, chairman and managing director of the White Star Line, encouraged Captain Edward J. Smith to sail the *Titanic* as fast as possible in order to get into New York earlier than scheduled. Cameron's 1997 movie *Titanic* plays up that rumor, but the reality is that the *Titanic*'s top speed was not fast enough even to contend for the Blue Riband.

White Star Advertised the Titanic as "Unsinkable"

Did the White Star Line advertise the *Titanic* — or any other ship, for that matter — as unsinkable? The answer is "yes and no." The White Star Line didn't blatantly advertise the *Titanic* as unsinkable, but it also didn't do anything to disabuse the world of the notion that its ships were incapable of sinking.

A brochure from the company said this about the sister ships the *Olympic* and the *Titanic:* "these two wonderful vessels are designed to be unsinkable." Is there a difference "unsinkable" and "*designed to be* unsinkable"?

There was a perception on the part of the public and the shipbuilding industry that the *Titanic* had been built to achieve an invulnerability heretofore unimagined and that there was no way the ship could sink. Even Captain Smith weighed in when he said, "I cannot imagine any condition which would cause a ship to founder. I cannot conceive of any vital disaster happening to this vessel. Modern ship building has gone beyond that." Further fueling the fire was this comment (after the collision with the iceberg) by White Star Line Vice President Phillip Franklin: "There is no danger that the *Titanic* will sink. The boat is unsinkable and nothing but inconvenience will be suffered by the passengers."

A 1911 issue of *Shipbuilder* magazine carried an article about the *Titanic*'s construction. When describing the watertight compartments and doors, the article said that the *Titanic* was "practically unsinkable."

The White Star Line's choice of words in its brochures and public statements promulgated the belief that the ship was unsinkable. But the White Star Line didn't come right out and say that the *Titanic* or any of its other ships was incapable of sinking.

Chapter 20

Ten Terrific Titanic Documentaries

. . . .

In This Chapter

▶ Exploring *Titanic* history

▶ Trying to raise the Big Piece

▶ Considering alternative theories about the sinking

. . . .

The *Titanic* documentaries I describe in this chapter provide a good sampling of the many available for your viewing pleasure. Some, like *Titanic: The Complete Story,* are must-see documentaries. Others, like *Titanic's Achilles Heel,* which focuses on one controversial theory about what caused the sinking (a broken expansion joint), are strictly for diehard students of the *Titanic* tragedy.

Many of these documentaries are available from public libraries. YouTube (www.youtube.com) also has an extensive selection of *Titanic* documentaries (enter "Titanic" as a search term at YouTube to see what you can find). Most of the documentaries are available on DVD for purchase or rental as well.

At the end of this chapter, I briefly describe documentaries that didn't make my Top Ten list.

Secrets of the Titanic (1986)

"Her name is a synonym for tragedy," says narrator Martin Sheen in *Secrets of the Titanic,* an excellent overview of the discovery of the *Titanic* wreck in 1985 by Dr. Robert Ballard and IFREMER (the French Research Institute for Exploration of the Sea); see Chapter 15. One of the earliest documentaries about the search for the great ship, *Secrets of the Titanic* boasts full participation by Dr. Ballard and his team. It shows footage that they captured before, during, and after the discovery of the wreck.

Also notable in this documentary are scenes from a Titanic Historical Society convention of several survivors still alive at the time. The survivors signed autographs, posed for pictures, and were treated like celebrities by the convention-goers.

Much of the footage in this documentary appears in other documentaries, and for those who have seen newer documentaries about the *Titanic,* the difference between this original footage and the high-definition video now being taken is astonishing.

The documentary ends poignantly with a few heartfelt comments by Dr. Ballard, who speaks of the *Titanic* with great respect and describes her "nobly" sitting upright on the ocean floor and "at rest."

This documentary is well worth seeing.

Titanic: The Complete Story (1994)

Titanic: The Complete Story first aired on the A&E Network in 1994. For its initial airing, the documentary was presented in two parts, *Titanic: Death of a Dream* and *Titanic: The Legend Lives On.* Later, the two parts were combined and packaged for DVD as *Titanic: The Complete Story.*

Many people feel that this *Titanic* documentary is the best ever made. No one can deny its comprehensive coverage of the disaster, its superb production values, and its meticulous attention to details and historical accuracy. *Titanic: The Complete Story* is well worth owning (or at least viewing) for foundational information that tells the tragic story of the *Titanic* as clearly and accurately as possible. This documentary is a good one for people who are new to the *Titanic* story.

However, this documentary, made in 1994, is a little out of date. Obviously, it doesn't include new information learned in the years since it was made. For example, it doesn't cover the existence (and raising) of the Big Piece: a 20-ton piece of the *Titanic*'s hull measuring approximately 15 by 25 feet (see Chapter 16). It doesn't discuss recent findings about the rivets (see Chapter 11) or cover recent debates about the angle of the ship's rise out of the water as it went down. It also doesn't cover the discovery of the six small holes totaling about 12 square feet that sank the *Titanic,* which disproved the long-held belief that a 300-foot gash sank her (see Chapter 11).

Titanic: The Investigation Begins (1996)

Titanic: The Investigation Begins is about the first (failed) attempt to raise the Big Piece from the ocean floor. As I detail in Chapter 16, this first expedition was organized and helmed by the late George Tulloch, one of the original founders of the company RMS Titanic, Inc., which was granted *salvor-in-possession* (ownership) rights to the wreck and its artifacts. The Big Piece was eventually raised successfully, but this documentary looks at Tulloch's first failed attempt to bring the walls of two C-deck cabins up from the ocean floor.

This documentary provides a great deal of detail about the attempt to raise the Big Piece. For example, it shows how Tulloch's team used lift bags fueled by diesel power. When the gear begins to fail, the scene is quite dramatic, especially when the Big Piece reaches the surface, the cables break, and the Big Piece planes down to the bottom 10 miles away from where it was originally salvaged.

As I explain in Chapter 16, some controversy surrounded Tulloch's expedition. To help fund it, Tulloch booked two cruise ships to accompany the mission. He charged passengers $5,000 a ticket to come and watch the Big Piece being raised to the surface. Casino gambling and other entertainments were available on the two cruise ships, which rubbed many people the wrong way because they saw it as disrespectful.

The producers and crew of *Titanic: The Investigation Begins* say that the passengers were along to help with the mission. Their help included attending an on-deck memorial service and throwing flowers into the water at the site of the sinking. (During the memorial service, the names of each and every one of the more than 2,200 souls on board were read aloud.) There were also numerous *Titanic* presentations aboard both cruise ships given by *Titanic* scholars. Plus the two cruise ships did an experiment to ascertain whether the *Californian* could have been the ship seen by the *Titanic* on the night of the disaster (see Chapter 7): One of the ships sailed to the most commonly accepted of the *Californian*'s possible positions, while the other remained at the wreck site and fired rockets similar to those from 1912. There was no question that the ships could see each other on the horizon and that the *Titanic*'s rockets would have been seen by the *Californian*.

Titanic: Anatomy of a Disaster (1997)

This excellent Discovery Channel documentary uses computer animation to investigate what caused the great ship to sink. This documentary also spends a great deal of time highlighting the recovered artifacts and was the public's first in-depth look at many salvaged items.

This documentary features scientists and researchers who combine underwater archaeology, forensic science, metallurgy, microbiology, and sonar imaging to present a complete investigation of the sinking. It also includes interviews with survivors.

Titanic: 90 Years Below (2002)

Titanic: 90 Years Below provides a comprehensive review of the many attempts to find the wreckage of the ship. It reveals details about Dr. Robert Ballard's top-secret Navy missions. It also offers incredible side-by-side views showing the original black-and-white footage of the wreck taken in 1985 beside the new high-definition color footage.

The documentary provides a balanced discussion of arguments for and against salvaging the wreck, including excellent commentary by Ballard and his team and an array of *Titanic* historians. Ballard is adamantly opposed to salvaging; he states his case with passion and conviction. However, the folks from RMS Titanic, Inc., the company named salvor-in-possession of the wreck, make equally convincing cases for salvaging. They believe that salvaging serves history, recovers important artifacts, and helps to chronicle the disaster for all time. (It should be noted that RMS Titanic, Inc., restricts its recovery to the debris field and has not invaded the ship.)

Ghosts of the Abyss (2003)

Ghosts of the Abyss could almost be considered a sequel to *Titanic,* the 1997 blockbuster film (which I discuss in Chapter 17). This unscripted documentary was directed by James Cameron, the director of *Titanic.* Bill Paxton, who played treasure hunter Brock Lovett in the same movie, also appears in this documentary. So does the burly, bearded Lewis Abernathy, who played Bodine, Lovett's friend who doubted whether the elderly Rose told the truth about her passage on the *Titanic.*

In the documentary, Paxton, Abernathy, Cameron, and several *Titanic* experts board the *Keldysh,* a Russian deep submersible, for a trip into the depths of the *Titanic* wreckage. This documentary provides one of the most thorough and eye-opening tours of the *Titanic*'s interior ever filmed. Molly Brown's brass bed? Yep! The Marconi Room? Yep! Translucent, purple, winged fish? Yep!

In a genuinely eerie effect, you see actors playing the roles of the crew superimposed on actual footage of the *Titanic* wreck. It's a bizarre, enlightening, and illustrative experience to see *Titanic* officers moving about and working as they did that night, albeit on the destroyed wreck. After you get used to seeing waiters carrying their trays and firemen shoveling coal amongst the wreckage, the effect is quite thrilling. The side-by-side juxtapositions of the *Titanic* then and now provide a new and fascinating perspective.

I also like this documentary for the interesting tidbits it provides. For example, after pointing out that an elevator is labeled as such (rather than as a "lift," as it would be in the United Kingdom), Cameron reminds viewers that despite its British and Irish construction lineage, the *Titanic* was owned by an American company, so it used American lingo and terminology in its outfitting.

(We also find out how submersible-crew members go to the bathroom, thanks to self-described "nervous pisser" Bill Paxton, who finally tells his teammates that he can't hold it any longer. He is then handed a plastic bottle.

He looks at it a moment and then, in a funny scene, decides that he'll be the one to turn around for privacy.)

Paxton, as one of the only "civilians" on the trip, provides most of the *ooh*ing and *aah*ing. In a sense, he serves as a surrogate audience member. The rest of the crew, professionals all, are mostly unemotional about what they see. Paxton reacts the way someone who has never before dived miles beneath the ocean surface might react.

The documentary also discusses *Titanic* survivor Helen Candee, who wrote about visiting the bow of the *Titanic* before sunrise and who is said to have inspired the scene showing Jack and Rose "flying" at the bow of the ship in Cameron's blockbuster film.

Overall, *Ghosts of the Abyss* is a splendid look at areas of the *Titanic* that many people have never seen, combined with effects that truly make you feel like you're there.

Titanic Tech (2003)

Titanic Tech is a one-hour documentary that focuses on the technical aspects of the biggest ship in the world rather than on the human drama of the sinking or the ship's luxurious accommodations.

The documentary begins with a discussion of the competition between the Cunard Line, the British-American–owned shipping company that concentrated on building the fastest ships, and the White Star Line, which challenged Cunard by building the biggest and most luxurious ships instead of the fastest ones.

Titanic Tech uses a wonderful analogy that truly serves to explain the ship's design:

- ✔ The keel is the spinal cord.
- ✔ The support rods, 3 feet apart, are the ribs (and are commonly referred to as such).
- ✔ The metal hull plates are the skin of the body of the ship.

The documentary features Ken Marschall, an artist known for his portraits of ocean liners, Edward Kamuda of the Titanic Historical Society, Navy engineers, and *Titanic* historians. These experts talk about how the propellers were made, how the *Titanic* created her own electricity, how the ship was the first to carry the Marconi wireless system, and how steam was continually recycled in a closed system to serve a multitude of purposes.

Titanic Tech is a balanced representation of what the *Titanic* was. As one of the interviewees makes clear, the *Titanic* was a state-of-the-art ship but not a cutting-edge one. The documentary argues that the *Titanic*'s seeming sophistication and magnificence of appointment actually masked the vulnerabilities that ultimately destroyed it.

Last Mysteries of the Titanic (2005)

Last Mysteries of the Titanic begins with an amazing sequence: James Cameron in a MIR submersible parked on the *Titanic*'s deck, operating an underwater ROV (remotely operated vehicle) camera and taking viewers on a tour of the ship (his 35th tour, by the way). What makes this scene so amazing is that it happens in real time. Cameron is broadcasting a signal to a ship on the surface live as he explores the *Titanic,* and the feed is being broadcast on live TV.

To illustrate different aspects of the ship, the documentary uses dissolves from photos alongside pictures of the wreck today and clips from Cameron's 1997 *Titanic* movie. (A *dissolve* is when a photograph slowly fades away and beneath it is the new photo of the same scene. Dissolves provide a very dramatic "before and after" perspective.)

In the documentary, camera bots go deep into the wreckage of the *Titanic* to show the Strauss first-class suite (Cameron said it was the model for Rose's cabin in his movie), the Marconi Room, Captain Edward J. Smith's cabin, and other specific locations on the ship. And as the bots tour the wreck, you see visuals of the ship before sinking. This is the technique that Cameron used in his 1997 movie when he dissolves from Jack and Rose standing on the bow, to Jack and Rose standing on the bow of the wreck, and finally to the wreck today. He makes excellent use of this technique throughout his entire tour of the ship.

Titanic's Achilles Heel (2007)

Titanic's Achilles Heel, a History Channel documentary, explores the expansion joint theory, one of the newer theories as to why the *Titanic* sank. The idea behind this theory is that the expansion joint in the middle of the ship, which was designed to allow the hull to flex in the waves, failed, and because it failed, the angle of elevation out of the water was far less than experts and historians first believed. The argument that the ship experienced a low-angle break hinges on the crushed condition of the stern half and the clean break of the bow half.

In Brad Matsen's book *Titanic's Last* Secrets (published by Twelve), Dr. Robert Ballard, commenting on this new theory, said it's essentially irrelevant. James Cameron said it was interesting but not persuasive enough to change his mind about a high-angle break.

Titanic's Achilles Heel explains why the expansion-joint theory is important. However, it ultimately doesn't provide proof that the expansion joint failed and that if it did fail, its failure had anything to do with the angle at which the ship lifted out of the water.

Rebuilding the Titanic (2011)

In *Rebuilding the Titanic,* a team of a half dozen British builders constructs a third of the *Titanic*'s bow to scale, using 1910 building practices and equipment. If you take nothing else away anything from this documentary, you will feel unqualified awe at the skills, determination, work ethic, and commitment of the *Titanic*'s original builders. Almost everything was done by hand. Watching the builders in this documentary hammer in rivets and bend steel using their own brute strength, you realize the epic nature of building giant ships like the *Titanic, Olympic,* and *Britannic* (see Chapter 2).

The general rule in the early 1900s was that one life lost for every $500,000 spent to build a ship was acceptable. The *Titanic* cost approximately $7.5 million, which meant that Harland and Wolff would have accepted 15 deaths during the ship's construction. Only eight men died, so the company was pleased. One can't help but wonder what shipbuilders from a century ago would think of today's zero-tolerance policy for workplace injuries. It truly was a different time.

Rebuilding the Titanic is an educational program that children in particular will be blown away by. It prods adults and children alike to imagine what work was like a hundred years ago. Workers were young, old, and mostly unprotected by workplace safety laws and protective gear and equipment.

As of this writing, the bow section that was built for this documentary is on display in Belfast, Northern Ireland, near the Harland and Wolff dry dock and pumphouse.

Other Documentaries Worth Watching

Many documentaries have been made about the *Titanic* besides the ones I describe in this chapter. Here are a handful of others you may want to watch:

- ✔ *Treasures of the Titanic* (1987): Hosted by Doug Llewelyn, this made-for-TV documentary focuses on artifacts lost aboard the *Titanic.*
- ✔ *Titanica* (1998): This documentary, which was created from an IMAX film, uses robot cameras to explore the *Titanic* wreckage.

✔ *Deep Inside the Titanic* (1999): This Discovery Channel documentary features underwater footage of the wreck and testimony from survivors. You can view this documentary online; look for it on YouTube (www.youtube.com).

✔ *Titanic: Answers from the Abyss* (1999): This Discovery Channel documentary focuses on why the ship broke apart after colliding with the iceberg.

✔ *Titanic Revealed* (2004): This National Geographic documentary features Dr. Ballard and covers the two top-secret nuclear-sub missions Ballard had to carry out before being allowed to hunt for *Titanic*.

✔ *Return to Titanic* (2005): From National Geographic, this TV documentary follows Dr. Ballard as he returns to see the wreckage.

✔ *Titanic: How It Really Sank* (2009): This documentary from National Geographic explores theories as to why the ship sank, beginning with the first inquiries in 1914 and continuing to the present time.

Appendix

A Titanic Timeline

*T*his appendix presents a timeline of events surrounding the *Titanic,* starting with the birth of its captain in 1850 and ending with the centennial celebrations in 2012.

1850

January 27 Edward John Smith, the ultimately doomed commander of the *Titanic,* is born in England in Hanley, Staffordshire, Stoke-on-Trent.

1869

Edward Smith, 19, begins his seafaring career as an apprentice on a clipper ship.

1880

At the age of 30, Edward Smith joins the White Star Line as fourth officer on the *Celtic.*

1887

Edward Smith, 37, having attained the rank of captain, takes command of the White Star steamship the *Republic.*

1898

Morgan Robertson's seemingly prophetic novella *Futility* (later renamed *The Wreck of the Titan)* is published. In this tale, the world's largest steamship — the *Titan* — hits an iceberg and sinks on its third voyage. (See Chapter 13 for more about the novella.)

1907

April 30 At a dinner at the Downshire House in London, J. Bruce Ismay, chairman and managing director of the White Star Line, and Lord William James Pirrie, a partner in the shipbuilding firm of Harland and Wolff, agree to build two giant ocean liners: the *Olympic* and the *Titanic.*

July 1 The order is officially placed with Harland and Wolff for the construction of the *Olympic* and the *Titanic.*

1909

March 31 The first keel plate for *Titanic* is laid in the Harland and Wolff shipyards in Belfast.

1910

October 19 Plating of the *Titanic* is completed. Hydraulic riveting is used to give the best-quality plating for the ship.

October 20 The *Olympic* is launched in a 62-second "voyage." The Lord Lieutenant of Ireland, Lord William James Pirrie, and J. Bruce Ismay are present at the launch.

1911

May 31 The *Titanic* is officially launched from Harland and Wolff Slip Number 3. The launch lasts 62 seconds and is witnessed by more than 100,000 people.

June Captain Edward J. Smith, 61, is appointed master (commander) of the *Olympic* for its maiden voyage.

June 14 The *Olympic* departs Southampton, England, for New York. She averages 21.17 knots on her journey to New York and 22.32 knots on her return voyage.

1912

January Sixteen wooden lifeboats and four collapsible Englehardt boats are fitted on board the *Titanic*.

March 31 The outfitting of the *Titanic* is complete.

April 1 Scheduled sea trials for the *Titanic* are postponed due to strong northwest winds.

April 2 Five tugs tow the *Titanic* down Victoria Channel to Belfast Lough for sea trials. The trials include maneuvering the ship at different speeds, evaluating the performance of the helm, and performing an emergency stop.

April 2 After successful sea trials, the British Board of Trade awards the *Titanic* her passenger certificate.

April 2 The *Titanic* departs Belfast under the command of Captain Smith and proceeds to Southampton.

April 3 The *Titanic* arrives in Southampton and docks at Berth 44.

April 7 Hundreds of people come to the docks to view the *Titanic*.

April 8 Foodstuffs are loaded onto the *Titanic*.

April 9 The *Titanic* spends her final day in Southampton. All the officers spend the night on board and keep regular watches.

Wednesday, April 10, 7:30 a.m. Captain Smith boards the *Titanic* for her maiden voyage.

Wednesday, April 10, 9:30 a.m. to 11:30 a.m. Three boat trains from Waterloo Station near London arrive at the *Titanic* carrying first-, second-, and third-class passengers.

Wednesday, April 10, 11:45 a.m. *Titanic*'s mighty triple-toned steam whistle blows three times. The great vessel casts off 20 minutes later, accompanied by six tugboats, and has a near collision with the *New York* (see details in Chapter 5).

Wednesday, April 10, 1:30 p.m. After its departure was delayed by the near collision with the *New York,* the Titanic leaves Southampton.

Wednesday, April 10, 6:30 p.m. After an 89-mile trip across the English Channel, the *Titanic* arrives at Cherbourg, France, where she takes on 274 more passengers.

Wednesday, April 10, 8:10 p.m. The *Titanic* departs from Cherbourg, bound for Queenstown (now Cobh), Ireland.

Thursday, April 11, 11:30 a.m. After an uneventful journey down the English Channel and into St. George's Channel, the *Titanic* drops anchor in Queenstown harbor off the coast of Queenstown, Ireland. She takes on 120 more passengers. Prior to leaving Queenstown, the *Titanic* raises the American flag above her deck, signifying her next port of call: New York Harbor.

Thursday, April 11, 1:30 p.m. The *Titanic* raises her starboard anchor for the final time and departs Queenstown harbor for New York.

Friday, April 12, 12 p.m. Between now and noon Saturday, April 13, the *Titanic* covers 519 miles, with 24 of her 29 boilers in use.

Saturday, April 13, 12 p.m. Between now and noon Sunday, April 14, the *Titanic* covers 546 miles.

Sunday, April 14, 9 a.m. The *Titanic* receives a message from the *Caronia*: "Captain, *Titanic* — West-bound steamers report bergs, growlers and field ice in 42° N. from 49° to 51° W., 12th April. Compliments — Barr." (A *growler* is an iceberg of small mass.)

Sunday, April 14, 1:42 p.m. The *Titanic* receives a message from the *Baltic*: "Captain Smith, *Titanic* — Have had moderate, variable winds and clear, fine weather since leaving. Greek steamer *Athenai* [sic] reports passing icebergs and large quantities of field ice to-day in lat. 41° 51' N., long. 49° 52' W. Last night we spoke German oiltank steamer *Deutschland,* Stettin to Philadelphia, not under control, short of coal, lat. 40° 42' N., long 55° 11' W. Wishes to be reported to New York and other steamers. Wish you and *Titanic* all success. — Commander."

Sunday, April 14, 7:30 p.m. Harold Bride on the *Titanic* picks up a message from the *Californian* to the *Antillian:* "To Captain, Antillian, 6:30 p.m. apparent ship's time; lat. 42° 3' N., long. 49° 9' W. Three large bergs five miles to southward of us. Regards. — Lord."

Sunday, April 14, 9:40 p.m. The *Titanic* receives a message from the *Mesaba:* "From Mesaba to Titanic and all east-bound ships. Ice report in lat. 42° N. to 41° 25' N., long. 49° to long. 50° 30' W, saw much heavy pack ice and great number large icebergs. Also field ice, weather good, clear."

Sunday, April 14, approximately 11 p.m. *Californian* wireless operator Cyril Evans sends a message to the *Titanic:* "Say, old man, we are stopped and surrounded by ice." Evans receives the reply, "Shut up, shut up, I am busy; I am working Cape Race" from *Titanic* wireless operator Jack Phillips.

Sunday, April 14, 11:40 p.m. In the crow's nest, Frederick Fleet sees an iceberg looming directly ahead in the *Titanic*'s path. He rings a 16-inch brass bell three times and picks up the telephone that connects to the bridge. Sixth Officer James Moody answers. Fleet shouts into the phone, "Iceberg right ahead."

First Officer William Murdoch immediately orders maneuvers to avoid the iceberg. He sounds a bell alarm for ten seconds to warn crew below decks that the watertight-compartment doors are about to be closed. Murdoch then pulls the switch to slam the doors shut.

Sunday, April 14, 11:40 p.m. A mere 37 seconds after Fleet spotted the danger, the *Titanic* collides with an iceberg.

Monday, April 15, 12:05 a.m. Captain Smith orders the *Titanic*'s lifeboats uncovered and the crew and passengers assembled.

Monday, April 15, 12:15 a.m. The *Titanic* sends out her first distress call, a CQD (meaning "All stations: distress"), that's picked up by the *La Provence* and the *Mount Temple.*

Monday, April 15, 12:45 a.m. The *Titanic*'s first distress rocket is fired. The first lifeboat, No. 7, is lowered from the starboard side.

Monday, April 15, 1:40 a.m. The *Titanic*'s last distress rocket is fired.

Monday, April 15, 2:05 a.m. Collapsible D, the last lifeboat to hold passengers and crew, is lowered from the port side. Collapsibles A and B, free from their tie-downs, are swept from the deck.

Monday, April 15, approximately 2:17 a.m. The *Titanic*'s last wireless distress call is transmitted: "We are sinking fast."

Monday, April 15, 2:18 a.m. The *Titanic*'s lights fail. People in the lifeboats hear an enormous crashing sound as things in the ship — from grand pianos to engines — break free and plunge toward the ocean.

Monday, April 15, 2:20 a.m. The *Titanic*'s stern rears up out of the ocean, poises upright for a moment or two, and then plunges downward, splitting in two and sinking 2.5 miles to the bottom of the ocean. More than 700 survivors watch the nightmarish tragedy from lifeboats.

Monday, April 15, 3:30 a.m. *Titanic* survivors adrift in the lifeboats first see the *Carpathia*'s rockets.

Monday, April 15, 4:10 a.m. The *Carpathia* arrives at the site of *Titanic*'s foundering and begins taking on survivors. The rescue operation continues for four hours.

Monday, April 15, 8:10 a.m. Crew members of the *Carpathia* pick up Lifeboat No. 12, the last one afloat.

Monday, April 15, 8:30 a.m. The *Californian* pulls up alongside the *Carpathia*.

Monday, April 15, 8:50 a.m. Captain Arthur Rostron of the *Carpathia* sets sail for New York with the *Titanic*'s survivors.

April 17 U.S. Senator William Alden Smith of Michigan proposes a special investigation into the sinking of the *Titanic*. His resolution is unanimously approved.

April 18 The *Carpathia* arrives in New York and docks at Pier 54, North River, with *Titanic*'s survivors. More than 10,000 people line the docks.

April 19 The opening session of the U.S. Senate Subcommittee *Titanic* Hearing takes place at the Waldorf-Astoria Hotel in New York City.

April 20 The cable ship *Mackay-Bennett* arrives at the site of the *Titanic*'s foundering to retrieve bodies. A total of 328 bodies are recovered.

April 23 The British Lord Chancellor appoints a Wreck Commissioner under the Merchant Shipping Act to investigate the sinking of the *Titanic*.

April 26 The British Home Secretary appoints five assessors for a *Titanic* inquiry.

May 2 The British Board of Trade's Commission of Inquiry into the loss of the *Titanic* begins in the Scottish Hall, Buckingham Gate, Westminster, England.

May 13 The last lifeboat belonging to the *Titanic* is found adrift in the Atlantic by the *Oceanic*. Three bodies in the boat are buried at sea.

May 18 More than 30,000 mourners attend the burial of the *Titanic*'s bandmaster Wallace Hartley in his hometown of Colne, Lancashire, England.

May 28 The U.S. Senate Subcommittee *Titanic* Hearing issues its final report.

July 3 The British Board of Trade's inquiry into the loss of the *Titanic* is concluded.

1914

The International Ice Patrol (IIP) is founded with the purpose of monitoring icebergs in the Atlantic and Arctic oceans. The sinking of the *Titanic* was the impetus to create the organization. Every year on April 15, the IIP drops several wreaths in the North Atlantic at the place where the *Titanic* sank.

1955

November Walter Lord's history of the *Titanic* disaster, *A Night to Remember,* is published. It goes on to become the bible for *Titanic* historians.

1985

September 1 A joint French-American scientific expedition led by Robert Ballard discovers the wreckage of the *Titanic* 2.5 miles below the surface of the North Atlantic. Ballard states that he'll keep the precise location of the wreck a secret to prevent scavengers from desecrating the site.

1987

August An expedition by IFREMER (the French oceanographic institute that co-discovered the wreckage in 1985) to the site of the *Titanic* retrieves some 1,800 artifacts. IFREMER claims salvor-in-possession rights to the wreck and everything around it.

1994

June 7 A Norfolk, Virginia, court names RMS Titanic, Inc., the salvor-in-possession of the *Titanic* and any and all artifacts the company recovers. In order for possession to remain in effect, RMS Titanic, Inc., must remain "in possession" of the ship, thus requiring periodic visits to the site, some of which have been solely for photography.

1996

August RMS Titanic, Inc., fails to raise a piece of the *Titanic*'s hull from the ocean floor.

1997

December 19 James Cameron's film *Titanic* opens in the United States to excellent reviews and extraordinary business. It goes on to become the highest-grossing film of all time and the winner of 11 Academy Awards.

1998

August RMS Titanic, Inc., successfully raises a 20-ton piece of the *Titanic*'s hull, known as the Big Piece, to the surface. (See Chapter 16 for more on the raising of the Big Piece.)

2009

Elizabeth Gladys Millvina Dean, the last *Titanic* survivor, dies in England at the age of 97.

2012

Titanic centennial commemorations are held in Belfast, Southampton, Halifax, and other cities important to the *Titanic*'s history. Commemorative cruises to the North Atlantic are launched as well.

Index